D1271317

Jura Separatism
in
Switzerland

John R. G. Jenkins

CLARENDON PRESS · OXFORD

1986

Oxford University Press, Walton Street, Oxford OX2 6DP

Oxford New York Toronto
Delhi Bombay Calcutta Madras Karachi
Kuala Lumpur Singapore Hong Kong Tokyo
Nairobi Dar es Salaam Cape Town
Melbourne Auckland

and associated companies in
Beirut Berlin Ibadan Nicosia

Oxford is a trade mark of Oxford University Press

Published in the United States
by Oxford University Press, New York

British Library Cataloguing in Publication Data

Jenkins, John R. G.
Jura separatism in Switzerland.—(Oxford
research studies in geography)
1. Jura (Switzerland)—History—Autonomy and
independence movements
I. Title
322.4'2'094943   DQ360
ISBN 0–19–823247–0

Library of Congress Cataloging in Publication Data

Jenkins, John R. G. (John Robert Graham), 1928–
Jura separatism in Switzerland.
Bibliography: p.
Includes index.
1. Jura (Switzerland)—History—Autonomy and
independence movements. 2. Jura (Switzerland)—
Ethnic relations. I. Title.
DQ356.J46 1985   949.4'5   85-18734
ISBN 0–19–823247–0

Photoset by Enset (Photosetting)
Printed and bound in
Great Britain by Biddles Ltd,
Guildford and King's Lynn

To
Betty

PREFACE AND ACKNOWLEDGEMENTS

I owe a debt of gratitude to many individuals who assisted me in one way or another in the research which preceded this work, and in the preparation of this volume itself. Included in this group are many Swiss citizens—too numerous to name individually—both in the Bernese Jura itself and elsewhere in Switzerland. I wish to express my thanks to them collectively. They include Jurassian separatists, anti-separatists, and interested observers of the Jurassian scene.

At the start of my research study Mr Paul A. Ramseyer, then First Secretary of the Swiss Embassy, London was of great assistance and encouragement to me, and arranged my initial contacts with Pro Helvetia, the highly regarded Swiss cultural organization. I am most grateful to him for his help.

I next wish to express my thanks to three distinguished scholars. Firstly, Professor Christopher Hughes, Emeritus Professor of Politics at the University of Leicester, and a leading British authority on Switzerland, has been of great assistance to me on a number of occasions. During the early stages of my research he kindly suggested a number of valuable sources of data to me in Switzerland, and put me in touch with several knowledgeable contacts in that country. He subsequently read a preliminary draft of the manuscript of this book, and made a number of useful suggestions. Finally, Professor Hughes has given me invaluable advice on a number of subsequent occasions.

Professor Kurt Mayer, Emeritus Professor of Sociology at the University of Berne, has also been of great help to me throughout my research. Professor Mayer's own earlier research on the 'Jura problem', his perceptive comments on the subject in personal conversations with me, and his thought-provoking publications on the topic were most informative and useful.

Professor Kenneth D. McRae, Professor of Political Science at Carlton University, Ottawa, Canada, is a leading Canadian expert on various facets of society in bilingual and multilingual states, and the author of two excellent works on Switzerland. Professor McRae was kind enough to read the manuscript of this work and make a number of valuable suggestions.

Throughout my Jura research, and subsequently, Vice-Chancellor J. Etter, Miss J. Mekacher, and Mr D. Jaccottet of the Secrétariat du Conseil-exécutif pour les affaires jurassiennes (The Executive Council for Jurassian Affairs, Government of Canton Berne), were extremely helpful in personal discussions and in responding to my many enquiries. So, too, was Mrs Hanne Zweifel of Pro Helvetia, Zurich in putting me in touch with a number of knowledgeable authorities on Jurassian and Swiss affairs, and in providing me with invaluable background material. I also wish to thank Dr Marius Hammer, of the Swiss National Library, and Mr Hans Wernli, of the Swiss Federal Statistical Office, for their assistance on a number of occasions.

Preliminary research funds for my D.Phil. study were provided by Oxford University grants from the Zaharoff Fund, the Vaughan Cornish Bequest, the Committee for Graduate Studies Special Research Fund, and the Jesus College Research and Advance Study Fund. I wish to express my thanks and appreciation to the officers of these funds for their support during the critical early stages of my research.

Subsequently, Pro Helvetia of Zurich assisted me with a generous research grant to enable me to conduct extensive field research in the Bernese Jura for my D.Phil. degree. At a later stage, when further field research was required to complete this work, Pro Helvetia kindly assisted me with a further grant. Pro Helvetia's assistance and encouragement throughout my Jura research are greatly appreciated.

I particularly wish to express my thanks to my D.Phil. supervisor, Emeritus Professor Jean Gottmann, FBA, formerly Head, School of Geography, Oxford University. Professor Gottmann, a distinguished, world-renowned geographer who is still extremely active, faced heavy demands on his energies in both the field of scholarship and administration while he was supervising my thesis. Nevertheless, he generously devoted substantial amounts of time and energy in patiently guiding me through all stages of my research. Professor Gottmann's incisive comments and suggestions were of very great value to me, and he has encouraged me further in the writing of this work. I owe him a deep debt of gratitude.

Thanks are also due to my Oxford D.Phil. examiners, Mr Norman Pollock (Emeritus Fellow of St. Edmund Hall and formerly Tutor in Geography), and Mr Vernon Bogdanor, (Fellow and Tutor in Politics at Brasenose College) for encouraging me to continue with my Jura research and to produce a book on the subject.

I also wish to express my profound thanks to Dean Andrew Berczi, Director of Research, and the Wilfrid Laurier University Research Grants Committee for the award of a book preparation grant to enable me to complete this work. Dean Berczi himself, the University's senior administration, and members of the University Research Grants and other research-oriented committees, have played key roles in helping to establish Wilfrid Laurier University, over the past decade, as an important centre of Canadian scholarship. My university is to be especially commended for its encouragement of *interdisciplinary* research in recent years.

In addition, I wish to express my appreciation to Dr Paul Griffiths, of the Oxford University Computing Service, for his advice while I was using the Oxford computer facilities during my D.Phil. research. Subsequently, Mr Bob Ellsworth, of the Wilfrid Laurier University Computing Service, was also of great help to me during the later stages of the research I conducted in connection with this work.

I also wish to thank Mrs Lillian Peirce and Miss Judy Lankowski, who typed the final manuscript of this work, Mrs Margaret Wilson (Oxford

University), and Mrs Pam Schaus (Wilfrid Laurier University) who produced the maps. In addition, I wish to thank Dr Barry Boots, (Chairman, Department of Geography), Dr Russell Muncaster, formerly Chairman of the Department of Geography and now Vice-President: Academic, and Dr Alex Murray, Dean, School of Business and Economics, Wilfrid Laurier University, for their assistance and encouragement.

In a wider sense, this book is dedicated to the people of Switzerland, a country in which I have long had an interest, and for which I have developed a deep admiration and affection during the past twenty years. In particular, I should like to express my thanks to my Swiss friends Alfred and Elisabeth Brönniman and Heiner Henny, of Ziefen, Baselland for the kindness and hospitality they have shown me on many occasions.

Last but not least, I wish to thank my son John C. Jenkins, for some valuable comments on an earlier draft of the manuscript of this book, and my wife Betty for her patience throughout the several years of research and writing which have resulted in this work.

August 1985   J.R.G.J.

CONTENTS

LIST OF PLATES

LIST OF FIGURES

LIST OF TABLES

1

The Bernese Jura as a Subject for Study

Investigators . . . have discovered that the making and breaking of nations
is a process which is now occurring in most parts of the world and that it is a
process which must be studied in its general and uniform aspects, especially if the unique features of each country . . . are eventually to be
understood better than they have been thus far.

KARL DEUTSCH AND WILLIAM FOLZ (1966)

On 24 September 1978 the people of Switzerland, representing their various
cantons, voted in favour of the establishment of a new self-governing Swiss
administrative unit, to be known as *la République et Canton du Jura*, or 'Canton
Jura', in English. The subsequent proclamation of Canton Jura, in 1979, was a
direct result of the existence of a phenomenon known as 'Jura separatism', a
phenomenon which had manifested itself, in part, through the political
activities of individuals referred to as 'Jura (or Jurassian) separatists'. The
major purpose of this work is to consider the degree to which, if at all,
geographic factors may have influenced Jura separatism. A further, secondary
purpose is to relate the resultant findings to the Swiss Confederation as a whole
and, to the extent that this is possible, to other modern states which are
confronted with separatist movements.

The Establishment of Canton Jura

Canton Jura, which officially came into existence on 1 January 1979, is
situated in the extreme north-west of Switzerland (Fig. 1). Between the
Vienna Settlement of 1815 and 1978 the new canton formed a part of the Swiss
canton of Berne,[1] and the specific region within which the new canton is
situated was known, from 1815 to 1978, as the 'Bernese Jura' (Fig. 2). 41·5 per
cent of qualified Swiss electors voted in the national referendum which was
required to establish Canton Jura, representing a somewhat higher-than-
average Swiss voter turn-out. 82·3 per cent of those voting favoured the
establishment of the new canton. Table 1 provides further details of voting
patterns in this referendum.

Canton Jura is the twenty-third canton of the Swiss Confederation, and the
sixth Swiss canton in which French is the official language. At the time of the
1980 census it had a population of approximately 65,000; by 1984 its
population was approximately 67,300. Perhaps Canton Jura's most
noteworthy feature is that it is the first truly new Swiss canton to have been
established since 1815.[2]

Fig. 1. Canton Jura in Relation to Switzerland and Western Europe.

Terminology

Because of the various meanings of the word 'Jura', it is desirable to define the terminology to be used in this work at the outset. Traditionally, the term 'Jura'

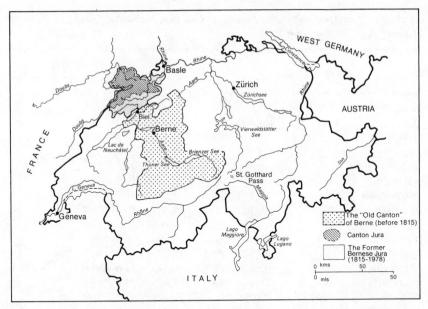

Fig. 2. The Geographical Location of the Bernese Jura in Relation to the Old Canton and the Rest of Switzerland.

has been used by geographers to describe that range of mountains which extends for approximately 245 kilometres (150 miles) in a south-westerly to north-easterly direction, from near Lyons in France through several Swiss cantons into the southern part of the Federal Republic of Germany. Specifically, within Switzerland, the Jura mountain range crosses Cantons Vaud, Neuchâtel, Berne, Solothurn, Baselland, the Aargau, and Schaffhausen. From the latter three Swiss cantons, the Jura range continues in a north-easterly direction into the Federal Republic of Germany where, beyond the Black Forest, it is known as the 'Swabian Jura' (Fig. 3). The words 'Jura' and 'Jura range' will be used in this traditional sense in this work.

The north-western region of Canton Berne, as it existed prior to 1979, consisted of seven districts. These districts were Courtelary, Delémont, Franches-Montagnes, Laufen, Moutier, La Neuveville, and Porrentruy (Fig. 4). All these districts were predominantly French-speaking except for Laufen, which was German-speaking. All seven districts were situated within the Jura range; for this reason the region was known, between 1815 and 1978, as the 'Bernese Jura'.

In 1974 a majority of voters in each of the three northern and western districts of the Bernese Jura voted to break away from Canton Berne to form Canton Jura, while a majority of voters in the remaining southern districts,[3] together with the Laufen district[4] in the north-east, voted to remain a part of Canton Berne. In effect, the latter region (i.e., the South Jura together with

Table 1. *Switzerland: Voting Patterns by Canton in National Referendum to Establish Canton Jura: 24 September 1978*

Canton	'Yes'	%	'No'	%	% qualified voters participating
Zurich	267,680	82·4	57,112	17·6	48·0
Berne	187,555	69·6	82,050	30·4	44·0
Lucerne	65,420	88·5	8,495	11·5	41·0
Uri	8,023	85·4	1,367	14·6	45·2
Schwyz	19,897	85·9	3,279	14·1	41·0
Obwalden	5,038	89·3	603	10·7	36·3
Nidwalden	6,446	86·5	1,005	13·5	42·3
Glarus	6,488	80·5	1,557	19·5	35·7
Zug	19,270	87·1	2,863	12·9	51·8
Fribourg	38,648	90·1	4,228	9·9	38·0
Solothurn	49,929	80·1	12,377	19·9	46·8
Basel-Stadt	42,697	86·0	6,976	14·0	35·6
Baselland	50,939	84·9	9,025	15·1	46·1
Schaffhausen	22,951	79·2	6,024	20·8	71·7
Appenzell Outer Rhodes	9,442	73·1	3,480	26·9	43·5
Appenzell Inner Rhodes	2,551	87·0	380	13·0	36·5
St Gallen	74,590	83·0	15,327	17·0	40·0
Graubünden	28,811	82·9	5,941	17·1	35·0
Aargau	79,475	80·2	19,566	19·8	38·0
Thurgau	41,059	81·1	9,546	18·9	49·0
Ticino	50,941	95·1	2,650	4·9	36·9
Vaud	94,660	88·6	12,193	11·4	35·0
Valais	41,254	91·9	3,643	8·1	34·3
Neuchâtel	35,098	84·7	6,343	15·3	42·7
Geneva	60,859	91·2	5,886	8·8	37·4
Total	1,309,722	82·3	281,917	17·7	41·5

Laufen) formed a 'new' Bernese Jura significantly reduced in area. In this work the terms 'North Jura' and 'South Jura' will be used to denote the two major French-speaking subregions of the former Bernese Jura, i.e., excluding the Laufen district.

The terms 'Bernese Jura' and 'former Bernese Jura' will refer to the seven-district region which was known by that name between 1815 and 1978 (Fig. 4). The term 'Canton Jura' will be used to describe the new canton, made up of the great majority of communes in the North Jura, together with a limited number from the South Jura, which came into existence in 1979. The term 'Jurassian' will be used to describe any inhabitant of the former Bernese Jura (i.e., of the North Jura, the South Jura or Laufen), who is a Swiss citizen. Finally, the term 'Old Canton' will be used to describe that part of Canton

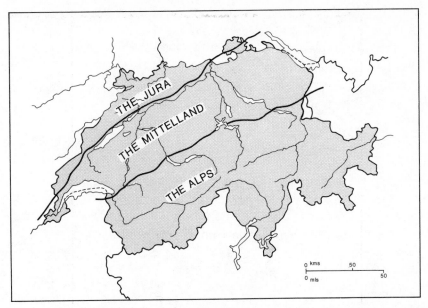

Fig. 3. The Major Physical Divisions of Switzerland.

Berne other than the Bernese Jura, i.e., the 'old part' of Canton Berne which existed prior to 1815, but excluding its pre-1815 subject territories of Vaud and the Aargau (Fig. 4).

The Phenomenon of Jura Separatism

The very existence of Jura separatism is puzzling to some observers for two reasons. Firstly, they are surprised that the phenomenon exists in Switzerland at all. Switzerland is not only regarded by many Swiss, and most non-Swiss, as a peaceful and tranquil state. It is also regarded as having been remarkably successful in maintaining a political structure (the Swiss Confederation) in which peoples of two major religious and four major language groups co-exist relatively harmoniously. A number of Swiss writers, including, among others, Feller (1965) and Fabre (1961) have stressed what they perceive to be the efficient working of the 'Swiss system'. An even greater number of non-Swiss observers, including Armattoe (1944), Gilliard (1955), Jordan (1973), and McRae (1983) have echoed these sentiments. Jordan, in fact, contrasts Switzerland with Belgium, to Switzerland's advantage.

In spite of the opinions of such writers as those listed, a growing number of other writers have, in recent years, expressed some doubt that the Swiss political system does, indeed, function very effectively. Certain Swiss, including Béguelin (1973) and Ziegler (1979), are bitterly critical of many aspects of Swiss government and Swiss life. Other Swiss and non-Swiss

Fig. 4. The Bernese Jura in Relation to Canton Berne as a Whole (1815–1978).

observers, including Mayer (1968), Deutsch (1969), Hughes (1975), Obler, Steiner, and Dierickx (1977), and McDonald (1978), while acknowledging the many achievements of the Swiss, cite the 'Jura problem' specifically as an exception to the rule, and caution the reader against assuming that it can be solved quickly and satisfactorily.

Secondly, certain other observers are intrigued because Jura separatism appears, to them, to be running counter to various efforts to unite Western Europe. These latter efforts have already met with a modest degree of success. The European Community (consisting of France, The Federal Republic of Germany, Italy, the Benelux countries, the United Kingdom, Ireland, Denmark, and Greece) has, at the time of writing (1985), successfully concluded negotiations to bring Spain and Portugal into its ranks in January 1986. Moreover, the Community's parliament, elected on the basis of popular suffrage within its member states, seems likely to strengthen the bonds between the latter.

The 'Minority Problem' in Europe

However, in spite of such developments, and in contrast to them, Europe is still beset with problems which involve such factors as language, religion, and perceived inequitable economic treatment. As McDonald (op. cit.) has put it:

Europe is . . . witnessing a remarkable revival of regionalism. Within the regions or local districts of nearly every country, pressures are mounting for greater recognition of cultural uniqueness, demands for redress of economic injustices are increasingly strident, and calls for various forms of regional autonomy—ranging from independence to more effective regional parliaments—are punctuated by widely publicised debates, demonstrations, and occasional acts of violence.

The years since the end of World War II have, indeed, witnessed an increasing degree of political unrest among the so-called 'minority nations' of Western Europe; peoples such as the Basques, Catalans, Scots, Welsh, and Corsicans. As McDonald (op. cit.) has suggested, this political unrest has often been related to a concern for the survival of the particular languages and cultures of the peoples in question, but with economic considerations also being of considerable importance as a rule. Esman (1977) has suggested that separatist feelings existed in the early post-World War II years but were quiescent because, presumably, more pressing concerns occupied the attention of the peoples of the regions in question.

The word 'minority', used in this connection, can sometimes be misleading in that the peoples in question may constitute a *majority* of the inhabitants of their particular region. (Thus, to quote one example, the Catalans form a majority of the population of Catalonia. In this example, however, the minority nation involved lives within a larger political unit i.e., the Catalans live within the Spanish State). In certain other areas, however, the original inhabitants of a region may, indeed, have been reduced to the status of a minority in regions to which they feel they have a historic right (e.g. Breton-speakers in Brittany), thus adding to their sense of grievance.

Further Terminology

The title of this work is 'Jura Separatism in Switzerland'. The word 'separatism' was, however, selected by the writer only after careful consideration of a number of factors. To begin with, there is no doubt that the words 'separatist' and 'separatism' are in common use, and that, for example, those who have been active in Catalan-oriented political activity in Catalonia have usually been referred to as 'separatists'. Moreover, there is no doubt that in each of the regions in question there are some so-called 'extremists'—individuals who desire to break away, or 'separate' completely from—the larger political unit of which they form a part (for example, Switzerland, Spain,

France, or the United Kingdom), and establish new, completely independent states.

On the other hand, it would appear, at the time of writing, that the majority of political activists in each of the regions in question merely seek to obtain a greater degree of autonomy for their particular region *within* the larger political unit. These individuals do not consider themselves to be separatists but federalists, believing that the larger political unit (Switzerland, Spain, France, or the United Kingdom) will be strengthened, not weakened, if their region is granted a greater degree of control over its own affairs. Moreover, in the writer's discussions with a number of Europeans who favour a greater degree of autonomy for their respective regions, most of these individuals made it clear that they disliked the term 'separatists' and 'separatism' because the words, for example, in each of their French, German, and English versions were often used in a negative, derogatory sense by their political opponents.

For these reasons the writer gave serious consideration to the use of the less emotionally-charged words 'autonomist' or 'devolutionist' (and 'autonomy' or 'devolution') in this work. However, it was finally decided to use the words 'separatist' and 'separatism' in discussing the political situation in the Bernese Jura for two reasons. Firstly, the words 'separatist' and 'separatism' enjoy widespread usage in the English, French, and German languages, and are readily understood. By contrast, the English words 'devolutionist' and 'devolution' (together with their French equivalents) tend to be applied primarily to political events in the United Kingdom. Secondly, within the specific context of the Bernese Jura, the word 'separatist' has, in recent years, been applied to those who have advocated, as a minimum concession, the 'rearrangement' of the political map of Switzerland through the establishment of a new Swiss canton in the Bernese Jura. The word 'autonomist', on the other hand, has been applied to those who have, on various occasions in recent years, merely proposed that the peoples of the Bernese Jura obtain varying degrees of autonomy *within* the boundaries of Canton Berne as they existed until 1979. Because of the greater relative strength of the separatist cause (as opposed to the autonomist cause) the writer believed that a study of Jurassian separatism would produce more fruitful results.

It must be emphasized, however, that the decision to use the terms 'separatist' and 'separatism' in this work should not, in any way, be interpreted in a negative sense. The writer simply recognizes that there has existed, and still exists, in the former Bernese Jura region of Switzerland a phenomenon which is most commonly referred to as 'Jura' (or 'Jurassian') separatism and seeks, as a politically unbiased, neutral observer to determine, in this work, why the phenomenon exists.

Centralism vs. Regional Self-government

Central government attitudes toward the aspirations of regional politicians have varied greatly. In Canada, for example, the various provinces, including the predominantly French-speaking, predominantly Catholic province of Quebec, were given their own legislative assemblies and a remarkable degree of control over their own affairs as early as 1867. Quebec, moreover, unlike the other Canadian provinces, was also allowed to conduct its affairs in the French language. Moreover, the Catholic Church was recognized, by the British government, as playing a significant role in the social life of the province, and its rights were protected. The French Civil Code of Law was also retained in Quebec. In recent years, moreover, the Quebec provincial government has passed legislation which has greatly increased the use of the French language—at the expense of the English—in the province.[5]

In Europe itself, the nineteenth century gave birth to a number of nationalist movements, most of which were related to linguistic and/or religious concerns. Hungary, for example, won a substantial amount of autonomy from the Austrian Empire with the establishment of the 'dual monarchy' in 1867. The Bernese Jura itself was, as we shall discuss later in this work, the scene of political unrest on a number of occasions between 1815 and the end of the nineteenth century. In the early twentieth century a number of new (or reborn) nation-states whose *raison d'être* was primarily linguistic (e.g., Czechoslovakia and Yugoslavia) were created at the end of World War I.

In more recent years, too, growing separatist feeling has begun to result in political change. In Spain, the central government has granted a degree of self-government to a number of regions, including Catalonia and the Basque Provinces. In the United Kingdom, the results of a referendum in March 1979 (in which a narrow majority of those voting in Scotland—but not an absolute majority of those *eligible* to vote—supported Scottish devolution, and a majority of those voting in Wales opposed it) have, at least temporarily, delayed the granting of any further degree of self-government in these countries. In Canada, in May 1980, the Quebec provincial government sought the voter's permission to open negotiations between Quebec and the Canadian federal government to obtain 'sovereignty-association' (i.e., political independence together with economic association). The proposal was defeated by a 60:40 margin. In none of these regions, however, is the phenomenon of separatism likely to disappear in the near future.[6]

It appears, in fact, that attempts to resolve the issues posed by separatism are only rarely successful. Such attempts often result, it would seem, in measures which please neither of the parties involved in the dispute. Many separatist-inclined groups (such as ETA in the Basque provinces of Spain) feel that any proposed changes are not sweeping enough, whereas many inhabitants of the larger political unit believe that too much autonomy has already been granted. Dissatisfaction may also arise from the delimitation of new boundaries, since many separatists feel that their new political unit should include certain other, adjacent territories which are rightfully 'theirs'. Both Ireland and the former Bernese Jura are examples of the latter situation.

The phenomenon of separatism, then, results in political problems which are, at best, difficult to solve. It is the writer's belief that any contribution to a greater understanding of the phenomenon of separatism may be of some value, since it is necessary to understand a phenomenon itself before the problems caused by it can be dealt with effectively.

Separatism in the Bernese Jura

The phenomenon of separatism in the former Bernese Jura (as opposed to separatism in some other regions of the world), is of interest for several reasons. To begin with, we have already seen that Switzerland is highly regarded by many other countries as a model of political stability. The Swiss Confederation, by its very nature as an association of semi-autonomous states (cantons) which jealously guard their individual rights, has, it would seem, recognized the differing needs of differing communities. It can be argued that if even a 'model democracy' such as Switzerland faces separatist problems, it is highly desirable that these problems be studied. As suggested above, if the factors causing separatism in Switzerland—and the efforts made by the Swiss to deal with separatism—can be better understood, it may be easier for other governments to deal more effectively with separatism in their respective countries.

Secondly, a search of the literature suggests that Jura separatism, as a specific topic, has been examined previously, in detail, by only a limited number of scholars. This may be because Switzerland is a small and, perhaps to some observers, rather uninteresting country. The relative lack of literature on the subject of separatism in the Bernese Jura may also be due to the fact that the phenomenon, in its present form, dates only from 1947.

Thirdly, observers of the Jura separatist phenomenon who have written on the subject have usually touched upon it in the course of a wider discussion of Switzerland as a whole, and have tended, with a few exceptions, to confine their remarks to a few paragraphs or pages.

Fourthly, the majority of those observers and/or writers who have discussed Jura separatism in some detail (either directly or indirectly) have been historians, political scientists, or sociologists. The latter include, among others, historians such as Amweg (1974), Ruffieux and Prongué (1972), Prongué (1972, 1973, 1974, 1975, 1976, 1978), and Bessire (1977). Political scientists include Hughes (1954, 1962, 1975) and McRae (1964, 1982). Sociologists include Mayer (1951, 1952, 1968), Henecka (1974a), and Bassand and Fragnière (1976). The writers listed have naturally examined the phenomenon of Jura separatism from the viewpoints of their respective disciplines. In this study, by contrast, the writer sought to ascertain the degree to which *geographical factors* might be related to the phenomenon of Jura separatism. If such relationships did, indeed, exist, the writer sought to determine their precise nature.

The Geographical Significance of the Bernese Jura

The Bernese Jura (as it existed up until 1978) is of geographical interest for several reasons. To begin with, an observer cannot fail but be struck by the region's peripheral position in the extreme north-west of Switzerland, on the French border (Fig. 2). Because of this peripheral geographical location, the Bernese Jura lies some distance from the most densely populated region of Switzerland, the gently undulating *Mittelland* (Middle-Land) or Swiss plateau, which extends from Geneva in the south-west to Lake Constance in the north-east. The Bernese Jura lies even further from the third major physical region of Switzerland, the Alps (Fig. 3). It is the Mittelland which has occupied centre stage in the history of the Swiss Confederation. By contrast (and as will be outlined subsequently in this work), the Bernese Jura has played a relatively minor role in Swiss history.

The Topography and Physical Appearance of the Region

Secondly, because the greater part of the Bernese Jura is occupied by a portion of the Jura mountain range, much of the region has a somewhat unusual physical appearance. It is because the Jura range differs so much from other areas of Switzerland that, together with the Mittelland and the Alps, it has been classified as one of the three major physical divisions of the country.

If an observer were to fly over the greater part of the Bernese Jura, moving from the north-east to the south-west (or vice versa) along the ridges of the Jura chain, he or she would see longitudinal cultivated valleys dotted with occasional villages and small towns. An observer would also see dark green wooded slopes, with occasional limestone escarpments and some open pastureland at higher altitudes. In places, the longitudinal south-west–north-east ridges have been cut through by rivers flowing in a generally north–south direction. These rivers flow through gorges flanked by spectacular limestone crags. In the upland plateau, country typical of much of the district of Franches-Montagnes in the western Bernese Jura, settlements are often found on higher ground.

From the Mittelland, looking northwards from the Berne–Biel *autoroute* (motorway), the Jura mountain chain rises sharply above the Swiss plateau. It is densely forested; coniferous woods extend all the way to the skyline, and few upland settlements are visible from the Mittelland. The Jura chain's precipitous crags and dark green natural vegetation give it a rather remote, forbidding appearance to the inhabitant of the Swiss plateau. To the latter, the Jura range seems to be a different world to the Mittleland, with a different way of life.[7]

An observer studying a communications map of Switzerland is also likely to be struck by the limited number of internal road and rail routes in the Bernese Jura, when compared to the relatively dense system of communications which

exists in the Mittelland. This topic will be discussed in more detail subsequently, but it is difficult not to conclude, tentatively, that it is associated
both with the difficult topography of much of the Bernese Jura and its
peripheral location in the Swiss state.

It is further suggested that the Bernese Jura is of interest because it differs
linguistically from the greater portion of the population of the adjacent Mittelland. The region is predominantly French-speaking and, in much of its area,
forms in fact a mountainous, eastward-pointing, French-speaking 'promontory' surrounded on three sides by German-speaking peoples. The latter
consist, in turn, of German-speakers in the Alsatian Sundgau[8] to the north of
the Bernese Jura, German-speakers in the Laufen district, in the half-canton of
Baselland and in Canton Solothurn to the east, and German-speakers in the
Old Canton of Berne, to the south (Fig. 5).

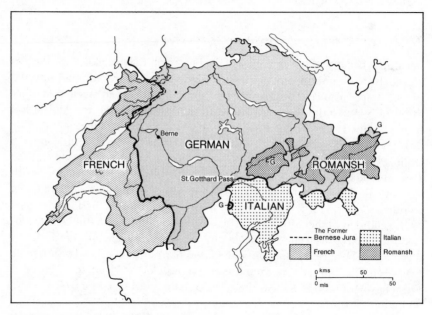

Fig. 5. Linguistic Map of Switzerland, 1980.

This topic, too, will be discussed in more detail subsequently. However,
once again, it is difficult for the observer to avoid noting that there appears to
be a striking similarity between the topographical and linguistic maps of this
part of Switzerland in that to the west of the Laufen district, in the extreme
north-east of the Bernese Jura, the 'high ground' is largely French-speaking
while the 'low ground' is German-speaking. Germanic peoples were apparently only able to settle the Jura range itself as far west as the Laufen district.

Finally, the Bernese Jura is of interest because it has been—and still is—politically unstable. The degree of this instability makes it, in fact, unique in Switzerland. In Swiss cantons, as Fig. 6 indicates, boundaries between linguistic regions (for example, between German-speaking areas and French-speaking areas) do not coincide, as a general rule, with boundaries between religious regions (i.e., areas in which Protestantism or Catholicism is the religion of the majority of the inhabitants).

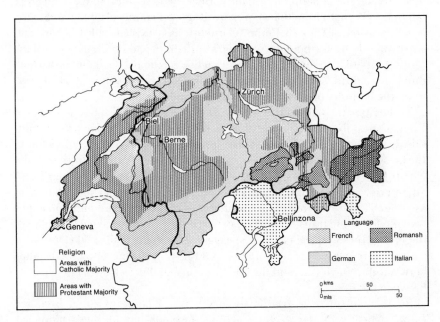

Fig. 6. Switzerland: A Comparison of Languages and Religions, 1980.

On the contrary, the observer of the Swiss scene almost invariably finds that, in cantons in which there are distinct French-speaking and German-speaking regions (such as Canton Fribourg or Canton Valais), both groups of people are of the same religious persuasion (i.e., Catholic in the two cantons mentioned). They may also share certain other characteristics, such as a rural (as opposed to an urban) economy, which increase the interests each has in common with the other. This serves to reduce the number of points of tension between them.

Similarly, when two groups of people of different religions live in adjacent areas within the same Swiss canton (such as is the case, for example, with Protestants and Catholics in the Aargau), they share a common language, i.e., German in the example cited. Weigandt (1979) expresses the situation prevailing in most areas of Switzerland thus: 'Antagonisms, rather than being compounded, cross-cut each other.' Henecka (op. cit.) refers to these cross-cutting antagonisms as *Zick-Zack Loyalitäten* (zig-zag loyalties).

With the exception of certain areas of Canton Graubünden (French: Grisons) the canton of Berne is unique, however, in that it is, today, the only Swiss canton within whose boundaries conflicting loyalties of language and religion exist. Moreover, in Graubünden the linguistic tensions which *do* exist have not, as yet, caused serious political problems. In Canton Berne, however, they have. As will be explained more fully in the chapters which follow, a majority of the inhabitants of the former Bernese Jura speak a different language (French) from that spoken by the great majority of inhabitants of the larger portion of Canton Berne (German), as it existed both prior to, and subsequently to, the boundary changes of 1979. In addition, a majority of the inhabitants of the North Jura also practise a religion (Catholicism) which differs in doctrine, practice and tradition from the Protestant religion adhered to by the majority of the population of Canton Berne.

To complicate matters still further, the South Jura, which lies between the French-speaking, Catholic, North Jura and the German-speaking, Protestant, Old Canton (and whose communes largely elected to remain with Canton Berne at the time of the 1974 referendum), shares its French culture with the North Jura but shares its Protestant tradition with Berne. It thus constitutes an intermediate cultural zone. It might appear logical, at first glance, to assume that the existence of such an intermediate zone as the South Jura might provide for a safe transition region between the French-speaking Catholics of the North Jura and the German-speaking Protestants of the Old Canton—a transition region whose inhabitants could help in the mediation of disputes between the North Jura and the Old Canton, and thus help to defuse tensions between them.

Such, unfortunately, has not been the case. The new Canton Jura (the former North Jura) has sought to acquire the South Jura; the Old Canton has sought to retain it and a majority of the peoples of the South Jura presently (1985) wish to remain a part of Canton Berne. This, in fact, appears to have been the position of the majority of South Jurassians throughout recent history, except on those occasions when linguistic concerns have been foremost. At such times the allegiance of many South Jurassians has been given to the Bernese Jura rather than to Canton Berne. Such occasions, however, have been relatively rare.

As mentioned at the beginning of this chapter, it is the primary aim of this work to identify geographical factors which may have resulted in the appearance of the phenomenon of separatism, prior to 1978, in the Bernese Jura. This task will be undertaken in the chapters which follow.

Notes

1. After careful consideration, the author has decided to use those spellings of Swiss towns and cities which are most familiar to the English-speaking reader. For this reason, the spelling 'Berne', is used rather than the German-Swiss 'Bern', and 'Basle' rather than the German-Swiss 'Basel'.

2. It should be noted that two already existing Swiss cantons (Basle and Unterwalden) each

divided themselves into two half-cantons during the nineteenth century, and remain as half-cantons to the present day. These changes did not *add* a new canton to the Swiss Confederation as did the creation of Canton Jura, however.

3. As will be discussed later, the boundaries of some of these districts have been adjusted since Canton Jura came into existence.

4. Laufen can be considered distinct from both the North and South Jura subregions, for reasons to be explained subsequently.

5. Some of this legislation, however, was ruled illegal by the Supreme Court of Canada in 1984.

6. In Quebec, in fact, close to 50 per cent of the purely French-speaking population voted in favour of opening negotiations on sovereignty-association with the federal government in Ottawa.

7. It should be emphasized, however, that the appearance of a considerable part of the extreme north-western Ajoie area of the Bernese Jura, which protrudes into France around the town of Porrentruy and forms a part of the district of Porrentruy, differs significantly from that of the remainder of the region. This 'Table Jura' area, by contrast, is gently undulating and relatively low-lying (see Chapter 2).

8. While the French language is used increasingly in Alsace today as a result of French government policy, the traditional speech of Alsace is a Germanic dialect which is still in relatively widespread use.

2

The Physical and Human Geography of the Bernese Jura

> The physical environment . . . like the wicket in cricket . . . has some
> bearing on the course of the game.
>
> GORDON EAST (1948)

Any attempt to analyse the phenomenon of separatism in the former Bernese
Jura can only be facilitated by an examination of the physical and human
geography of the region.

The Physical Geography of the Region

The reader was reminded in Chapter 1 that modern Switzerland consists of
three physical regions,[1] namely the Jura mountain range of the north-west
(which includes the region of the Bernese Jura), the plateau region or Mittelland of the centre, and the Alps of the south and south-east (Fig. 3). The
Alpine massif, almost invariably, seems to be the region of which visitors tend
to think first when Switzerland is mentioned, since it is the scenery of the Alps
which first attracted tourists to Switzerland from other countries, and which
continues to attract the majority of foreign visitors to Switzerland. Nevertheless, the more densely populated Mittelland has played a greater role in Swiss
political and economic life, since the Middle Ages, than have either the Jura or
Alpine regions.

Geology

The geology and physical features of the Jura[2] mountain range have been
discussed in detail by a number of writers, including Früh (1932), Gutersohn
(1958), and Monkhouse (1974), Rees (1974), and Monbaron (1974). Because
the geology of the Jura range has been a major determinant of the physical
geography of the Bernese Jura, it is necessary to discuss the former briefly.

The Jura range itself is of Mesozoic origin, and consists primarily of Jurassic
rocks. Because the limestone formations of the region have so impressed
visitors during the past two centuries or so, the term 'Jurassic' has passed into
standard geological usage. That section of the Jura chain which consists of
severely folded Jurassic formations, and which accounts for the greater part of
the Swiss (including the former Bernese) Jura region is known as the 'Folded
Jura' (le Jura plissé in French, and the Faltenjura in German). The most extreme
folding is to be found in Switzerland, along the inner edge of the Folded Jura
and especially in the former Bernese Jura (Fig. 7).

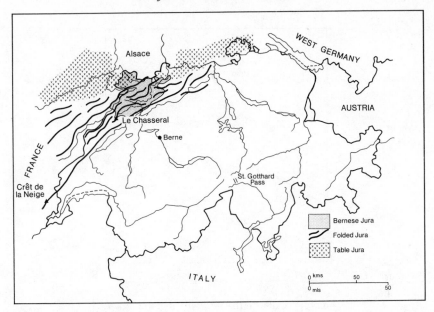

Fig. 7. The Jura Range in Relation to the Bernese Jura and European Frontiers.

To the west and north-west of the Folded Jura lies a distinctive plateau area of Jurassic rocks which have been divided into a number of blocks by fault-lines. This region is known as the 'Plateau Jura' or 'Table Jura' (*le Jura tabulaire* in French, and the *Tafeljura* in German). The Table Jura forms the greater part of the French Jura region, but also includes the Ajoie region of the Bernese Jura, which protrudes into France around the town of Porrentruy (Fig. 7).

The strata which were subsequently folded to become the Jura mountain range are separated by the Mittelland (Fig. 3) from that region which experienced more severe (though related) earth movements, and which became the Alps. Following the folding which took place in west-central Europe during the Alpine period and which, in addition to the Alps, also produced the Jura range, a long period of erosion occurred. There were, of course, variations in the extent of the denudation from area to area, but geologists estimate that the Jura mountains are now less than half their original height. Erosion completely removed the Tertiary and Cretaceous sediments in many areas, and consequently, the greater part of the surface of the present-day Jura region consists of Jurassic deposits. Among the latter, limestones are the most prominent. Rees (op. cit.) cites the landscape of the commune of Sonvilier (Figs. 8 and 9) which lies in the St-Imier Valley (vallon de St-Imier) in the southern Bernese Jura district of Courtelary, as being fairly representative of Jura geology.

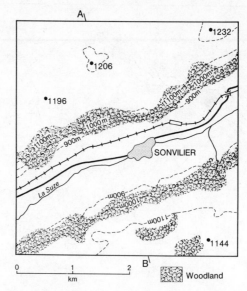

Fig. 8. A Valley in the Jura (adapted from Rees).

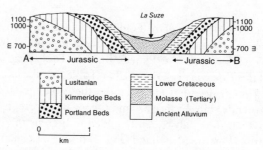

Fig. 9. A Geological Section Across a Jura Valley (adapted from Rees).

Climate

The climate of the Bernese Jura warrants a brief comment because, in combination with the geology of the Jura mountain range, it has interacted with the
Jura's topography to produce the somewhat unusual drainage system of the
region. The Jura range, which is exposed to rain-bearing south-westerly
winds, receives a substantial annual rainfall. The highest peaks receive a mean
precipitation of close to 2,000 millimetres (70 inches). Even the valleys of the
Jura receive an annual rainfall which is substantially greater than that of the
more populated areas of the Mittelland.

Winters in the Jura range are long and quite severe compared to most areas of the Mittelland, especially in the western areas along the French frontier. The topography of the region is such that, during the winter months, the cold northerly *bise* wind sweeps down many of its valleys, while the Jura's ridges exclude the warm, southerly *Föhn* wind. A number of observers have commented unfavourably on the climate of the Jura, including Hughes (1975), who, referring particularly to the Jurassian winters, has described the region as 'climatically the most disagreeable inhabited part of Switzerland'.[3] Summers in the Jura range are sunny and relatively pleasant, however, with cooler temperatures than those prevailing in the Mittelland.

Topography and Drainage

The topography and drainage of the Bernese Jura deserve our attention because, historically, they have made communications, both between the region and the Swiss Mittelland, and between different areas within the region, difficult.

At its widest, in Canton Vaud, in Canton Neuchâtel, north of Lake Neuchâtel, and in the Bernese Jura, north of the Bielersee (French: lac de Bienne), the Jura range consists of five or six parallel anticlinal ridges running in the generally south-westerly to north-easterly direction already noted (Fig. 10). Compared to the Alps, the peaks of the Jura chain are of modest height. The

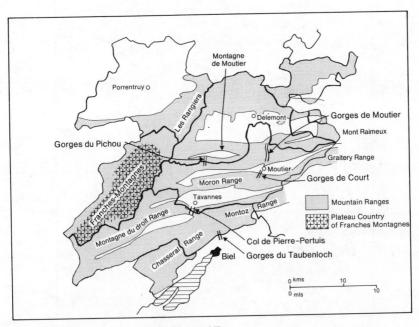

Fig. 10. The Bernese Jura: Major Physical Features.

highest point of the Jura, the Crêt de la Neige (1,718 metres or 5,653 feet) lies in France; the highest peak in Switzerland is Le Chasseral (1,607 metres or 5,287 feet) (Fig. 7).

Rees (op. cit.) in discussing the Jura range, has emphasized that there is usually a 'simple relationship between structure and relief'. In the Folded Jura, in most cases, the anticlines (outer folds) still correspond to the ridges (French: *monts*), and the synclines (inner folds) form the valleys (French, singular: *val, vallée,* or *vallon;* plural: *vaux*). Longitudinal sections of rivers, for the most part, follow these synclinal valleys.[4] Streams (French: *ruzes*) which flow down the sides of the anticlines into the longitudinal valleys of the Jura have, in some areas, cut back into an anticline to form a high-altitude depression or *combe*. These combes are surrounded on three sides by scarps or *crêts,* which frequently form sheer limestone cliffs, called *corniches calcaires*.

The above remarks do not apply to the whole of the Bernese Jura. We earlier noted that the relatively undulating Table Jura country of the Ajoie district, around Porrentruy, in the extreme north-west of the Jura, is in sharp contrast to the rest of the region. Within the Jura range itself, the relatively wide and relatively flat basin of the Sorne, Birse, and Scheulte rivers to the south-west, south and south-east of the town of Delémont also contrasts with the narrow longitudinal ridges and occasional gorges of the region as a whole (Fig. 10).

Fig. 11. Major Drainage Systems of the Bernese Jura.

Because of its relatively high rainfall, the Jura mountain range appears, at first glance, to be more favoured by nature than are certain other limestone regions of Europe. While this is true to some degree, water supply is unquestionably a problem in a number of areas within the Jura chain, and the local architecture reflects this.[5] As is typical of many limestone regions, rivers and streams often suddenly appear on the surface, flow for some distance and then, just as suddenly, disappear again.

In the north-west and west of the Bernese Jura, the rivers and streams flow into the Doubs, and thence into the Rhône and the Mediterranean. Within the Bernese Jura itself two major river systems, that of the Birse (German: Birs) and Suze dominate the drainage pattern of the region. The Birse, rising in the south-central part of the region, flows in a generally northerly and north-easterly direction to join the Rhine near Basle. In sharp contrast, the Suze rises in the extreme south-west of the Bernese Jura, near the border of Canton Neuchâtel, and flows in an easterly direction for many miles until it turns southward to join the Bielersee and, subsequently, the Aare and the Rhine (Fig. 11).

For the most part, these rivers and their tributaries flow along the longitudinal, south-westerly to north-easterly synclinal valleys discussed earlier.[6] However, on occasions, the rivers of the Folded Jura range, both in the Bernese Jura and in neighbouring regions, change direction and cut across nearby anticlines, forming transverse valleys known as *cluses*. These rivers existed before the anticline was formed by folding, and continued to flow (and erode) as the anticlinal uplift proceeded. Many *cluses* consist of narrow, tortuous gorges walled in by precipitous limestone cliffs (Plate 1).

Because of the existence of the *cluse* phenomenon, the drainage of the Jura range (including the region of the Bernese Jura) provides a study in contrasts. A river which has been flowing placidly in a longitudinal valley suddenly enters a steep, winding gorge, often changing its direction dramatically at the same time. For example, the Sorne suddenly swings northwards and flows through the gorges du Pichou, and the Birse also turns northwards to flow, firstly through the gorges de Court and, subsequently, through the gorges de Moutier (Figs. 1, 2, and 3). Such gorges are few and far between, however and, as indicated earlier, this meant that communications *within* the Bernese Jura were particularly difficult in past times.

A third element of the topography and drainage of the Jura chain in general is its south-western to north-eastern alignment. This means that the ridges of the Jura lie, dramatically, at right-angles to travellers approaching the Bernese Jura from Berne (Fig. 7). Moreover, because most Jurassian rivers flow parallel to the mountain ridges, a traveller—or an army—could only enter the Bernese Jura via one of the few *cluses* which cut across these ridges, or across the Pass (French: *col*) of Pierre-Pertuis, to which reference will be made later in this chapter. We shall also need to take this 'difficulty of entry' factor into account in our study.

In summary, it is suggested that, in geographical terms, the Bernese Jura differs fundamentally from the Mittelland and Alps (in which regions the Old Canton of Berne is located), in its geology, in its climate, in its topography and drainage, and in the south-westerly to north-easterly alignment of its ridges. This has had a profound influence on the history of the region.

The Human Geography of the Region

Amweg (1928), Bessire (op. cit.), and a number of others have written extensively on the history of human settlement in the Bernese Jura. A great deal of the background material in the sections which follow is based upon the writings of these authorities. The geographical conclusions drawn are those of the author, however.

Early Settlement

Amweg suggests, on the basis of archaeological evidence, that the Bernese Jura was inhabited by hunters prior to around 4000 BC, and by agriculturalists after that date. Celtic-speaking peoples appear to have occupied both the Bernese Jura and the Swiss plateau from the fifth and fourth centuries BC onwards. They consisted of three tribes; the Helvetii, the Rauraci, and the Sequani. It is interesting to note that, according to Amweg (op. cit.) and others, the settlement boundaries between these Celtic tribes coincided with distinct geographical features. The Helvetii, from whom the Latin *Helvetia* ('Switzerland') derives, appear to have occupied the greater part of the Mittelland, together with that area of the present-day Bernese Jura which lies to the south of the Montagne du Droit and Montoz ridges (Fig. 10) and includes the valley of the Suze river, which eventually flows into the Rhine. The Rauraci appear to have occupied the drainage basin of the Birse which, as we have seen, is also part of the Rhine drainage system, and its tributaries in addition to areas to the east (Fig. 11).

The western areas of the future Bernese Jura were occupied, it would seem, by the Sequani, whose territory included the Ajoie around Porrentruy, the valley of the Doubs river and its tributaries, in addition to an adjoining area of France. All of these areas are a part of the Rhône drainage basin (Fig. 11).

In summary, the east–west mountain ridges of the Bernese Jura which, as we have seen, separate various drainage areas, seem to have been major factors in the settlement patterns of the three distinct (and, at times, mutually hostile) Celtic tribes of the area as early as the fifth century BC.

Settlement During the Roman Period

Present-day Switzerland was a march, or border country for an extensive period of time during the life of the Roman Empire, with the Rhine forming the boundary of the Empire from about AD 100–250. It would appear that the Romans, making use of existing Celtic and pre-Celtic trails in some instances, first developed the formal road network which exists in the Bernese Jura today. This includes the roads which follow the longitudinal river valleys in which early settlements appear to have been concentrated, and which traverse such north–south *cluses* as the gorges de Moutier and the gorges de Court to connect neighbouring valleys. These early communication routes are significant because they helped to determine the basic pattern of human settlement in the Bernese Jura.

Accomplished engineers and road-builders though the Romans were, they must have found the physical geography of the region a formidable barrier to communications, both within the Bernese Jura itself and between the Bernese Jura and other areas. One of the most significant geographical barriers in the region—and one not traversed by a cluse was—and is, to this day, the massive range of Montoz, running in an approximately east–west direction and separating the upper Birse Valley (la vallée de Tavannes in the present-day Bernese Jura district of Moutier) in the central Jura from the Suze Valley (le vallon de St-Imier in the present-day district of Courtelary) in the south (Fig. 10). The Romans opened up a tortuous, winding route between these two valleys by piercing a huge rock which blocked their way near the summit of the pass. The route has been known ever since as 'le col de Pierre-Pertuis' (which is usually translated as 'The Pass of the Pierced Stone') near the present-day town of Tavannes (Fig. 10).

The Post-Roman Period

Following the end of the Roman period (by which time the Celtic peoples of the Bernese Jura appear to have become Latinized in speech), the greater part of the present-day Bernese Jura formed, at various times, a part of the First Kingdom of Burgundy (AD 407–534), the Empire of the Franks (AD 534–888), and the Second Kingdom of Burgundy (AD 888–1032). During the Frankish period, Christian missionaries were active in the region. Saint Ursanne established a convent and a church in the valley of the Doubs and Saint Imier settled in the Suze Valley (le vallon de St-Imier). Saint Germain established the great monastery of Moutier-Grandval (near the present-day town of Moutier) around AD 640. The settlements of St-Ursanne, St-Imier, and Moutier gradually developed around these religious establishments. Small communities also began to grow up around other religious centres established in the region.

The Early Days of the Bishopric

In AD 999, the then reigning bishop of Basle (whose ecclesiastical seat, at Basle (German: Basel), was situated nearer to the North Jura than was any

Mittelland town or city) was recognized as enjoying some feudal privileges in certain areas of the future Bernese Jura, under the suzerainty of the kings of Burgundy. The area nominally subject to successive prince-bishops' authority gradually grew until, by the beginning of the fourteenth century, it extended from the Porrentruy area in the north to La Neuveville on the Bielersee (French: lac de Bienne) in the south. Thus, in AD 999, began a relationship between the prince-bishops of Basle and the people of the Bernese Jura which lasted for almost 800 years.

It should be emphasized, however, that during the centuries which followed, *l'evêché de Bâle* (the bishopric of Basle), over which the bishop was feudal ruler (or prince) comprised merely a part of the much larger *diocèse de Bâle* (diocese of Basle), of which the bishop was spiritual leader.

In AD 1032 the bishopric of Basle became associated with the Holy Roman (i.e., German) Empire. Henceforth the prince-bishops paid allegiance to the German emperors rather than to the kings of Burgundy. During the succeeding centuries, while Basle (situated as it is at the bend of the Rhine) and certain towns of the predominantly German-speaking Mittelland, such as Zurich and St Gallen, became important industrial and trading centres, Amweg (op. cit.), Bessire (op. cit.), and other historians suggest that the bishopric of Basle (the future Bernese Jura)—a mountainous area situated some distance from the main trade routes of this part of central Europe—was influenced by the outside world to only a very limited extent.

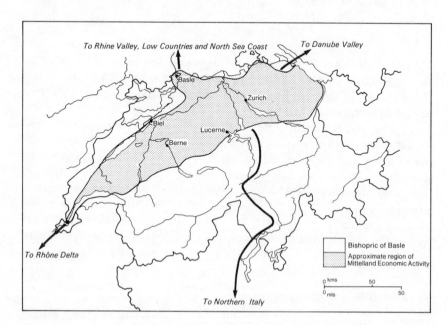

Fig. 12. Switzerland: Major Medieval Trade Routes.

All indications are, in fact, that the topography and geographic location of the bishopric discouraged the establishment of significant north–south trade routes through the region. Easier routes connecting the more thickly populated Mittelland to other populous regions of Europe lay to the north-east, via the Basle area (Alsace, the Rhine Valley, and the Belfort Gap), and to the south-west, via Lake Geneva and the Rhône Valley to the Mediterranean (Fig. 12).

Settlement Between 1528 and 1815

It must be emphasized that the suzerainty enjoyed by successive bishops of Basle was only nominal in certain areas of the bishopric, such as the *seigneurie* of Erguel in the south and the *prévôté* (prefecture) of Moutier in the central region.

In 1528 the Reformation in the city of Basle forced the incumbent bishop of Basle (whom, as we have seen, was also nominal 'prince' or secular ruler of the bishopric) to flee the city permanently. The prince-bishop moved with his court to Porrentruy, in the extreme north-west of the bishopric. As a result of this development, the population of the town of Porrentruy grew substantially. Not only did the prince-bishop's civil administrators and their families accompany their ruler to Porrentruy, but a number of artisans and tradespeople also moved there from Basle.

Other existing settlements in the bishopric of Basle (namely, St-Ursanne, Moutier-Grandval, and St-Imier) grew slowly in size as the overall population of the region grew during the period from 1527 to 1815. Place-name evidence suggests that additional settlements were established in the region from time to time to exploit natural resources such as trees for charcoal, or minerals of various kinds. Many of these settlements were established by immigrants from other areas—usually German-speaking regions to the east.[7] Such settlements were often short-lived, however, since the resources being exploited by the new settlers were usually limited.

A major socio-economic development occurred in the bishopric in the eighteenth century—a development which had a permanent effect on the settlement geography of the region. This development was the establishment of the watch-making industry,[8] which spread from Neuchâtel and Geneva to many communities in the Jura range. It caused a number of settlements in the bishopric (including Porrentruy, Moutier, and St-Imier) to grow substantially in size.[9]

Settlement from 1815 to the Present Day

The reigning prince-bishop of Basle was deposed in 1792 by the French authorities, who had previously occupied the region. In 1815, following the Congress of Vienna, the end of the rule of the prince-bishops was officially confirmed by the cession of the greater portion of the bishopric (with very

minor frontier adjustments along the French border in the Ajoie) to a somewhat unenthusiastic Canton Berne,[10] as compensation for the latter's loss of
Vaud and the Aargau; the latter becoming new Swiss cantons.

The years following the cession of the 'Jura territory' to Canton Berne in
1815 witnessed great changes in the human geography of what was henceforth
known as the 'Bernese Jura'. For what appears to have been the first time in
the recorded history of the region, substantial numbers of people from other
regions of Switzerland began to settle there.

Certain rural areas of the original Canton of Berne (the Old Canton), such
as the Emmental, had a very high birthrate, resulting in severe pressure on the
limited amount of agricultural land. This, in turn, led to heavy emigration. In
earlier times, such emigrants from rural areas settled in larger Swiss towns and
cities both in Canton Berne and in other parts of the Mittelland, or emigrated
abroad. After 1815, however, because the former bishopric of Basle now
belonged to Canton Berne, increasing numbers of Bernese from the Old
Canton began to settle in the region. This Bernese immigration to the Bernese
Jura became increasingly heavy in the years after 1860. The new settlers found
themselves in a region which, because of the geographical characteristics
discussed earlier, differed significantly from their home districts in the Old
Canton both in physical features and language. In the northern districts of the
Bernese Jura, moreover, a different religion (Catholicism) was practised.

Several parallel movements of population took place within the Bernese
Jura, and each will be described separately.

The Entrepreneurial Invasion. There was, firstly, an 'entrepreneurial' invasion of
the Bernese Jura. The watch-making skills which the inhabitants of the region
had developed during the eighteenth century were found to be similar to the
skills required by workers in light precision engineering. Consequently, while
the traditional watch-making centres such as Porrentruy, Moutier, St-Imier
(and, outside the Bernese Jura proper, Biel) continued to grow in size, light-
engineering factories were also established in these centres and in other
Jurassian settlements such as Delémont, Bévilard, Malleray, and Tavannes.
Although some of the new factories in the Bernese Jura were established by
native Jurassians and other French-Swiss, others were established by
German-speaking Swiss from Baselland, the Aargau, the Old Canton of
Berne, Solothurn, Zurich, St Gallen, and elsewhere.

Jurassian rural—urban population movements. Partly because of the activities of the
entrepreneurs mentioned earlier, significant employment opportunities were
generated in the Bernese Jura. St-Imier in the region itself, La Chaux-de-
Fonds and Le Locle (both in nearby Canton Neuchâtel), and Biel, among
other centres, continued, in addition, to grow steadily in importance as
watch-making centres. These towns attracted very large numbers of French-
speaking Jurassians from rural areas to work in the larger settlements. Any
community in the Bernese Jura which boasted a small factory assembling

watch components, or producing precision machinery, served as a magnet for the French-speaking inhabitants of the rural areas of the region. The populations of a number of towns and villages grew rapidly. By 1910 Biel, originally an entirely German-speaking town situated on the Mittelland at the southern edge of the Bernese Jura, had a French-speaking population which accounted for 32 per cent of its total population.[11]

Table 2 provides Swiss federal census data with respect to the population for each of the seven districts of the Bernese Jura, and for the district of Biel, for a 120-year period from 1850 until 1970. (Appendix C: Table 1 provides comparable data for each individual commune in the six French-speaking districts of the Bernese Jura. It can be seen from these figures that the urbanized communes containing the towns of Porrentruy and Delémont in the North Jura, and the similarly urbanized communes of Moutier, Tavannes, Bévilard, and Malleray in the South Jura grew substantially during the latter part of the nineteenth century.)

It was indicated above that these urbanized communes attracted large numbers of rural French-speaking Jurassians to work in watch-making and precision engineering establishments. This rural–urban migration was a major reason for the decline in population of a number of rural communities in the Bernese Jura during this period.[12] The result of this massive French-speaking native Jurassian exodus from rural communes to the towns of the region, and to Biel, was that a substantial amount of agricultural land became available in the Bernese Jura.

Bernese Peasant Immigration. The massive nineteenth-century Bernese immigration flow from the Old Canton to the Bernese Jura (to which reference was made earlier), was predominantly agricultural in nature. It was facilitated by the large-scale movement, noted earlier, of native French-speaking Jurassians to the watch-making and engineering centres of the region. Large numbers of farms in the Bernese Jura—farms which had previously been occupied by native, French-speaking Jurassians—were thus purchased by German-speaking immigrants from rural areas of the Old Canton.

The majority of Bernese immigrants settled in the southern districts of the Bernese Jura. It is suggested that there were three, interrelated geographic reasons for this migration. Firstly, the southern districts of the Bernese Jura were adjacent to the Old Canton and easier of access from the latter. By contrast, the northern districts were more distant, and were made even more difficult of access by reason of the rugged topography of the region and the latter's poor internal communications. This simple geographic fact meant that a Bernese immigrant family needed to travel for only one or two days from its old home in, say, the Emmental, to its new home in, say, the St-Imier Valley in the South Jura. By contrast, it would have taken the same family three, four or five days to have moved to a new home in the North Jura.

Secondly, the southern districts of the Bernese Jura were industrialized to a

Table 2. *Bernese Jura: Population by Districts, 1850–1970*[a]

District	1850	1860	1870	1880	1888	1900	1910	1920	1930	1941	1950	1960	1970	Population change, 1970 vs. 1960
Courtelary	16,406	21,665	22,702	24,879	27,003	27,538	26,745	26,093	24,381	21,703	23,435	25,536	26,442	3·5
Delémont	12,320	12,441	13,018	13,561	13,935	15,976	17,925	18,564	18,542	19,143	20,796	24,019	27,549	14·7
Franches-Montagnes	8,974	10,251	10,789	10,872	10,750	10,511	10,614	9,933	8,753	8,399	8,496	8,727	8,303	-4·9
Moutier	10,988	12,413	13,722	14,812	15,933	19,378	23,017	23,475	24,050	24,852	26,701	29,786	31,909	7·1
La Neuveville	3,838	4,116	4,412	4,436	4,473	4,267	4,237	4,546	4,503	4,266	4,536	5,045	5,756	14·1
Porrentruy	20,565	21,890	23,988	24,209	25,419	26,578	25,611	25,324	23,679	24,263	25,212	25,651	26,135	1·9
Total: 6 French-speaking districts	73,090	82,776	88,681	92,769	97,513	104,250	108,149	108,205	103,958	102,566	109,176	118,764	126,094	6·2
Laufen	5,203	5,195	5,677	5,989	5,985	7,491	8,383	8,487	9,137	9,512	10,585	12,089	14,033	16·1
Total: 7 districts of Bernese Jura	78,293	87,791	94,358	98,758	103,498	111,741	116,532	116,692	113,095	112,078	119,761	130,853	140,127	7·1
Biel	5,974	8,138	12,166	17,087	21,630	30,117	32,769	35,415	38,596	42,125	49,454	60,683	66,247	9·2
Total: Bernese Jura and Biel	84,197	96,109	106,524	115,845	125,128	141,858	149,301	152,107	151,691	154,203	169,215	191,536	206,374	7·7

[a] The figures cited in this table include both Swiss citizens and others.

Source: Swiss Federal Bureau of Statistics.

greater degree than were the northern districts during the nineteenth century. This greater degree of industrialization appears to have been due, at least in part, to the South Jura's geographical proximity to (and, thus, its better communications links and lower transportation costs to and from) the more densely populated and industrialized Swiss Mittelland. This industrialization made more agricultural land available to new settlers in the southern, rather than the northern, districts of the Jura.

Thirdly, as will be outlined in more detail in Chapter 5, there were historic ties of friendship[13] between the southern districts of the Bernese Jura and Berne which, after the Reformation, extended to include a common Protestant religion. The immigrants from the Old Canton were thus likely to have felt more at home in the South Jura than in the North Jura.

These interrelated factors (geographical proximity; greater industrialization leading to a greater amount of available farmland; historical ties of friendship and a common Protestant religion) meant that the South Jura was thus more attractive to the Bernese as a settlement area. Interestingly, however, it appears that certain high-altitude communities, even in the South Jura, were not settled by Bernese to any appreciable extent—possibly because of their relative remoteness and/or greater difficulty of access, in addition to their (perhaps resultant) lack of industrialization. These communities included Nods and Diesse in the southern district of La Neuveville, and Plagne in the southern district of Courtelary.

Even more interestingly, these particular communes, even though all three are situated quite close to the boundary between the Bernese Jura and the Old Canton, registered quite strong pro-separatist votes in both the 1959 Jura initiative and the 1974 Jura referendum. It is at least conceivable that both their remoteness (based on their altitude) and their 'purer' Jurassian populations tended to make these communities relatively less pro-Bernese than the majority of other South Jura communes. We shall return to this theme subsequently.

Other Immigration. The construction of a railway network, the establishment of customs posts on the French border and other developments led, in addition, to the establishment of other smaller, but still significant, pockets of settlement in the Bernese Jura by Bernese and other German-Swiss.

It has already been indicated that the massive German-speaking population flow to the Bernese Jura, which began after 1815, but which became particularly heavy between 1860 and 1914 (and which continued, though to a lesser degree, up to the 1960s), had a marked effect on almost every aspect of life in the region. It will be discussed at length in Chapters 4 and 7.

Communication Developments in the Nineteenth and Twentieth Centuries

While the roads of the Bernese Jura were improved somewhat during the
nineteenth century as a result of the substantial population growth of the
region as a whole, railways were rather late in appearing on the scene in this
part of Switzerland. Moreover, the only direct railway line between the
Bernese Jura and France, and (in the other direction) between the Bernese
Jura and the Swiss Mittelland, was constructed in 1871, many years after
railways had been built in *other* regions of Switzerland (Fig. 13). Significantly,
it appears only to have been constructed at all because France had recently lost
Alsace to the German Empire, and needed an alternative railway route from
Paris to Berne (the Swiss federal capital in addition to the administrative
centre of Canton Berne), which did not pass through German territory.[14]

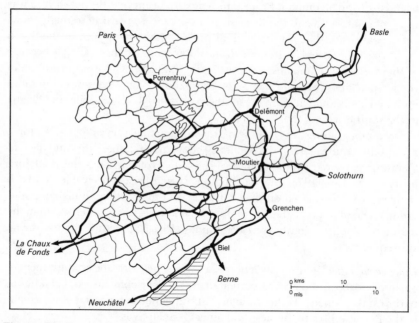

Fig. 13. The Bernese Jura: Present-day Rail Network.

Twentieth-century Depopulation

During the twentieth century a 'population haemorrhage' (which began, as we
have seen, in some rural communes in the nineteenth century) continued, and
in some cases intensified, in certain communes of the Bernese Jura. Following
World War II, in particular, significant numbers of Jurassians, especially
younger men and women, emigrated from rural communes. Some of them

settled in larger centres in the Bernese Jura itself, but many left the region altogether and settled elsewhere. Betweeen 1960 and 1970 (i.e., during the period immediately preceding the 1974 Jura referendum) more than half the communities in the Bernese Jura recorded a population decrease, as did also the North Jurassian district of Franches-Montagnes as a whole (Table 2).

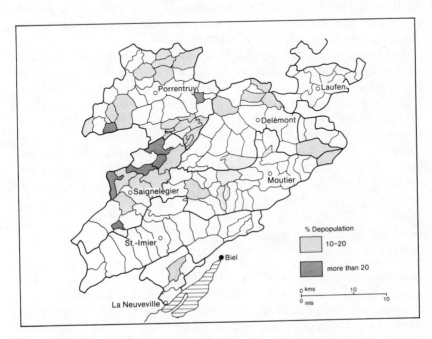

Fig. 14. The Bernese Jura: Communes Experiencing Serious Depopulation, 1960–1970.

Significantly, approximately two-thirds of these communes with declining populations were situated in the North Jura (Fig. 14). This was the area in which separatist feeling, historically, has been most strongly in evidence, and which has become the new Canton Jura. The seriousness of the population decline is evidenced by data for the communes of Bourrignon in the Delémont district and Le Bémont in the district of Franches-Montagnes (Appendix C: Table 1), which experienced population declines of 14 per cent and 15 per cent respectively between 1960 and 1970. Certain other communes, such as La Peuchapatte in Franches-Montagnes (Appendix C: Table 1), with a 40 per cent decline, experienced even more dramatic reductions in population. Since the 1970 census, moreover, the economic crisis confronting the Swiss watch industry[15] has caused serious unemployment even in urban centres of the Jura range as a whole. This led to further emigration from the Bernese Jura.

The Development of the Laufen District

During the same period under discussion (1815–1970), the overall population of one district of the Bernese Jura—the German-speaking district of Laufen— grew steadily in spite of some emigration (primarily from its rural communes) to nearby Basle. Laufen, situated as it is in the extreme north-eastern corner of the Bernese Jura, has always had much stronger social and economic ties with the nearby city of Basle and its environs than with the six French-speaking districts of the Bernese Jura to its west and south-west.

The Laufen district's links with Basle (which include historical ties, inter-related industrial enterprises and the common German-Swiss culture of the two regions), appear to be due primarily to the geographical proximity of the Laufen valley (German: Laufental) to the Basle district, and to the fact that the topography and drainage of the district, with the Birse flowing through the area to the Rhine at Basle, have facilitated close contacts with the Basle region. Table 2 indicated that the total population of the Laufen district increased from 5,203 in 1850 to 14,033 in 1970. Today, a substantial number of in-habitants of the Laufen district are employed in Basle and its nearby industrial suburbs.

Twentieth-century Communications Developments

Twentieth-century developments in the communications field also require some discussion. Since World War II, hundreds of miles of autoroute have been built in various regions of Switzerland, including one which tunnels through the eastern Folded Jura to connect the cities of Basle, Solothurn, and Berne. In addition, other autoroutes have been built in order to connect the Swiss autoroute system with the systems of other countries, notably those of France, West Germany, and Italy. Even by 1970, however, practically no autoroutes had been constructed in the Bernese Jura (Fig. 15). This suggested, to many Jurassians prior to the 1974 referendum, that the region was considered by Canton Berne and the Swiss federal authorities to be a relatively unimportant part of Switzerland. A 'Transjurane Highway' (Fig. 15) was proposed by Jurassians on a number of occasions, but was only approved by Swiss federal authorities in 1984.

Summary and Conclusions

In this chapter it has been stressed that because of its geology, climate, topography, and drainage, the Jura mountain range differs markedly in its physical characteristics from either the Mittelland or the Alps. It has also been stressed that its mountain ridges lie at right-angles to a traveller approaching the Bernese Jura from the Mittelland, with only limited points of access either to the region as a whole or, within the region, from one valley to another.

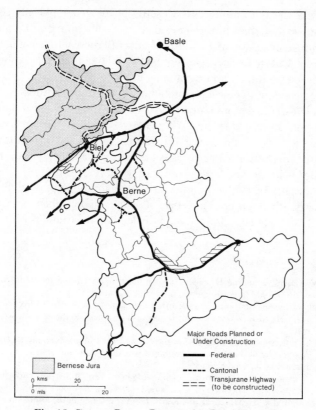

Fig. 15. Canton Berne: Present-day Road Network.

There have been several consequences of this. Firstly, in earlier times it was difficult for the German language, Bernese armies, and new religious philosophies to penetrate the Jura mountain range and, more particularly, the North Jura. Secondly, the peripheral geographic location of the bishopric of Basle (on the north-western boundary of the Swiss Mittelland) and its rugged topography served, in combination, to discourage the construction of good internal and external road communications which might have served to strengthen the economy of the region.

Thirdly, the population mix of the pre-1979 Bernese Jura resulted from certain massive nineteenth-century population movements which followed the union of the Bernese Jura with Canton Berne in 1815. Rural pressures in the Old Canton, the industrialization of the valleys of the Bernese Jura, and the consequent availability of Jurassian farmland led to a massive German-speaking and predominantly Bernese population influx—especially into the South Jura.

The heavy Bernese settlement in the South Jura occurred, in part, because of the topographical and communications problems which made it relatively easy for the Bernese immigrants to settle in the geographically contiguous South Jura rather than in the more distant North Jura, and because of the greater industrialization of the south. Heavier Bernese settlement in the South Jura also took place because of other factors related to its geography, namely its historic friendship with Berne and its Protestant character.

Finally, economic developments during the nineteenth and twentieth centuries led to the depopulation of many rural Jurassian communities. This depopulation continued to the 1970s, where it assumed haemorrhage proportions in some villages, predominantly located in the North Jura. It may thus have contributed to a greater degree of resentment against the government of Canton Berne in the North (as contrasted to the South) Jura.

It will already be evident to the reader that a number of possible causes of Jurassian political unrest have been touched upon, albeit briefly, in this chapter. These will be examined in more detail in the chapters which follow.

Notes

1. Some writers, including Hughes (op. cit.), have suggested that the southern slopes and valleys of the Alps should be considered as a fourth physical region.

2. Monkhouse (op. cit.), has suggested that the name 'Jura' is derived from a Celtic word meaning 'forest'. He further suggests that it may also be related to the Slavonic word *gora*, also meaning 'forest'.

3. We can only speculate as to whether the climate of the Jura mountains, together with the forbidding topography of the region, discouraged would-be Germanic settlers coming from the Mittelland, but it may well have done.

4. It should be emphasized that the valley–ridge structure of the Jura range is not always simple or regular, however, because the long periods of erosion mentioned earlier have worn away parts of the original folds. Moreover, the fourth Ice Age resulted in the formation, especially in such districts of the Bernese Jura as Franches-Montagnes, of a large number of small lakes which lie in uneven depressions in the boulder clay, or which have been created by mounds of clay which have blocked the flow of streams (Fig. 11).

5. Rees (op. cit.) has reminded us that the typical stone farmhouse of the Jura has a wide roof which is specially designed to collect rainfall 'and conduct it to a watertight cistern for storage'.

6. This is particularly true of the Suze during a considerable part of its course.

7. It was during the sixteenth century that Anabaptist (Mennonite) settlements were first established in the Jura. These settlements, which have played a role in the political history of the Bernese Jura far greater than their relatively small population would seem to warrant, are discussed at greater length in subsequent chapters.

8. A more detailed discussion of the watch industry in the Bernese Jura will follow in Chapter 3.

9. The growth of one other settlement also deserves mention, even though, strictly speaking, it is situated beyond the boundaries of the Bernese Jura. Just as Porrentruy grew in size and importance during the two and a half centuries under discussion, so also did the town and trading centre of Biel (French: Bienne), lying in the German-speaking Mittelland at the foot of the Jura range. Biel, while situated outside the Bernese Jura proper (Fig. 4), has been closely associated with the region through the greater part of its history, and will be discussed further in subsequent chapters.

10. As indicated in Chapter 1, although, for purposes of clarity and consistency, the region being examined has been referred to as the 'Bernese Jura' it was, in fact, only known by this name after 1815, when it was awarded to Berne.

11. For a more detailed discussion of the linguistic history and present-day linguistic situation in Biel, see Chapter 4.

12. One example out of many is the commune of Montfavergier in the district of Franches-Montagnes. The population of this commune declined from 174 in 1850 to 80 by 1910 (Appendix C: Table 1).

13. The historical ties of friendship with Berne, and the shared Protestant religion were, as will be emphasized later, themselves due to the geographical proximity of the South Jura to the Old Canton and the rugged topography and relatively poor communications of the region as a whole. These characteristics made the North Jura quite remote to the newcomers.

14. In a brochure (Brocard, 1977) published to commemorate the centenary of the opening of the line between Delémont (in the north-east Bernese Jura) and Delle, on the French side of the frontier bordering the north-western Porrentruy district of the Bernese Jura, the following statement (reflecting, even today, the bitterness and resentment of at least some Jurassians) occurs: 'It seems rather strange to us, as Jurassians, that the decision to build a railway in the Jura was not made until after the Franco-Prussian War, and then only because a new direct link between Paris and Berne was deemed to be desirable.'

15. See Chapter 3 for a more detailed description of this topic.

3

The Economic Geography of the Bernese Jura

> The (European) regions in which autonomous feeling is strong are mainly those in which a substantial share of the population feels economically disfavored as compared to their fellow citizens in other parts of the larger nation.
>
> JAMES MCDONALD (1978)

Having discussed the physical and human geography of the Bernese Jura, it is also necessary for us to examine the economic geography of the Bernese Jura, and relate it, too, to what one observer has called 'this peculiarly un-Swiss aberration', Jura separatism.

Table 3 indicates the percentages of the working population of the seven districts of the Bernese Jura employed in the three basic sectors of economic activity, namely agriculture, manufacturing, and service industries prior to the establishment of Canton Jura. In order to highlight trends, comparisons are made between data for 1910, 1941, and 1970, respectively.[1] Some comments follow.

Table 3. *Bernese Jura: Percentage of Working Population Employed in Agriculture, Manufacturing and Service Industries for Selected Years*

District	Agriculture			Manufacturing			Service Industries		
	1910	1941	1970	1910	1941	1970	1910	1941	1970
Courtelary	17	15	8	69	65	71	14	20	21
Delémont	35	26	8	44	45	62	21	29	30
Franches-Montagnes	37	37	20	48	38	58	15	25	22
Moutier	23	16	7	64	65	72	13	19	21
La Neuveville	42	31	9	37	32	55	21	37	36
Porrentruy	33	30	11	46	44	60	21	26	29
Laufen	29	19	5	55	60	69	16	21	26
Total: 7 districts	28	23	9	55	54	66	17	23	25

Source: Swiss Federal Bureau of Statistics (adapted from Prongué).

Agriculture in the Bernese Jura

Table 3 makes it clear that the most agricultural district in the Bernese Jura in 1970 was Franches-Montagnes in the north-west of the region, where 20 per cent of the employed work-force, in the district as a whole, was engaged in some form of agriculture. In fact, 40 per cent or more of the work-force was employed in agriculture in eight of Franches-Montagnes' seventeen communes (Appendix C: Table 1, and Fig. 16). In one commune (Le Peuchapatte) the figure was 83 per cent, and in a second (Epiquerez) it was 73 per cent. With the exception of the district of Porrentruy, where 11 per cent of the employed population was engaged in agriculture (Appendix C: Table 1), no other district of the Bernese Jura had more than 9 per cent of its work-force employed in agriculture in 1970. The figure for the Bernese Jura as a whole (i.e., for all seven districts) was 9 per cent (Table 3). This, interestingly, compared to 9 per cent for the whole of Canton Berne (including the Bernese Jura), and 8 per cent for Switzerland as a whole.

Overall district figures, however, tend to mask the fact that, quite apart from Franches-Montagnes, each of the other districts of the Bernese Jura (with the exceptions of the highly industrialized Laufen district near Basle and the district of La Neuveville bordering on the Bielersee), contained several communes where 40 per cent or more of the work-force was still employed in agriculture at the time of the 1970 census.[2]

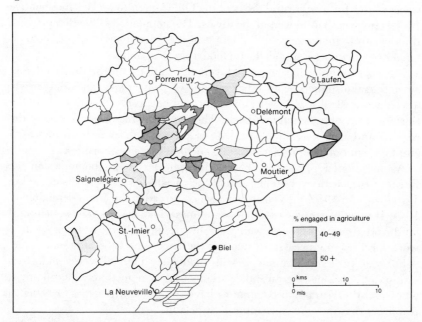

Fig. 16. The Bernese Jura: Communes with 40% or more of their Working Population Engaged in Agriculture in 1970.

Nevertheless, Table 3 clearly indicates that the percentages of the work-forces engaged in the agricultural sector decreased dramatically in some districts of the Bernese Jura in the years after 1910. The most startling decrease, from 42 per cent in 1910 to 9 per cent in 1970, was in the district of La Neuveville where the relative employment shares accounted for by both the manufacturing and service sectors increased markedly. However, Delémont, Porrentruy, and Laufen also experienced steep declines. Courtelary and Moutier were already heavily industrialized in 1910, so that the relative decline in the agricultural work-force in these districts was not as great in the years after 1910 (Table 3).

The reasons for the decline in the relative importance of agricultural employment in the Bernese Jura—a decline which began in the mid-nine-teenth century—do not seem difficult to pin-point. To begin with, in the subsistence economy which existed in Switzerland, as in most parts of Europe, in earlier times, agricultural activity was necessary in every community to feed the local population. Moreover, in many communes of the Bernese Jura there were no alternative employment opportunities. The situation began to change toward the middle of the nineteenth century, however. As was recounted in Chapter 2, the industries which were established in a number of Jurassian communities attracted large numbers of French-speaking rural people to the larger population centres in the Bernese Jura, and to Biel. We have also noted that, in addition, significant numbers of German-speakers moved to rural areas of the Jura from rural areas of the Old Canton to replace those native Jurassians who had moved to the towns. The population of the Bernese Jura thus began to increase, resulting in a growing urban market which could no longer be adequately supplied with food from local sources.

Moreover, somewhat improved communications meant that food and agricultural products from other regions of Switzerland, and from newly developed agricultural regions abroad, could now compete with those of the Bernese Jura on a favourable basis. The growth of the urban centres of the region, and various technological developments led, in turn, to increased employment opportunities in retailing and other service industries.

As mentioned previously, Figure 16 indicates those communes in the Bernese Jura with over 40 per cent of their respective work-force engaged in agriculture in 1970, the census year which preceded the Jura referendum of 1974. It must be emphasized that communes which possess good agricultural land and those communes which are highly agricultural in terms of their work-force are not necessarily one and the same. This is because some large, urbanized Jurassian communes with manufacturing and service industries originally developed because they were situated in good agricultural areas, whereas other Jurassian communes have, traditionally, been so lacking in resources that they are 'agricultural' by default.

In the relatively few areas where good agricultural land exists in the region (as in the Sorne basin to the west, south-west and south-east of Delémont) it is used to produce arable crops and dairy products. In the more mountainous, remote areas (such as most of Franches-Montagnes), timber is grown for commercial purposes. Moreover, the nature of the terrain (open pastureland, with occasional stands of pine trees, but largely free of underbrush) is such that horses are reared and riding is an important tourist attraction. The Ajoie region around Porrentruy has a good deal of agricultural land, but this is also a district where industry provides a substantial number of job opportunities.

Jurassian separatist spokesmen have, traditionally, associated the population decline of many Jurassian communities with Bernese mismanagement of the economy of the Bernese Jura. If this perception was widely shared, in the region, during the period from 1945 to the Jura referendum of 1974, we might expect to find that resentment among those living in the most agricultural communities and/or those communities (and they were not, of course, necessarily the same in all cases) from which emigration had been heaviest in the 1960s and early 1970s, would have resulted in particularly strong Jurassian separatist feeling. We shall investigate this possibility in due course.

Industry in the Bernese Jura

Table 3 also provides data on the percentage of the Jurassian population employed in the manufacturing sector, by districts, for the years 1910, 1941, and 1970.[3] It is clear from the figures that the results of the Great Depression were still being felt in the southern, watch-making district of Courtelary in 1941, in that the percentage of workers employed in industry dropped from 69 per cent in 1910 to 65 per cent. By 1970, however, the percentages of workers employed in industry were higher, in the case of all districts (including Courtelary), than in 1910. The 1910 percentage figure for the region as a whole was 55 per cent, whereas the 1970 figure was 66 per cent (Table 3).

The major industries of the Bernese Jura, as it existed prior to 1979, were the watch, light engineering, and metallurgical industries. Smaller industries included resource-based enterprises such as quarrying and cement manufacture, forest-based industry (timber, pulp, and paper), food and tobacco industries, textiles and clothing. Each of the leading industries of the Bernese Jura will be discussed in turn.

The Watch Industry

The history of the development of the Swiss watch industry has been recounted by Amweg (op. cit.), Bessire (op. cit.), and Prongué (op. cit.), among others, and was touched upon briefly in Chapter 2. As the population of the remote, poverty-stricken valleys and uplands of the Jura range gradually grew during the seventeenth and eighteenth centuries, it became increasingly important that the inhabitants of these rural areas obtain subsidiary employment. Because of the harsh mountain climate of most regions of the Jura chain, little agricultural work could be done during the long winter months. The watch-making industry provided an opportunity for year-round employment.

As the watch-making industry developed in the Bernese Jura, in Biel,[4] and elsewhere (e.g. Cantons, Geneva, and Neuchâtel) in the Jura range of Switzerland during the eighteenth and nineteenth centuries (leading, as we have already noted, to the depopulation of many rural communities in the Bernese Jura), it gradually became more and more specialized. For example, the case, the face, the hands, and the spring were manufactured in separate small workshops, each often situated in a small village. The separate watch parts were assembled subsequently in yet another large workshop or factory, usually situated in a larger population centre, such as St-Imier, Tavannes, Moutier, or Biel.

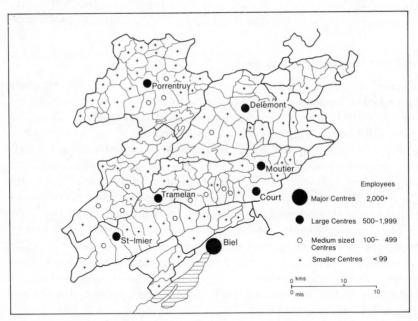

Fig. 17. The Bernese Jura: Watchmaking Centres, 1970.

Although the largest watch-manufacturing centres of Switzerland (Geneva, La Chaux-de-Fonds, Le Locle, and Biel) are not, in fact, situated in the pre-1979 Bernese Jura but in other areas in, or adjoining, the Jura range, the watch industry is still of great importance to the region. Figure 17 indicates the major regional centres of the industry in 1970, among which St-Imier (Plate 2), Tramelan, Court, Moutier, Delémont (Plate 3), and Porrentruy

(Plate 4) were the most important. Many smaller establishments were located in other, smaller communities, however.

As is widely known, the Swiss watch industry has been confronted by a series of crises during the twentieth century. Each of these crises has led to large-scale unemployment in the Bernese Jura, a reduction in the number of establishments through mergers and closures, eventual losses of workers to other types of industry, and emigration from the region. Bessire (op. cit.) has shown that between 1912 and 1933 alone the percentge of Swiss watch production accounted for by the Bernese Jura and Biel fell from 52 per cent to 24 per cent. Other regions of Switzerland, including the cantons of Geneva, Neuchâtel, and Solothurn, were the prime beneficiaries of this decline in relative terms.

The most recent crises to confront the industry began in the early 1970s,[5] and was caused both by the increase in value of the Swiss franc and by growing competition from Japan and other countries, especially in the all-important US market.[6] The Japanese enjoyed the advantage of certain economies of scale; for example, in 1978 the two leading Japanese watch-makers accounted for 88 per cent of all Japanese production. By contrast, the leading Swiss manufacturer (SSIH) accounted for only 9 per cent of Swiss production in the same year (1978), even after a number of mergers with other firms.

As a result of the most recent Swiss watch industry crisis, employment dropped from 75,824 to 55,539 workers between 1965 and 1975. These developments caused further serious economic problems in certain smaller communities in the Bernese Jura and, in the case of some individuals, may have resulted in increased resentment toward the Bernese government and the 'outside world'. Another cause of concern in the Bernese Jura was that wages in the watch industry did not compare favourably with those paid in other industries. The average monthly pay for skilled or semi-skilled workers in the watch industry, for example, was 2,464 Swiss francs in 1977, compared to 2,606 francs in engineering and 3,021 francs in the chemical industry.

The Light Engineering and Metal-working Industries

Figure 18 indicates the location of the light engineering and metal-working industry in the Bernese Jura in 1970. The major centres in the region itself were Moutier and a number of medium-sized towns in both the North and South Jura. Biel, just outside the region, was also an important centre. The watch industry, with its need for precision machine tools and its reserve of workers with experience in precision work, influenced the location of these Jurassian light engineering establishments. The engineering industry in the Bernese Jura, in spite of export difficulties arising from increases in the Swiss franc's value, was reasonably prosperous in the years following World War II and made a significant contribution to the economy of the region. The metallurgical industry in the Bernese Jura, as in certain other parts of Switzerland,

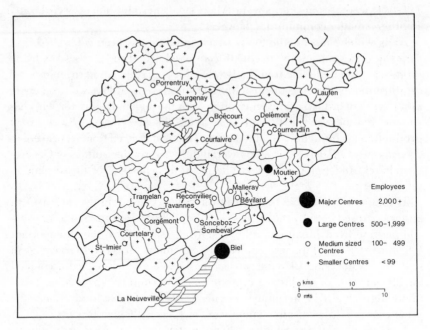

Fig. 18. The Bernese Jura: Light Engineering and Metal-working Centres, 1970.

developed logically from much older foundries, forges, and workshops. The largest foundry in the Bernese Jura was at Choindez, in the gorges de Moutier, but lying just within the communal boundary of Courrendlin.[7]

Other Industries

Other manufacturing and processing industries of some importance in the Bernese Jura include food and tobacco factories in the Porrentruy district, and small timber, pulp, and paper mills in Franches-Montagnes.

Service Industries in the Region

Table 3 also provides certain basic data on employment in the tertiary (service) sector in the Bernese Jura between 1910 and 1970. It can be seen that, as has occurred in many regions in many countries, the percentages of those employed by service industries have, for the most part, increased during the twentieth century. The highest percentage of workers employed in the tertiary sector was in the district of La Neuveville, which contains the town of the same name.[8]

Tourism, an important industry in the Alpine region of Switzerland, remained relatively unimportant in the economy of the Bernese Jura until the 1970s. This was in part due to the fact that the scenery of the region is not as dramatic as that of, say, the Bernese Oberland in the Alpine massif. Nevertheless, much attractive scenery is to be found in the Jura and, in recent years, *Pro Jura*, the Jura Tourist Authority, has begun an energetic campaign to attract more tourists, both Swiss and foreign, to the region. A guide to Jurassian hotels and restaurants is now published each year, and an effort has been made to publicize the availability of horse-riding and farm holidays in the district of Franches-Montagnes.

The Work of the ADIJ

The economic problems of the Jura began to arouse concern among Jurassians themselves as early as the mid-nineteenth century. The first of what was to prove to be several crises developed in the Swiss watch industry in the early 1920s and, as was discussed earlier, caused serious unemployment in the Bernese Jura. In addition, Jurassians were especially angry about the re-establishment of the Paris–Basle–Berne rail route which followed the return of Alsace-Lorraine to France in 1919.[9] This latter event was specifically referred to as a cause for grave concern to Jurassians in the 'Statement of Objectives' of *l'Association pour la défense des intérêts du Jura* (The Association for the Defence of Jurassian Interests, or ADIJ) which was established in 1925.

Since its establishment, ADIJ has made repeated representations to both the government of Canton Berne and to the Swiss federal government on behalf of Jurassian economic interests. It draws its membership from all districts of the former Bernese Jura. It is non-political and, interestingly, includes both separatists and anti-separatists among its members. The ADIJ was officially neutral in the 1974 referendum and has stated that it will continue to fight for the economic interests of the pre-1979 Bernese Jura as a whole, regardless of new cantonal boundaries.

Present Day Communications in the Bernese Jura

Reference was made in Chapter 2 to the limited road network of the Bernese Jura. It was also stated, in Chapter 2, that the existing high level of concern developed, following World War II, into anger among some Jurassians when it became clear that no new highways were planned for the region. As a result of the federal and cantonal governments' programmes, a modified autoroute had penetrated a short distance into the Bernese Jura from Biel by 1970. Apart from this limited highway, however, the closest autoroute to the former Bernese Jura, at the time of writing (1985), runs from Biel to Neuchâtel. The Swiss autoroute network thus barely touches the region at all (Fig. 15).

Summary and Conclusions

In studying the economic geography of the Bernese Jura, an outside observer can hardly fail to conclude that, in the years leading up to the 1974 referendum, the region faced a number of serious economic and social problems.[10] Agriculture and forest resource industries have never been able to provide employment for large numbers of Jurassians. We have noted that the watch industry has been confronted by a number of crises over the past century, and its most recent crisis (like earlier crises) has led to severe unemployment and factory relocation.

The engineering and metal-working industries, which developed from the watch industry during the nineteenth century, brought some degree of economic stability and occupational diversification to the Bernese Jura. Even these industries, however, are likely to be threatened by the effects of the increased value of the Swiss franc overseas, which makes all Swiss exports more expensive and thus less competitive in foreign markets. Furthermore, the tourist industry of the region is still relatively underdeveloped when compared to that of the Alpine regions of Switzerland.

In the 1970s, in the eyes of at least some Jurassians, the economic problems of the region, including the depopulation of rural communes, mass unemployment in the watch industry and emigration of native Jurassians to other regions of Switzerland may seem to have been caused by the neglect and misrule of the government of the Canton of Berne. It is suggested, therefore, that as observers of the Jurassian political scene, we must ask ourselves: In the 1970s, did a relationship exist between economic hardship, on the one hand, and Jura separatism on the other? Were Jurassian 'have-not' communes more likely to vote separatist in the 1974 referendum than Jurassian communes which were still relatively prosperous?

A similar question can be asked with respect to depopulation. Was a Jurassian commune which had experienced a population loss more likely to vote separatist in 1974 than a commune which had a stable population, or which had experienced population growth? Finally, did a relationship exist between a predominantly agricultural community (which might have been agricultural by default because it had not developed strong secondary and tertiary economic sectors) and Jurassian separatism?

Notes

1. Appendix C: Table 1 provides more detailed data for 1970, on a commune-by-commune basis, for each of the six French-speaking districts of the region.

2. Ibid.

3. Ibid.

4. It also, incidentally, spread eastwards from Biel to certain adjacent, German-speaking Mittelland communities at the southern edge of the Jura range, such as Grenchen in Canton Solothurn.

5. In 1970 the Swiss watch industry consisted of approximately 1,000 different firms and 74,000 employees. It was Switzerland's fourth largest industry, accounting for 12 per cent of total Swiss exports. Approximately 97 per cent of total production was exported, and Switzerland accounted for 42 per cent of the world's total ouput. By 1982, primarily because of competition from Japanese- and Hong Kong-made digital watches, Switzerland's share of the world watch market had declined to about 20 per cent. (Source: John Parry, *Advertising Age*, 17 December 1984.)

6. Other reasons for the problems confronting the Swiss watch industry include low industry research and development expenditure (which made the industry slow to recognize the potential of such technological advances as digital watches), ultra-conservative marketing practices and a reluctance to diversify.

7. As a result, it falls just within the boundary of the new Canton Jura.

8. The town of La Neuveville is a popular lakeside holiday resort. It also attracts many retired German-Swiss as permanent residents.

9. The result of this development was that the Paris–Porrentruy–Berne railway, constructed (as mentioned previously in Chapter 2), as an alternative route in 1871, was under-utilized.

10. The Union Bank of Switzerland publishes annually a list of the largest industrial firms, commercial enterprises and service firms in the country using annual sales as its criterion of size. In 1983, not a single firm from the French-speaking districts of the Bernese Jura appeared among the first 145 firms listed. The French-owned Burrus tobacco firm, located at Boncourt in the Porrentruy district of the region, was no. 147 in 1983. (Source: *Les principales entreprises de Suisse*, Union de Banques Suisses, Zurich, 1984 edition.)

4

The Geography of Language of the Bernese Jura

Any linguistic area has the right to preserve and defend its own linguistic character against all outside forces that tend to alter or endanger it.

WALTER BURCKHARDT (1931), quoted by KENNETH MCRAE (1964)

It was suggested in Chapter 1 that one of the reasons why the Jura region is of interest to geographers is that it forms an eastward-thrusting, French-speaking linguistic promontory which borders German-speaking regions to the north, east, and south (Fig. 5). The geography of language of the region is also significant in a study of Jura separatism, because one of the major arguments of separatist spokesmen has been that the people of the pre-1979 Bernese Jura represent a French-speaking cultural group which, since 1815, has been threatened by 'germanization'.

The Present-day Situation

In this chapter the geography of language of the pre-1979 Bernese Jura will be examined in detail. As discussed in Chapter 1, six of the seven districts of the Bernese Jura (namely Courtelary, Delémont, Franches-Montagnes, Moutier, La Neuveville, and Porrentruy) were predominantly French-speaking in 1970 (i.e., at the time of the census which immediately preceded the Jura referendum of 1974). Only the north-eastern district of Laufen, which was contiguous to the half-canton of Baselland and to Canton Solothurn, was (like Baselland and Solothurn) German-speaking.[1]

A number of writers, including Weilemann (opp. cit.), Gutersohn (op. cit.), Früh (op. cit.), McRae (op. cit.), Müller (1965), Lobsiger (op. cit.), Doka (1973), and Mayer (op. cit.), have examined the relative positions of the German and French languages both in Switzerland as a whole and, in some cases, in the Bernese Jura specifically. However, in order to obtain a better understanding of the present-day geography of language of the Bernese Jura, we must also review the region's linguistic history.

The Period of the Alemannic Invasion and Settlement

It will be recalled from Chapter 2 that Celtic-speaking tribes occupied the region of the Bernese Jura as well as the Mittelland during the first two and a half centuries of Roman rule. Früh (op. cit.), Amman and Schib (op. cit.), and others have suggested that around AD 260, however, the linguistic situation

changed and the present-day linguistic map of Switzerland, including the
linguistic map of the Bernese Jura, began to take shape.

About this time German-speaking tribes reached, and penetrated, the
Roman defensive fortifications (the 'limes') between the Danube and the
Rhine. The Alemanni, one of these German-speaking tribes, appear to have
dispersed themselves widely over a large area of the Mittelland to the south of
the Jura mountain range. During the first period of their expansion they may
have settled an area as far west as the Aare river (on which the city of Berne
now stands). At the southern edges of the Swiss plateau, in what is now
west-central Switzerland, the Alemanni would appear to have penetrated the
upper valleys of all rivers flowing northward across the Mittelland from the
Alpine massif.[2]

Moving outwards from the bend of the Rhine near the present-day city of
Basle, the Alemanni also appear to have occupied the most easterly areas of
the Jura chain (i.e., those areas lying in present-day Baselland, the Aargau,
and Solothurn) and that eastern portion of the Birse valley which forms the
present-day, German-speaking Laufen district of the Jura region. To the north
of the Jura chain, the Alemanni also crossed the Rhine and occupied the plain
of present-day Alsace as far west as the crests of the Vosges Mountains. As a
result of these Alemannic invasions, the latinized Celts of the Jura also found
themselves confronted by German-speaking tribes to their north.

During this same period (i.e., about AD 300–50), another German-
speaking tribe, the Burgundians, settled in the Gallo–Roman regions to the
west, south-west, and south of Lake Geneva in present-day France. In this
area, however, they became latinized in their language and culture fairly
rapidly. Partly because they were encouraged to do so by their Roman allies,
and partly because they were under military attack from a neighbouring
Gaulish tribe, the Burgundians moved in a north-easterly direction about AD
500. The Burgundians settled in what is now the south-western part of
Switzerland, including the area around Lake Geneva and the moderately
undulating Mittelland region as far north as Lake Neuchâtel, and as far east as
the Aare river. Because the Burgundians had earlier settled and become
latinized in south-eastern Gaul, their Francoprovençal dialects appear to have
been related to the *langue d'oc*, the dialect of the south of France. The
Francoprovençal dialect of French subsequently came to be spoken by the
greater part of the population of what is now French-speaking Switzerland.
For a period of about 500 years, from AD 500 to 1,000, according to Früh (op.
cit.) and other writers, the Aare river appears to have formed the approximate
boundary between the German-speaking and latinized peoples who occupied
the whole of present-day Switzerland (Fig. 19).

What of the future Bernese Jura during this period of the 'barbarian
invasions'? We have already noted that, to the north of the region, there is
evidence that the German-speaking Alemanni occupied the plain of Alsace.
Similarly, to the south of the Jura, the Alemanni appear to have advanced

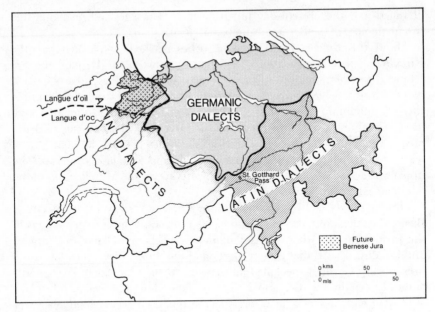

Fig. 19. Linguistic Map of Switzerland, *c.* AD 850.

westwards across the Mittelland at least as far as the present-day towns of Pieterlen and Büren (to the east of the present-day town of Biel). In between these two westerly thrusts of German-speaking Alemannic settlement (the Sundgau region of Southern Alsace and the Swiss Mittelland), the mountainous bulk of the Jura range interposed itself, and, it appears, was not settled by the newcomers. According to Bessire (op. cit.) and other writers, such limited evidence as is available suggests that that part of the Jura range which is known today as the Bernese Jura remained a scantily-populated area in which the Latin language of the Romans gradually replaced the longer-established Celtic language of the local tribes.

The latinization of the Jura was probably made easier by the fact that the Celtic inhabitants of the Jura—and especially the Sequani—remained in contact with other Celtic tribes to the west in present-day France. It appears that these latter Celtic tribes had, as a result of a lengthy Roman occupation, adopted a latinized tongue which gradually developed into the *langue d'oïl*, the northern dialect of French (Fig. 19).

In summary, geographers such as Früh (op. cit.) and historians such as Bessire (op. cit.) believe that, at the end of the first period of the Alemannic invasions, the present-day linguistic map of Switzerland was beginning to take shape, even though the Latin–Teutonic linguistic frontier, apparently then on the Aare, was subsequently to be pushed somewhat further to the west in the Mittelland.

As Figure 19 indicates, during this entire period the peoples of the region which, subsequently, became the bishopric of Basle and, still later, the Bernese Jura appear to have remained geographically and culturally distinct from the German-speaking peoples who occupied the Sundgau to their north, the extension of the Folded Jura range to the east, and the Mittelland to the south-east. To the extent that the predominantly Celtic inhabitants of the Jura, surrounded as they were on the north, east and south by German-speaking peoples, were influenced at all by any outside culture, such influences were, apparently, Latin influences from the inhabitants of romanized Gaul to the west. As indicated, these peoples appear to have spoken dialects of northern French, the *langue d'oïl*, as contrasted to the *langue d'oc* of the other latinized (and future French-speaking peoples) of Switzerland.[3]

Regional dialects in French-speaking Switzerland have practically disappeared since the end of the last century. However, some observers of present-day Swiss political life believe it is significant that, of all the regions of French-speaking Switzerland, the Bernese Jura *alone* once spoke a *langue d'oïl* dialect.[4] (The Burgundian Francoprovençal dialect of the *langue d'oc*, the language of southern France, appears to have penetrated only the extreme south-western corner of the region.) (Fig. 19)

The Period from AD 800 to the Reformation

The future Bernese Jura remained a stronghold of Latin culture throughout the period from AD 500–1,000, according to Bessire (op. cit.) and others, even though German-speaking peoples appear to have occupied territory to their north, east, and south-east. During this period the boundaries between Latin-speaking and German-speaking peoples (which, it will be recalled, seems to have followed the Aare river at least in part) in the region which constitutes present-day Switzerland were relatively stable.

In 1032, it will be recalled from Chapter 2, the bishopric of Basle itself became associated with the predominantly German-speaking Holy Roman Empire, acknowledging the overall authority of the emperor. At about this time the German–French linguistic boundary in the Swiss Mittelland (to the south and south-east of the Jura range) began to move westwards once again, according to Früh (op. cit.), Amman and Schib (op. cit.), and others. The reasons for this are not clear. Nevertheless, whatever the reason, it appears that the Mittelland region between the Aare and Saane (French: Sarine) as far west as Fribourg (German: Freiburg), which was founded by the German-speaking counts of Zähringen in the latter part of the twelfth century, Seeland as far west as Biel and the upper Valais (German: Wallis), all appear to have become German-speaking in the eleventh and twelfth centuries.

It is significant, however, that throughout this period the Bernese Jura appears to have remained predominantly French-speaking. The second westward thrust of German-speaking peoples, like its predecessor, appears to have *by-passed* the mountainous bishopric of Basle. Rather, it followed such natural east—west Mittelland communication routes as the Aare river between the present-day cities of Aaru, Biel, and Berne. Once again, compared to the mountainous, forested Jura range with its relatively limited arable land and harsh winter climate, the rich agricultural lands of the western Mittelland and the plateau's relatively moderate climate may have appeared more attractive to the new settlers. This second German-speaking westward movement, which ended about AD 1200, was followed by another period, lasting approximately 200 years according to Früh (op. cit.), of relatively little change in the linguistic map of Switzerland.

In examining the hypothetical linguistic maps of the area during the whole of the period under discussion (AD 500–1400), it is difficult not to conclude that the physical geography of the present-day Bernese Jura constituted the primary reason (and, perhaps, the *only* reason) why it remained a primarily French-speaking linguistic promontory. It was suggested in Chapter 2 that the south-westerly—north-easterly configuration of the Jura range (which results in its constituting a right-angled barrier to travellers approaching it from the Mittelland), together with the difficulty with which this barrier could be penetrated, preserved the French culture of the Bernese Jura. This theory cannot, of course, be proved. However, it is suggested that the topographical map of the Bernese Jura, on the one hand, and its linguistic map, on the other, are too strikingly similar to be purely coincidental.

We must not overlook, moreover, the fact that the Jura mountain range is not easy to penetrate even from the north-east. Müller (op. cit.) has pointed out that to the west of the present-day, German-speaking Laufen district of the Bernese Jura, and towards the present-day, French-speaking commune of Soyhières in the Delémont district of the new Canton Jura, the Birse enters a modest gorge which appears to have served as an approximate dividing line between the French and German languages throughout the Middle Ages and up to the present day. To the east and southeast, only a limited number of high mountain passes (such as the Scheltenpass) and narrow gorges (such as the gorge of the Raus linking Crémines in the South Jura and Gansbrunnen in Canton Solothurn) gave access to the Bernese Jura.

This is not to say that there were not some German-speaking areas, quite apart from the German-speaking Laufen district, in the future Bernese Jura during medieval times. A number of writers have, in fact, speculated as to the precise extent to which French and German, respectively, were spoken in the region during the Middle Ages. Müller (op. cit.) has suggested that, during the thirteenth century, the prince-bishops and the chief officials of the government of the bishopric were all German-speaking,[5] even though they ruled a population which would appear to have been predominantly French-speaking in the greater part of the region. Moreover, according to Müller (op. cit.), during the thirteenth century the abbots of the monasteries of Lucelle (German: Lützel) in the north of the Bernese Jura, of St-Ursanne in the north-west, and of Moutier-Grandval in the south-central area of the bishopric were also of German-speaking backgrounds.[6]

In the fourteenth century the bishopric of Basle came under the political influence of the kings of France. As a result, for a period of about one hundred years (i.e., from approximately 1315 until 1418), the prince-bishops and their officials came from French-speaking regions and appear to have spoken French as their first language. From 1418 onwards, according to Müller (op. cit.), German-speaking prince-bishops and officials once again occupied the key positions of power in the bishopric of Basle. This situation was, in fact, subsequently made self-perpetuating by a regulation which specified that all official positions, including that of the bishop, could only be occupied by members of the German-speaking noble families. In the event, almost all bishops and their officials came from one particular German-speaking region, the upper Rhineland.

The Period from the Reformation to 1792

As indicated in Chapter 2, as a result of the Reformation, Bishop Philippe de Gundelsheim and his officials decided to leave the city of Basle permanently in 1528. (This followed a hurried, but temporary, departure by his predecessor Christophe d'Utenheim the previous year.) Henceforth, the administration of the Bernese Jura was fragmented. The bishop, as temporal governor (prince) of the bishopric, established his seat of government in Porrentruy. The cathedral chapter moved to Freiburg in the Black Forest of present-day West Germany, and the church court established itself in Altkirch in Alsace.

We noted in Chapter 2 that many officials and their families accompanied the prince-bishop to Porrentruy in 1528, and that these officials were German-speaking. Porrentruy itself, however, appears to have been French-speaking to such an extent that, in 1567, the reigning bishop found it necessary to appoint a governor who, while originally German-speaking, could also speak, write, and understand French. Müller (op. cit.) has suggested that in the South Jura, however, the senior officials continued, for the most part, to be French-speaking natives of the region throughout this period.

Nevertheless, in these centuries, language did not appear to be a very important issue in the minds of the inhabitants of the bishopric. It seems to have been quite common for oaths of allegiance to have been administered in German in predominantly French-speaking areas (Müller, op. cit.). The bishops' officials at Porrentruy, while they sent their sons to France to learn both French and courtly manners, nevertheless married German-speaking wives and continued to speak German among themselves. The widespread use of German as the successor to Latin as the administrative language of the bishopric, and the lesser (and perhaps shorter-lived) influence of German tradesmen and artisans is suggested by the large number of communes in the French-speaking districts of the Bernese Jura which have German as well as

French names. (Sixty-eight of the 133 communes of the six French-speaking districts of the Jura, or more than 50 per cent of the total, fall into this category.)

In spite of this administrative and commercial use of the German language in the Ajoie (German: Elsgau) region around Porrentruy, the use of French as an *official* (as well as a popular) language appears to have become increasingly widespread in the Bernese Jura during the sixteenth, seventeenth, and eighteenth centuries. Bessire (op. cit.) and others conclude that by the eighteenth century, to all intents and purposes, the widespread use of German was confined, as it is today, to the Laufen district in the extreme north-west of the region.

The Period from 1792 to 1900

As Chapter 7 will outline in more detail, from 1792 onwards Revolutionary France began to exert increasing political pressure on the bishopric of Basle. The rule of the incumbent prince-bishop was ended in 1792 and, for a number of years thereafter, France controlled the region, first establishing the 'Rauracian Republic'. France subsequently annexed the region, renaming it *le département de Mont-Terrible*. French continued to be the official language of the region during this period, as it had been for the previous two-and-a-half centuries. As discussed in Chapter 2, following the final defeat of Napoleon, the territories of the former bishopric of Basle were awarded to Canton Berne[7] at the Congress of Vienna in 1815.

While language still does not appear to have been a source of political friction during the early years of the nineteenth century, the government of Berne did, nevertheless, guarantee the rights of the French language in its newly acquired territory. About the middle of the nineteenth century, however, the relative strengths of the French and German languages in the region began to change because of the immigration of German-speaking Swiss to the Bermese Jura; immigration to which reference was made in Chapter 2.

Table 4, based on data recorded in decennial Swiss Federal Government censuses, provides details of the extent to which French and German were spoken in each of the six predominantly French-speaking districts of the Bernese Jura, and in the district of Biel[8] from 1860 to 1970. (Appendix C: Table 1 provides similar data, on a commune-by-commune basis, for each of the French-speaking districts of the Bernese Jura, for selected years between 1860 and 1970.) German-speaking immigration to the Bernese Jura was not insignificant even prior to 1860.[9] Nevertheless it can be seen, from the figures, that German-speaking immigration became even more extensive in most districts of the Bernese Jura during the latter part of the nineteenth century.

It will be recalled from Chapter 2 that Bernese immigration was heaviest in the southern, more predominantly Protestant districts of the Bernese Jura which were closest to Berne, namely Courtelary, Moutier, and La Neuveville.

Table 4. *Bernese Jura: German-speakers as a Percentage of Swiss Citizens in French-speaking Districts and Biel, 1860–1970*

District	1860[a]	1870[a]	1880	1888	1900	1910	1920	1930	1941	1950	1960	1970
Courtelary	26	26	36	28	21	19	20	22	22	23	22	20
Delémont	14	16	23	25	25	26	22	22	19	18	16	12
Franches-Montagnes	1	2	5	5	5	5	8	9	10	12	12	9
Moutier	25	29	37	40	33	30	29	26	24	22	20	15
La Neuveville	20	21	29	26	21	21	23	24	26	26	27	26
Porrentruy	2	2	7	7	6	8	9	11	11	11	10	7
Total: 6 French-speaking districts	14	15	23	21	18	18	19	20	18	18	17	13
Biel	80	77	79	73	68	67	68	68	67	68	69	67

[a] Estimates based on the ratio of German- and French-speaking households.

Source: Swiss Federal Bureau of Statistics.

(For example, Table 4 indicates that in 1880, in the districts of Courtelary and Moutier, German-speakers accounted for 36 per cent and 37 per cent of the populations respectively.) The percentage of German-speakers subsequently increased still further in some districts. For example, in the census of 1888, 40 per cent of the residents of the Moutier district listed German as their mother tongue (Table 4). German-speaking immigration, however, was somewhat uneven in nature;[10] it tended to display a wave-like pattern over a period of time (Table 4 and Appendix C: Table 1).

This massive German-language immigration had an important impact on the educational system of the Bernese Jura. Some primitive German-language schools seem to have existed in the bishopric since the early Anabaptist settlements of the sixteenth, seventeenth, and eighteenth centuries. As a result of the heavy immigration of German-speakers during the latter part of the nineteenth century and the activities of the *Deutschschweitzerischer Sprachverein* (a German-Swiss cultural association), however, a large number of German-language schools were established in the Bernese Jura. These were scattered throughout the Bernese Jura from Charmoille (in the Porrentruy district in the north) to Frinvillier (in the district of Courtelary in the south). The geographic distribution of these schools is shown in Figure 20.

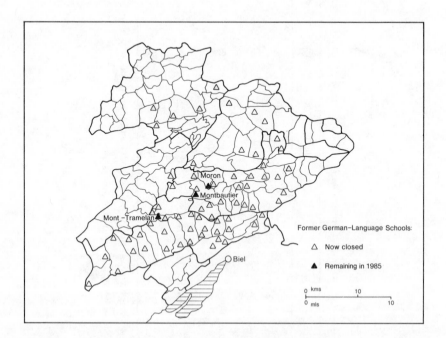

Fig. 20. The Bernese Jura: Distribution of Former and Present-day German-language Schools.

The Period from 1900 to 1913

Because of the appearance of large numbers of German-speaking (and predominantly Bernese) settlers in the quiet valleys of the region, language gradually became a sensitive issue in the Bernese Jura during the latter part of the nineteenth century, leading to friction between the original French-speaking inhabitants and the more recent German-speaking immigrants. Moreover, as was noted earlier, German-speakers from the Old Canton continued to settle in the Bernese Jura during the early years of the twentieth century, and their numbers were such that increasing tensions developed between French-speakers and German-speakers in the region.

In 1880 as many as twelve communes, out of a total of 134 communes in the six traditionally French-speaking districts of the Bernese Jura, recorded German-speaking majorities, and in many more the percentage of German-speakers exceeded 40 per cent of the total population. While—as indicated earlier—the percentage of German-speakers in some of these communes subsequently declined slightly, each subsequent census recorded *additional* communes in which, for the first time, German-speakers exceeded French-speakers.

There is no doubt that French culture in the Bernese Jura faced a serious threat during this period. Foreign observers tended to share the views of many French-speaking Jurassians regarding this threat. The English author Frank Webb, writing in the early years of this century, believed 'the onward march of the German tongue' to be 'irresistible' (Webb, op. cit.). In 1913 two incidents, the Schelten–Seehof crisis and the Anabaptist school affair, served to heighten linguistic tensions still further.[11] The outbreak of World War I exacerbated the tension, since it created a wide rift between French-Swiss (who were sympathetic toward the French cause) and German-Swiss, who generally favoured the German cause.

The Period form 1913 to the Present Day

German schools in more strongly French-speaking areas of the Bernese Jura received no support from the local Jurassian community and were forced to close, because of declining enrolments, even before 1914. In some areas, therefore, the linguistic threat to French culture proved to be less fearsome than it appeared at first glance. However, German schools continued to flourish for some years more in a number of areas of the region, and especially in the southern districts of the Bernese Jura (Fig. 20).

We earlier noted that during World War I German–French linguistic tensions, both in the Bernese Jura and elsewhere in Switzerland, heightened, due to the wider conflict between Germany and France. Gradually, however, with the defeat of Germany and the reduction of language tensions in Switzerland as a whole, the tide began to turn in favour of the French language. By

1919 the majority of German-language schools in the Bernese Jura had been closed. Because of protests and representations from French-speaking Jurassians, and declining enrolments in most German-language schools, the government of Canton Berne implicitly recognized the implications of Articles 27 and 116 of the Federal Constitution,[12] and of its own previous guarantees of support for the French language in the traditionally French-speaking part of the canton.

Subsequently, one by one, most of the remaining German-language schools in the Jura were closed during the decades which followed. This meant that the majority of children from homes in which German was the first language, in the traditionally French-speaking districts of the Bernese Jura, would henceforth receive their education in the French language. As a result, from 1918 onwards, the majority of German-speaking Jurassian children living in the six French-speaking districts of the region adopted French as their first language.[13]

We have seen, however, that German-Swiss immigration to the Jura continued not only up to World War I, but also during the 1920s, 1930s, and 1940s to such a degree that subsequent censuses recorded German-speaking majorities in a number of additional communes.[14] Observers such as Meylan, writing as late as the 1950s, believed French to be 'giving way' in the Bernese Jura (Meylan, op. cit.). An incident in 1947 which subsequently became known as *l'affaire Moeckli* (the Moeckli affair)[15] intensified feelings of discontent in the region, led to renewed protests by French-speaking Jurassians against the menace of germanization, and gave rise to the establishment, firstly, of the moderate *Comité de Moutier* (Committee of Moutier) and, subsequently, to the founding of the separatist organization, the *Rassemblement jurassien*. Nevertheless, the present-day facts, to this writer, do not appear to bear out these Jurassian language concerns. As Table 4 indicates, the overall percentage of German-speakers in the six French-speaking districts of the Bernese Jura declined more or less steadily from 1930 onwards, and by 1970 accounted for only 13 percent of the total. In 1930, a total of thirteen communes in the six French-speaking districts had German-speaking majorities. In 1941 there were ten such communes; in 1960 nine, and in 1970 only seven. (The location of predominantly German-speaking communes in 1880, 1910, and 1930 respectively is indicated in Figs. 21–3.)

By 1970 there were only three communes[16] *within* the French-speaking districts of the Bernese Jura which recorded German-speaking majorities (Fig. 24). All three of these communities, namely Mont-Tramelan in the district of Courtelary, Rebévelier in the district of Delémont, and Châtelat in the district of Moutier (Appendix C: Table 1), included significant Anabaptist settlements. By 1985, moreover, only three German-language schools survived in the whole of the French-speaking Bernese Jura. These were all situated in, or near, Anabaptist communities, and they served a total of approximately thirty-five children. The Mont-Tramelan school (the largest of the three) served the

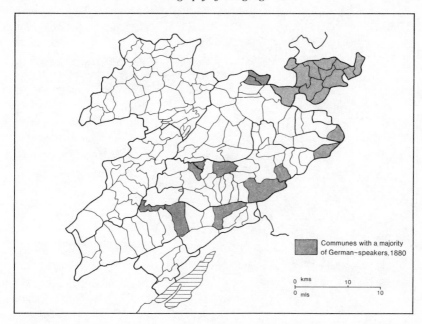

Fig. 21. The Bernese Jura: Predominantly German-speaking Communes, 1880.

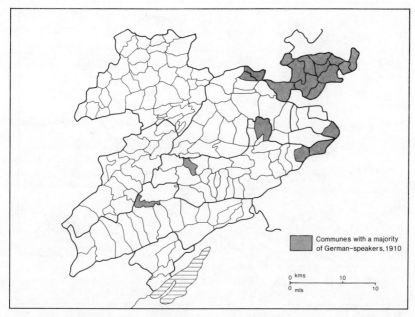

Fig. 22. The Bernese Jura: Predominantly German-speaking Communes, 1910.

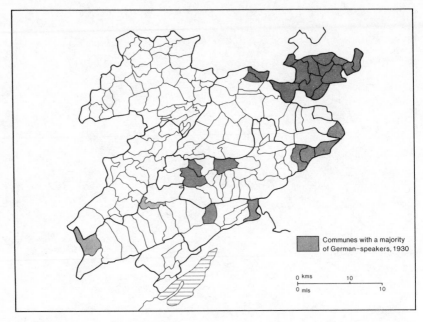

Fig. 23. The Bernese Jura: Predominantly German-speaking Communes, 1930.

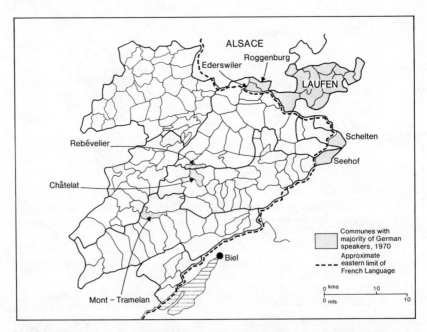

Fig. 24. The Bernese Jura: Distribution of French- and German-speakers, 1970.

commune of the same name, the Moron school served the German-speaking settlement of Moron in the commune of Châtelat (Plate 5), and the Mont-bautier school served other scattered Anabaptist families near the village of Le Fuet in the commune of Saicourt (Fig. 20).

The Present-day Language Frontier in the Bernese Jura

The approximate French–German linguistic frontier[17] in the pre-1979 Bernese Jura is depicted in Fig. 24. In the north, at the Swiss–French border in Alsace, the linguistic frontier separates the predominantly French-speaking commune of Movelier from the German-speaking communes of Ederswiler and Roggenburg.[18] The border then separates the French-speaking commune of Soyhières (in the Delémont district of the Bernese Jura) from the German-speaking commune of Liesberg (in the Laufen district of the region). To the south, the linguistic border follows the border of the Bernese Jura rather closely, except in the area of the Schelten pass, where the region includes the two easterly German-speaking communes of Schelten and Seehof, bordering German-speaking Canton Solothurn.

Summary

The historic and present relationships of the French and German languages in the Bernese Jura can now be summarized briefly. To begin with, following the Roman period when the Bernese Jura was inhabited by Celtic-speaking peoples, German-speaking Alemanni appear to have settled areas to the north of the region (Alsace) and to the south of the region (the Mittelland as far west as the present-day town of Pieterlen). They appear to have occupied those eastern portions of the Jura range which lie in the present-day Swiss cantons of Aargau, Baselland and Solothurn, and penetrated the Birse valley to settle the Laufen district of the Bernese Jura, which lay closest to the bend of the Rhine and the site of the future city of Basle.

During this period the predominantly Celtic Jurassians appear to have been gradually latinized through their contact with romanized Celts living to the north-west and west of of the Bernese Jura. The successors of these latter peoples appear to have spoken the langue d'oïl dialects of northern France and, consequently, the French dialects spoken through the greater part of the Bernese Jura were related to the langue d'oïl dialects, in contrast to the langue d'oc (Burgundian) dialects which were spoken in the other regions of present-day French Switzerland.

The Valley of the Birse in the north-eastern Jura district of Laufen (German: Laufental) represented the most westerly penetration of German-speaking peoples into the Jura range (Fig. 24). German-speakers were apparently unwilling and/or unable to settle the Jura chain to the west, even though it lay between German-speaking Alsace, to the north, and the predominantly German-speaking Mittelland to the south (Fig. 5). We have seen that the reasons for this appear to be closely related to the physical geography of the area in that, just beyond the most westerly German-speaking settlement in Laufental and to the east of Soyhières, the Birse valley forms a relatively narrow, winding defile which must have constituted a natural barrier to further settlement to the west.

The latinized Burgundians, while they settled Mittelland areas to the south-west of the Jura mountains, do not appear to have penetrated the Jura range itself to any marked degree. Consequently, as indicated earlier in this chapter, the Francoprovençal of the Burgundians (although spoken through-out the whole of the rest of present-day French Switzerland) appears to have been spoken only in the extreme south-west corner of the future Bernese Jura. Even during later periods of German-Swiss westward expansion (e.g., when the Mittelland was occupied as far west as the shores of the Lakes of Neuchâtel and Murten (French: Morat)), it does not appear that the French language spoken by the inhabitants of the greater part of the future Bernese Jura was seriously threatened (Fig. 5). This was so in spite of the fact that the bishops of Basle, the officials of the bishopric, and many traders and craftsmen in the region all spoke German as their first language. The Bernese Jura thus remained a stronghold of the French language—a latinized promontory jutting eastward into a German-speaking sea.

While German-speaking Anabaptists settled a few scattered communities (more especially in the South Jura) during the sixteenth and seventeenth centuries, they did not pose any serious threat to the French culture of the future Bernese Jura as a whole. A far more serious threat was posed by the heavy German-Swiss (and predominantly Bernese) immigration to certain Jurassian communes during the nineteenth and early twentieth centuries. As we have noted, this immigration was particularly heavy in the southern districts of the Bernese Jura.

Bernese immigration to some communes of the Bernese Jura continued, though to a lesser degree, until World War II. As already indicated, however, the threat of germanization receded. This was due to the hostility of many Jurassians, to a slackening of German-Swiss immigration during World War I, to declining enrolments in some schools, the implicit enforcement of Articles 27 and 116 of the Swiss Federal Constitution, and the recognition, by the government of Canton Berne, of earlier language guarantees it had made to its Jurassian population. As most of the remaining German-language schools in the region were gradually closed, the children of German-speaking immigrants became French-speaking. Many, in the North Jura, also became enthusiastic francophones. In spite of the concerns still expressed by some separatist spokesmen, therefore, the French-speaking Jurassians (both in Canton Jura and the South Jura, which has remained a part of Canton Berne) would appear to have won their linguistic battle against German during the course of the twentieth century.

In retrospect, however, if large-scale Bernese immigration had continued on the scale of the 1880–1910 period for two or three more decades, the French culture of the South Jura, in particular, might have been overwhelmed. It is interesting to speculate as to what might have occurred if the German-speaking population of large areas of the Jura had reached, say, the 55 per cent level. If such a degree of saturation had been reached, for example, throughout the length of the St-Imier valley in Courtelary, the cantonal government might well have been encouraged to resist francophone demands that the German-language schools of this area be closed. Events might then have taken a different course, and at least some southern areas of the Bernese Jura might have been overwhelmingly germanized if such a critical point had been reached.[19] Such, in the event, was not to be the case, however, and the present-day German–French linguistic border in the Bernese Jura itself thus appears, to all intents and purposes, to have remained relatively unchanged since the days of the Barbarian Invasions which began around AD 400.

Conclusions

It is suggested that there are three particularly significant conclusions which can be drawn from a study of the geography of language of the Bernese Jura as it relates to the separatist phenomenon. Firstly, and above all else, the geography of language of the Bernese Jura appears to be closely related to its *physical geography*. It seems to have been the mountainous nature of the region which enabled the Latin-derived French language to survive there when the latinized inhabitants of the areas to the north, east, and south were expelled or overwhelmed by German-speakers during the period from around AD 260 to 1200. The French language and culture, protected, it appears, by the rugged terrain of the Jura mountain range, was able to take root in the region.

Several points are worth re-emphasizing in this regard. Firstly, to the north, the German language established in Alsace did not succeed in penetrating the hilly foothills of the Jura range to any significant degree. To the north-east, German-speakers were unable to penetrate the gorge of the Birse leading from the German-speaking Laufen district to the French-speaking commune of Soyhières in the district of Delémont. To the east, high mountain ranges prevented German-speakers from moving westward, except to a limited degree in the communes of Schelten and Seehof. Along the south-east border of the Bernese Jura, the narrow gorge of the Raus separated French-speaking Crémines from German-speaking Gansbrunnen in Canton Solothurn. To the south, the Taubenloch gorge separated French-speaking Frinvillier from predominantly German-speaking Biel. To the south-west, the hilly Montagne de Diesse appears to have prevented German-speakers from establishing themselves beyond the north shore of the Bielersee (Lake of Bienne).

Secondly, in turn, the existence of a common French language and culture *did*, apparently, serve to develop (in spite of admittedly strong countervailing influences such as massive Bernese immigration to some areas) a certain 'Jurassian consciousness' among many of the inhabitants of the bishopric (the future Bernese Jura).

Thirdly, the germanization threat of the period between 1850 and 1918, even though it was not necessarily the result of official federal or Bernese government policy, was nevertheless a very real one. In retrospect, if it had continued at the same level, it might well have overwhelmed at least some southern areas of the Jura. It had a profound, traumatic effect on many francophones in the Jura, and it echoes today in the warnings of Jurassian separatist leaders that germanization still poses a real danger to the region.[20]

Our discussion of the geography of language of the Bernese Jura poses, it is suggested, the following question, among others. To what extent does the presence of the French language in the region correspond to the existence of present-day Jurassian separatist feelings? Were French-speaking Jurassians more in favour of the establishment of a new canton than German-speaking Jurassians in the years leading up to the 1974 referendum? This question will be discussed at greater length in Chapter 8.

Notes

1. Jurassian separatist spokesmen, in recent years, have not claimed the Laufen district for the new canton, presumably feeling that such a vigorous German-speaking district (which has strong links with Baselland and which clearly did not wish, in any event, to join a French-speaking canton) would be 'indigestible' and would create unnecessary problems for an enlarged Canton Jura. (See also Chapter 8, n. 1.)

2. The Alemanni did not settle in the areas south of the Alps, however. In this latter region the Lombards (originally a German-speaking tribe) settled and adopted the Vulgar Latin (later Italian) spoken in the Alpine valleys which led southwards. Nor did the Alemanni settle the eastern Alpine valleys of the Rhine and Inn in what is now Graubünden (Grisons), where the latinized inhabitants continued to speak a form of Latin which subsequently evolved into modern-day Romansh. (Much later, German-speaking 'Walsers' *did* settle both in Graubünden and in certain regions south of the Alps.)

3. It is suggested by these observers that this minor cultural difference, coupled with the Bernese Jura's somewhat remote geographical position in relation to the other French-speaking regions of the country, inhibited the development of close links between Jurassians and the inhabitants of the other French-speaking areas of Switzerland.

4. The North Jura remains one of the few French-Swiss regions in which a significant number of dialect speakers can still be found in 1985; for example, in the Val Terbi to the east of the town of Delémont. Christe's *A cârre di füe* (French: *Au coin de feu*) is an example of North Jurassian dialect literature.

5. This conclusion is based upon records both of the names of these individuals and of the areas whence they originally came. In Europe, up until the thirteenth century, all official documents were in Latin. In 1239, however, a Hapsburg document, written completely in German, was attested to before Bishop Witold von Roteln of Basle. This manuscript is believed to be the first official document in the German language. From this time onwards, German, French and other major European languages were used more and more frequently in such documents (Müller, op. cit.).

6. Further to the south-west (i.e., in that portion of the region which was geographically closer to the region of French language and culture to the north and north-east of the Lake of Neuchâtel) the relationship between those in authority and their subjects appears to have been different. In the present south-central district of Moutier, the abbots of the monastery of Bellelay (which had a

close connection with the monastery of Prémontre, near Laon in France) were apparently French-speaking (Müller, op. cit.).

7. As indicated in Chapter 2, the term 'Bernese Jura' first came into existence at this time. The term differentiated the new *Bernese* possessions in the Jura range (formerly belonging to the bishopric of Basle) from those regions of the Jura mountain range belonging to Neuchâtel (to the west), and to Baselland, Solothurn, and the Aargau (to the east).

8. The district of Biel consists predominantly of the town of Biel, but also includes the commune of Evilard. Chapter 2 has already described briefly how, following the 1815 settlement, substantial numbers of French-speaking Jurassians migrated from the communities of their birth to settle in larger communities within the Jura as well as communities lying outside the Jura proper, such as the city of Biel. In this latter town, they were treated with great tolerance by the German-speaking inhabitants, and were permitted to establish an extensive French-language school system. (A letter to the *Journal du Jura* (a Biel newspaper) by Merazzi (1979), suggests, in fact, that the French school system in Biel has been expanding at the expense of the German system in recent years.)

9. Appendix C: Table 1 indicates, for example, that 53 per cent of the population of the commune of Corgémont, in the Suze valley (vallon de St-Imier) in the southern district of Courtelary was German-speaking at the time of the 1860 census.

10. For example, the commune of Souboz, in the district of Moutier, first recorded a German-speaking majority in 1880. However, the commune recorded French-speaking majorities in several subsequent censuses with the German-speakers declining to 18 per cent of the total by 1910. A further heavy wave of German-speaking immigration occurred between 1910 and 1920, however. As a result, German-speaking majorities were subsequently recorded in Souboz (for example a 51 per cent majority in 1930 (Appendix C: Table 1)) and subsequently up to, and including, the census of 1941.

11. These incidents, and other linguistically related tensions of the period will be discussed more fully in Chapter 8.

12. Article 27 of the Swiss Federal Constitution states that the cantons are responsible for primary education. Article 116 of the same constitution states that French is both a national and official language of Switzerland. The Bernese Constitution recognizes French as an official cantonal language. In Switzerland, the 'territorial principle' of language is implicitly recognized by all authorities, i.e., that the official language of a region is the language spoken there, and that this language should be the one used in local schools.

13. Some individuals of German-Swiss background in the North Jura became, in fact, passionate Jurassian separatists, as the German surnames of some separatist leaders and of many separatist supporters attest.

14. Appendix C: Table 1 indicates, for example, that 38 per cent of the inhabitants of the commune of Goumois, in the district of Franches-Montagnes, were German-speaking in 1970, compared to 7 per cent in 1900 and 24 per cent in 1930. The reason was that this village on the French frontier included a number of German-Swiss government officials and their families in its population.

15. This incident will be discussed in greater detail in Chapter 8.

16. This did not include German-speaking communes such as Ederswiler and Roggenburg near Alsace, or Schelten and Seehof, near Solothurn. These four communes, although they officially belong to French-speaking districts, were all situated on the French-German language frontier (Fig. 24). See also n. 18.

17. This linguistic frontier is discussed by Müller (op. cit.), but has been personally verified by the writer.

18. These latter communes, which are contiguous with Alsace across the French border, speak an Alsatian dialect of German. This dialect has some similarities with that of Baselland. Früh (op. cit.) has suggested that Ederswiler and Roggenburg were French-speaking until about the middle of the seventeenth century when, following the devastating plague of their period, they were repopulated by settlers from Alsace.

19. Such an event, in fact, occurred *in reverse* in Canton Valais, where the French-speaking area expanded significantly at the expense of the German-speaking area between 1860 and 1920.

20. The latter present the 'threat' in geographical terms, in the form of maps showing German-Swiss arrows 'invading' the Bernese Jura from several points to the north-east, south-east and south of the region.

5

The Geography of Religion of the Bernese Jura

> The astonishing thing, considering the intense hatreds which the Reform-
> ation engendered, is not that the Swiss failed to achieve anything in unison,
> but that they stayed together despite these hatreds. The amazing thing is
> that the Confederation emerged whole.
>
> WILLIAM MARTIN (1974)

Just as a study of the geography of language of the Bernese Jura is essential to
any attempt to understand the phenomenon of Jura separatism, so, too, is a
study of the geography of religion of the region. Several historians have
described, at some length, the circumstances whereby certain areas of the
pre-1979 Bernese Jura became Protestant while other areas remained
Catholic. These writers include Martin (op. cit.), Amweg (op. cit.), and
Bessire (op. cit.). In addition, Früh (op. cit.), Gutersohn (op. cit.), and
Schindelholz (op. cit.) have discussed the relative strengths of Protestantism
and Catholicism in various areas of the region, while Schäppi (op. cit.) has
discussed legal aspects of religious practice in Switzerland, including the
Bernese Jura.

Pre-Reformation Military Alliances

Before we attempt to determine whether any relationship exists between
religious preference and the phenomenon of separatism in the Bernese Jura, it
is suggested that both the pre-Reformation and post-Reformation religious
histories of the region need to be examined. This must be done in order to
ascertain whether or not the physical geography of the Bernese Jura—which
appears to have so strongly influenced its linguistic history and geography,
also appears to be related to its *religious* history and geography.

Nominally, both before and after the Reformation, the bishopric of Basle
constituted one administrative unit under the temporal rule of successive
prince-bishops. Even prior to the Reformation, however, the geographical
proximity of Biel, and of certain southern districts of the bishopric to Berne
and the Mittelland, led to the development of close relationships both between
the towns of Biel and Berne, and between each of these two towns and the
various communities of the South Jura. In sharp contrast, the difficult topography of the Jura mountain range meant that contacts between these
southern districts of the bishopric, on the one hand, and the northern districts,
on the other, were limited. It is clear that the inhabitants of the South
Jura were sufficiently independent of their bishops' rule from Porrentruy,

even prior to the Reformation, to negotiate agreements on their own behalf with certain Mittelland states of the Swiss Confederacy, and with Berne in particular.

In Chapter 6 the important role which the town of Berne has played in the history of the Swiss Confederation as a whole will become obvious. At this point, it will suffice to say that, from the thirteenth century onwards, as Berne grew in size and importance, it began to expand its power and influence outwards in all directions. This caused Berne to develop certain formal relationships with the townspeople of Biel and the inhabitants of the South Jura lying to the north-west of Biel, even through both Biel and the South Jura were nominally subject to the rule of the prince-bishops of Basle.

Specifically, the Bernese felt threatened by the power of the state of Burgundy to the north-west, under its ambitious ruler, Charles the Bold. The Jura mountain range lay between the territories of Berne and Burgundy, and the Bernese felt it essential that they increase their influence in this frontier region. Berne therefore concluded a military alliance with Biel and the Erguel (the Courtelary district of the South Jura) in 1352 (Fig. 25). This was, significantly, a year before Berne joined the Swiss Confederation, and approximately *180 years before the Reformation.*

Before joining the Confederation in 1353, Berne continued to strengthen its relationships[1] with other towns and other regions which, at that time, were not themselves members of the Confederation. Military alliances were concluded

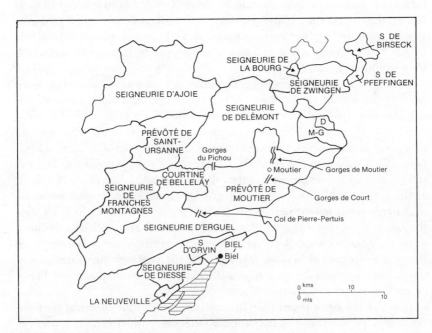

Fig. 25. The Bishopric of Basle: 1271–1792.

with Solothurn and La Neuveville in 1388 (Fig. 25). These latter alliances were cemented 140 years *before* the Reformation. In 1486, due to the rival claims of a cleric of Büren (a Mittelland town which was allied to Berne) and a Lucerner for the position of prefect of the *prévôté* (prefecture) of Moutier-Grandval, military action occurred. The following extract by Bessire (op. cit.) is quoted by Girard (op. cit.): 'In several days 1500 Bernese occupied the *prévôté* from Tavannes to Courrendlin. They even penetrated into the valley of Delémont, where they burnt several villages. The inhabitants of the *prévôté* had to swear allegiance to Berne.' Following this Bernese victory, according to Bessire (op. cit.), the reigning prince-bishop of Basle was obliged to negotiate with the Bernese at Courrendlin, at the northern exit of the gorges de Moutier, a winding *cluse* of the type described in Chapter 2. Following other negotiations, a treaty was signed later that same year (1486) in which the inhabitants of the prefecture (which lies primarily to the south of the gorges de Moutier), became allies of Berne (Fig. 25). This treaty, which was signed more than forty years before the Reformation, was subsequently renewed on a number of occasions during the two centuries which followed.

To a geographer, the references to these events, which it must be emphasized again, occurred *prior* to any division of the Bernese Jura along religious lines, are of considerable significance. It has been stated, on a number of previous occasions in this work, that the topography of the Jura mountain range must have made travel difficult in the Bernese Jura. It would seem only logical to assume that Bernese military forces, as they moved northwards from Berne, then along the narrow east–west longitudinal valleys, and then northwards again through the tortuous gorges of the Bernese Jura, would find their supply lines increasingly attenuated, until they reached a point beyond which they would hesitate to venture.

In this connection, it appears as if the area of Courrendlin (which lies, as we have indicated, at the northern exit of the gorges de Moutier, which itself extends to the north of the town of that name in the south-central Bernese Jura), was regarded by the Bernese as the limit of their sphere of influence, i.e., as a point beyond which they could not occupy territory on a permanent basis (Fig. 10). Expressing this somewhat differently, it would appear that Bernese troops were able to manoeuvre in the valleys of the South Jura (i.e., as far north as the gorges de Moutier) with considerable success. It would seem, however, that Berne regarded the narrow defile of the gorges de Moutier, together with the latter's northern exit at Courrendlin, as its logical northern military outpost or defence zone. Beyond this northern frontier, however, not only were Bernese armies at risk because of the adverse effects of their attenuated supply lines, but also because no traditional feelings of friendship towards Berne existed in this more distant territory.

It will have been noted that Bessire (op. cit.), in his comment that the Bernese '*even* penetrated in the valley of Delémont' (which lies to the north of Courrendlin) indicates that this military action was considered unusual.

Immediate Effects of the Reformation

At the time of the Reformation, which can be considered to have begun with Zwingli's sermons in Zurich in 1519, the city government of Basle took advantage of existing anti-clerical feeling, and ended the remaining feudal rights of the reigning bishop of Basle over the city. In 1525, the government of Basle also took advantage of the opportunity presented by a peasant revolt to persuade the communes of the nearby Birstal (the *seigneurie* of Birseck) to enter a permanent alliance with Basle. In this way, the city of Basle secured a foothold in that portion of the bishopric which lay immediately to the south-west of the city (Fig. 25). The Birseck area subsequently became a part of the canton of Basle.

It appears that the government of Basle did not attempt to take sides in the arguments between the disputing religious sects which came into being at this time. Rather, it allowed religious services of all kinds to be preached. Nevertheless, as was mentioned in Chapters 2 and 4, as a result of the city government's action the bishop, together with his see, left Basle permanently and went to Porrentruy in 1528. In fleeing with his court from Basle to Porrentruy, the bishop and his successors also replaced, as their seat of government, a cosmopolitan, German-speaking city and centre of important European trade routes on the Rhine with a small, relatively remote, French-speaking provincial town.[2]

The Geography of Religion from the Reformation until 1914

Following the Reformation, the bishops of Basle, from their new seat at Porrentruy, continued to govern the whole of their territory in a formal sense. This territory extended from the outskirts of the city of Basle in the north-east to La Neuveville in the south-west, and from Delle (on the French frontier in the north-west) to the outskirts of the town of Biel[3] in the south-east.

Earlier in this chapter we were reminded that, prior to the Reformation, close political and military relationships developed between the southern towns and districts of the bishopric of Basle, on the one hand, and the geographically adjacent Swiss Confederacy of the Mittelland—and especially Berne—on the other. Most significantly of all, at the time of the Reformation, these regions of the South Jura, as Mayer (op. cit.) puts it, '. . . followed Berne and its conversion of the new creed of Protestantism, while the northern parts of the bishopric . . . remained faithful to the Roman church.' An important new element was thus introduced into the geographical and social fabric of the future Bernese Jura. At the time of the Reformation the South Jura (that is, the area south of the gorges de Moutier), together with Biel, became predominantly Protestant while the North Jura, to the north of the gorges de Moutier, remained Catholic.

In examining Jura separatism and the claims of some observers that it is closely associated with the Catholic religion, it is essential that we ask the question: Why in fact did the South Jura become Protestant, and the North Jura remain Catholic? To begin with, there seems little doubt that two centuries of military alliances and friendly relationships (based, at least in part, on a geographical contiguity) with Berne made the peoples of the South Jura more willing than would otherwise have been the case to accept new beliefs and philosophies which reached them primarily from the Mittelland.

The extension of Protestantism to the South Jura has been well documented by such historians as Amweg (op. cit.), Bessire (op. cit.), and Prongué (1978). Swiss Protestantism was a Mittelland creed which originated in the Mittelland city of Zurich, and quickly spread to other towns and cities of the Swiss Plateau, including Geneva. Once it was accepted by the people of Berne, the new faith (preached enthusiastically, in the Jura region, by French-speaking missionaries from Geneva and elsewhere) was backed by Bernese military might, and supported by Biel.[4]

Bernese Protestantism can, perhaps, be compared to a massive wave which approached a series of ridges (the Jura mountain range) which, as we have earlier noted, faced it at right-angles and were difficult to penetrate. In spite of the height of the ridges, the size and force of the Bernese wave was such that it passed (via the gorges du Taubenloch) through and across the first ridge of the Bernese Jura, namely the Montagne de Diesse and the Chasseral–Montoz range (Fig. 26). The strength of the Bernese armies and the power of Bernese

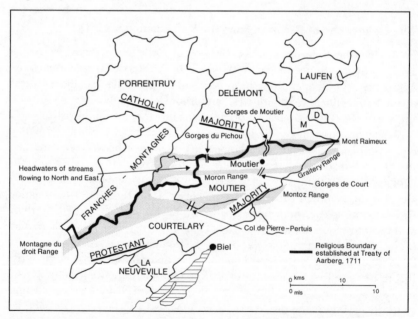

Fig. 26. The Bernese Jura: Distribution of Catholics and Protestants at Treaty of Aarberg, 1711.

and Genevese Protestantism were, indeed, such that they were subsequently able (by using the communications route which utilized the col de Pierre-Pertuis) to establish themselves a substantial distance to the north of the Montagne du Droit–Montoz range, which might at first appear to have been a formidable physical barrier to its northward movement (Fig. 26).

Bernese armies and Protestantism were subsequently able, by passing through the gorges de Court, to establish their power and influence in the town of Moutier and its environs, which lay to the north of the Graitery and Moron mountain ranges (Fig. 26). As it proceeded increasingly further from the point of its origin, however, Berne's militant Protestant wave appears to have lost both height and momentum. Moving northwards, it finally reached a point (the gorges de Moutier and the gorges du Pichoux) where it appears to have become exhausted, and unable to cross the subsequent obstacles which still confronted it, i.e., the Montagne de Moutier–Mont Raimeux barrier (Fig. 26).

South of this barrier, however, and from the town of Moutier, Bernese Protestant influences spread to the east (to the headwaters of the Raus river, which flowed through the Grandval) and as far as the mountainous border between the Bernese Jura and Canton Solothurn. South of the Montagne de Moutier and west of the town of Moutier, they also moved beyond the headwaters of the Chalière to the area where the infant Sorne flows northward through the gorges du Pichoux (Fig. 26). Protestantism and Bernese armies further maintained their momentum until they reached the somewhat remote upland areas around the abbey and settlement of Bellelay, where they met strong Catholic resistance.

To the south-west of Bellelay, to the west of Tavannes, Protestantism weakened when it reached the headwaters of the Trame beyond the town of Tramelan. To the south-west, Protestantism was unable to prevail, either, in the areas to the north-west of the Montagne du Droit–Chaux d'Abel mountain range. Beyond the gorges de Moutier (which lies to the north of the town of Moutier and bisects the east–west range of the Montagne de Moutier and Mont Raimeux) it appears, however, from the writings of Oechsli (op. cit.), Bessire (op. cit.), and others that the influences of the Catholic North Jura, radiating southwards from the bishop's seat at Porrentruy and such lesser centres as Delémont (and protected by the Montagne de Moutier–Mont Raimeux ridge), successfully resisted Protestantism. If, in fact, we pursue our wave simile further, the Catholic influences emanating from Porrentruy can be compared to an opposing series of waves which moved southwards to meet the Protestant waves head-on at the gorges de Moutier.

By contrast, the spread of Protestantism from Berne in certain other directions did not meet with such difficult topographical barriers as those which existed in the Bernese Jura. Bernese influences and armies alike could, for example, travel fairly easily in a south-easterly direction along the Aare and Emme valleys (which were already part of the Bernese state), and north-eastwards and north-westwards across the Mittelland. (All these areas were, of course, German-speaking in addition to being easy of access). By and large, the Bernese armies and missionaries met relatively little resistance in these regions.

During the years which followed the Reformation, the danger of renewal of the northward surge of Protestantism in the bishopric of Basle was combatted by a military alliance between the bishopric and the Catholic cantons of the Swiss Confederacy (Martin, op. cit.). This alliance was concluded without any demand on the part of the Catholic states that the bishopric should, in return, join the Confederacy. Nevertheless, the alliance helped to save the northern districts of the bishopric for Catholicism, since it forestalled a plan concocted by the Protestant towns of Berne, Biel and Basle to re-invade the bishopric, divide it between them, and introduce the Reformation throughout their new territories. The alliance, besides forestalling the Berne–Biel–Basle plot, also gave the bishop the courage to suppress religious reform movements in the northern districts of his territory.

Following further warfare in the Bernese Jura, the Treaty of Aarberg in July 1711 confirmed the geographical separation of Catholics (who, by now, were firmly established in the north of the region) and Protestants (who were similarly firmly established in the southern districts). In the prefecture of Moutier-Grandval, the greater part of the district (i.e., that position which lay to the south of the gorges de Moutier and south and south-east of the gorges du Pichoux) was confirmed as Protestant (Fig. 26).

The commune of Roches, in the gorges de Moutier itself, together with all communities to its south, was confirmed as being Protestant. This southern area of the future Bernese Jura was henceforth known as 'sur les Roches' ('above Roches' in the Birse Valley, since the Birse flows northwards through the gorges de Moutier to the Rhine). To the north of Roches, beginning with the commune of Courrendlin (which includes both the northern portion of the gorges and an area to the north of the gorges) is the area known as 'sous les Roches' ('below Roches' in the Birse Valley), which was confirmed as being officially Catholic.

With very minor exceptions, the present-day religious map of the Bernese Jura had essentially taken shape by 1560, a century and a half before it was officially confirmed at the Treaty of Aarberg in 1711. The northern districts (Porrentruy, Delémont, Franches-Montagnes, certain north-eastern, northern and western communes of the district of Moutier, and the German-speaking district of Laufen) remained Catholic. The southern districts (Courtelary, La Neuveville, and the greater part of Moutier) had become Protestant (Fig. 26).

Interestingly, in spite of this religious division of the bishopric, the region maintained a certain nominal cohesion. The sovereignty of the prince-bishops of Basle over their Jura territory continued to be recognized by Berne, by the Swiss Confederacy, and by the Great Powers. In the northern, Catholic,

Table 5. *Bernese Jura: Catholics as a Percentage of Swiss Citizens in French-speaking Districts, Laufen, and Biel, 1850–1970*

District	1850	1860	1870	1880	1888	1900	1910	1920	1930	1941	1950	1960	1970
Courtelary	6	9	10	10	11	11	12	13	12	11	15	19	20
Delémont	96	96	94	90	86	81	79	78	77	77	78	80	80
Franches-Montagnes	99	98	98	96	94	93	93	90	88	88	86	85	85
Moutier	39	40	38	36	34	33	33	31	30	31	33	35	38
La Neuveville	3	9	3	5	5	6	7	6	5	6	6	11	14
Porrentruy	99	97	92	93	91	91	90	88	86	86	85	85	85
Total: 6 French-speaking districts	63	61	60	57	55	54	54	52	51	54	53	54	56
Laufen	98	97	94	94	93	88	87	86	85	85	87	86	84
Biel	9	10	10	12	14	17	16	16	16	15	18	20	23

Source: Swiss Federal Bureau of Statistics.

'imperial' districts of the bishopric (i.e., in Porrentruy, Delémont, and Franches-Montagnes) the reigning bishop was, in effect, also the feudal monarch (prince) and ruled in a relatively authoritarian manner. In southern, Protestant, 'Swiss' districts the rule of the bishops was titular only. This was especially the case with the town of Biel. In the South Jura as a whole, the power of the bishops was, as Oechsli (op. cit.) puts it:

. . . greatly limited by the liberties of the subjects and by the support which these (subjects) secured from Berne and Bienne (Biel). This was the case in the valley of St-Imier, the manhood of which had from ancient days gone into the field under the banner of the town of Biel; in La Neuveville on the Lake of Biel; and in the val de Moutier, which had long been associated with Berne in a perpetual alliance.

Between 1711 and 1815 Bessire (op. cit.) and other historians of the region record no important religious developments in the bishopric. However, from the middle of the nineteenth century (i.e., the period which followed the 1815 cession of the former bishopric to Berne) to the present day we have access to more substantial information with respect to the geography of religion of the Bernese Jura, because of the availability of Swiss census data. Table 5, which is based on census figures, lists the percentages of Catholics among the populations of the various districts of the Bernese Jura, and of the district (including the town) of Biel from 1850 until 1970.[5] Figures 27 and 28 indicate the religious maps of the region in 1850 and 1970 respectively.

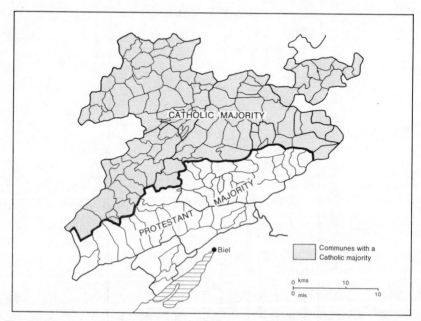

Fig. 27. The Bernese Jura: Distribution of Catholics and Protestants, 1850.

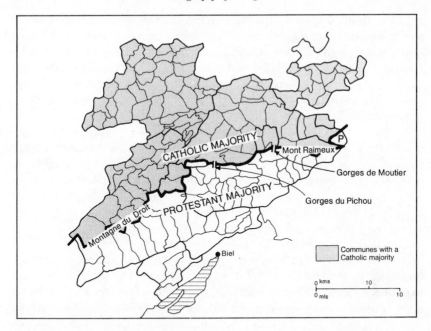

Fig. 28. The Bernese Jura: Distribution of Catholics and Protestants, 1970.

Figure 27 makes it clear that (with the exception of the sparsely populated eastern commune of Seehof, which had become predominantly Catholic by 1850) the dividing line between the predominantly Catholic communes of the North Jura and the predominantly Protestant communes of the South Jura in 1850 represented the situation which had prevailed in the region both 320 years earlier, at the time of the Reformation, and which continued to prevail approximately 190 years later at the time of the Treaty of Aarberg (Fig. 26).

Figure 28, summarizing the religious balance in the Bernese Jura in 1970, indicates that only three formerly Catholic communes on the religious border had changed their religious affiliation since 1850. One of these was Seehof, which recorded a Protestant majority (as was the case in 1711) again. Secondly, its neighbouring (and similarly German-speaking) commune of Schelten had a slight Protestant majority by 1970. Finally, significant German-speaking Anabaptist settlement in the commune of Rebévelier (to the west of the gorges du Pichoux) in the late nineteenth and early twentieth centuries had resulted in a Protestant majority in this commune by 1970.

It is thus interesting to note, from the census figures available to us, that even the massive immigration, discussed in Chapter 4, of German-speaking Swiss (primarily Protestants from the Old Canton) between 1850 and 1914 clearly did not disturb the religious balance of the Bernese Jura to any marked degree. There appear to have been several reasons for this: Firstly, it will be recalled, from Chapter 4, that the heaviest German-speaking Protestant immigration was to the southern districts of the region, i.e., Courtelary, Moutier, and La Neuveville. These districts were geographically closer to the Old Canton, were historical allies of Berne and Biel, and practised the same Protestant religion as the peoples of the Old Canton. In the district of Moutier as a whole, in fact, the Catholic proportion of the population fell from 40 per cent in 1860 to 30 per cent by 1930 (Table 5).

Secondly, not only was German-Swiss immigration to such northern, traditionally Catholic districts as Franches-Montagnes and Porrentruy lower than it was to southern, traditionally Protestant districts but, in addition, some of this immigration originated in predominantly Catholic German-Swiss cantons such as Solothurn. As a result, Protestants never constituted more than 7 per cent of the population of the district of Franches-Montagnes as a whole, or 10 per cent of the population of the district of Porrentruy prior to World War I. While Catholic Delémont did experience heavy German-Swiss immigration, even here Protestants constituted only 21 per cent of the population in 1910. This is not to deny that certain Catholic communes did experience extremely heavy Protestant immigration,[6] and the religious mix of a few communes was altered somewhat as a result. On the whole, however, for reasons listed earlier, the heavy Bernese immigration of the late nineteenth and early twentieth centuries had a greater influence on the *language* map of the Bernese Jura than on its religious map.

The Geography of Religion from 1914 to the Present Day

We saw earlier that migration from other parts of Switzerland to the Bernese Jura slackened, to some degree, in the period between the two World Wars. In spite of this, German-speaking Protestant immigration continued in some areas, and had certain minor effects.[7] In addition, because of increasing population mobility in Switzerland (as in other countries) since World War II, the formerly distinct geographic boundary between the two major religious groupings in the Bernese Jura had become blurred by the time of the 1974 referendum. The change was particularly marked in the central and southern districts of the region. In these latter districts significant numbers of individuals from the Catholic north found employment in industrialized, traditionally Protestant areas. As a result (and as Appendix C: Table 1 indicates), the percentage of Catholics in certain southern Jurassian communes had risen significantly by 1970.[8]

Anabaptist Settlements in the Region

Data on the Anabaptist (Mennonite) settlements in the Jura (which began in the latter sixteenth century and continued, in desultory fashion, until the twentieth century) have been provided by a number of writers, including Früh (op. cit.), Amweg (op. cit.), and Bessire (op. cit.). The majority of Anabaptist settlements in the Bernese Jura were, and are, situated in the southern, predominantly Protestant districts of the region, since the bishops of Basle did not wish to allow a fundamentalist Protestant sect to settle in the strongly Catholic north. In the period of rising political tension which followed the Moeckli affair in 1947, the relatively small, German-speaking Anabaptist settlements in the Bernese Jura began to face harassment from certain elements in the French-speaking Jurassian population who were particularly hostile to the German-Swiss culture.[9]

Summary and Conclusions

Observers differ in their views as to the degree which religious belief is related to separatist views in the Jura. A number of sociologists, including Mayer (op. cit.) and Henecka (op. cit.), together with a number of anti-separatist writers, including Aubry (op. cit.) and Flückiger (op. cit.) have suggested the existence of an extremely strong relationship between Catholicism and separatism. Other writers, including the sociologists Bassand and Fragnière (op. cit.) and Windisch and Willener (op. cit.) acknowledge the existence of a relationship but argue that other factors are of equal if not greater importance. At the other extreme, separatist writers, notably Béguelin (op. cit.), Charpilloz (op. cit.), and Fell (op. cit.) have denied that religion plays any significant role what-soever in the Jura problem. One thing which is clear is that the North Jura has been traditionally Catholic, and remains so to this day, while the southern part of the region, which was pro-Bernese and friendly towards Biel prior to the Reformation, became Protestant at the time of the Reformation, and has remained predominantly Protestant ever since.

Some writers, such as Amweg (op. cit.), have suggested that Protestantism was imposed by the military might of Berne and its ally, Biel. There is some truth to this, because there is no doubt that Bernese military power was a contributing factor in the spread of the Reformation to the South Jura. Other writers have argued, however, that, to the contrary, the southern areas adopted Protestantism readily because they are already on terms of friendship with Berne and Biel. There also appears to be some truth to this claim.

To this writer, the significant factors underlying both claims are, firstly, that the southern areas of the Jura are *geographically closer* to Berne than are those of the North Jura. Secondly, and compounding the effects of distance, is the fact that the Jura chain, in the Bernese Jura and elsewhere, is a high, forbidding mountain range whose ridges lie at right-angles to any traveller from Berne, and whose internal communication routes follow gorges (and occasionally, passes) which are few and convoluted.

The majority of the inhabitants of the southern valleys lived as close if not closer, in terms of travelling time, to the Mittelland as to the prince-bishops' seat at Basle and (subsequently), Porrentruy. This geographic fact of life encouraged the southern Jurassians to enter into close political and military relationships with the Swiss Confederacy and with Berne in particular. We have noted, moreover, that these close relationships *preceded* the Reformation by two centuries in some cases.

When the Reformation developed in Berne, the existing close relationships between Berne and the southern 'Swiss' districts of the bishopric facilitated the spread of Protestantism in the future Bernese Jura. The new religion preached by French-Swiss missionaries from Geneva and elsewhere, moved, in a north-ward and north-westward direction, over the southern districts of the Jura like a massive wave, in spite of the formidable east–west mountain ridges in its path. This Protestant wave was only stopped when it was confronted by the Montagne de Moutier–Mont Raimeux barrier, and by the Catholic armies of the North defending the gorges du Pichoux and the gorges de Moutier. It exhausted itself, in effect, when it travelled eastwards up the Grandval east of Moutier to the Solothurn border.

To the west of Moutier the Protestant wave weakened when it moved beyond the headwaters of the Chalière to the upper Sorne near the settlement of Bellelay, and when it moved to the headwaters of the Trame beyond Tramelan. In the south-west, Protestantism was unable to cross the Montagne de Droit–Chaux d'Abel barrier north of the Suze valley (vallon de St-Imier).

Thus, geographical factors influenced the spread of Protestantism in the Bernese Jura both indirectly and directly. Geographic proximity made it easier for friendships to develop between the South Jura and Berne, and these ties encouraged Protestant doctrines originating in Zurich and Geneva to spread to the South Jura. French–Swiss Protestant missionaries, preaching in the South Jura, were protected by the military power of Berne and, in addition, in the vallon de St-Imier, by Biel. Moreover, where necessary, the Reformation was imposed by military force in the South Jura.

Geographical proximity, similarly, was an important factor in the successful defence of the South Jura against Catholic efforts to retake the south. So, too, was the topography of the area and the south-westerly–north-easterly align-ment of its ridges. In fact, the two geographical dimensions of the topography and distance were, it appears, tacitly acknowledged by the powers of the day as limiting their respective freedoms of action in the present-day Bernese Jura. It would seem that the Bernese government was not prepared to extend its army's supply lines in a north-westerly direction *beyond* a certain geographic distance from Berne, because of the difficulties which might otherwise result.

The gorges de Moutier and the gorges du Pichoux—long, narrow and winding *cluses*—appear to have been regarded by the Bernese, at least implic-itly, as a suitable northern military frontier (Fig. 26). These gorges could certainly be readily defended, since attacking armies moving through a gorge in either direction could themselves be attacked by defending armies en-trenched on either side of the gorge. On the other hand, an attacking army could not easily deploy cavalry in flanking movements, because of the extreme narrowness of the gorges.

In summary, it appears that the human determinants (historical military alliances and military power) upon the present-day religious map of the Bernese Jura were *themselves* underlain by certain geographical variables—namely topography (including alignment) and distance. While, as we have seen, observers of the Jurassian scene differ in their opinions as to the degree to which Jurassian separatism is related to Catholicism,[10] even a cursory comparison between the 1970 religious map of the Bernese Jura and voting patterns in the 1974 referendum suggests, to the outside observer, a strong relationship between the two variables. Clearly, this relationship needs to be investigated further.

Notes

1. Mayer (op. cit.) describes these relationships as follows: 'In the fourteenth and fifteenth centuries the southern valleys of the Jura mountains and the towns of Biel and La Neuveville entered into a series of treaties and defensive alliances with the adjoining Swiss Confederacy and particularly with Berne, their immediate Swiss neighbour . . . Militarily they (i.e., the southern Jura valleys, Biel, and La Neuveville) were included in the Swiss defensive system, and were considered part of the Swiss zone of neutrality which protected them (subsequently) from the ravages of the Thirty Years War, in the course of which the northern territories of the bishopric suffered repeated occupations by the belligerents.'

2. As was indicated in Chapter 4, the bishops of Basle were to remain in Porrentruy until the arrival of French revolutionary troops in 1792.

3. While the bishopric of Basle did not include the town of Biel, the prince-bishops were, nevertheless, also titular overlords of the latter from the twelfth century onwards.

4. The influence and military power of Biel was particularly important in the vallon de St-Imier (Suze Valley) in the district of Courtelary. Both La Neuveville and Courtelary became Protestant in 1530, and Moutier followed in 1531. However, as indicated previously, the remoter northern areas of the district of Moutier (i.e., north of the gorges de Moutier) and its remoter western areas, remained Catholic.

5. Appendix C: Table 1 summarizes the Catholic percentages for each individual commune in the six French-speaking districts for selected years between 1860 and 1970.

6. For example, Appendix C: Table 1 indicates that the commune of Courrendlin, in the northern part of the district of Moutier, was 90 per cent Catholic in 1860. Because its boundaries included the foundry at Choindez, it attracted large numbers of immigrants. Many of these immigrants were German-speaking, Protestant Bernese. As a result, by 1930, 34 per cent of the population of Courrendlin was Protestant. So great was the German-speaking influx to the commune that Courrendlin recorded German-speaking majorities in the censuses of 1880, 1900, and 1910.

In the district of Moutier, the census of 1850 recorded no Protestants in the commune of Schelten, and only a handful in the commune of Seehof. It appears probable that both communes (which appear to have been predominantly German-speaking since at least 1650), were originally settled by Catholic peasants from the adjacent, predominantly Catholic (and German-speaking) canton of Solothurn. By 1900, however, the situation had changed dramatically. Protestants constituted close to 50 per cent of the population of both communes (Appendix C: Table 1) and, as we have seen, both communes subsequently recorded Protestant majorities. This change involving, as it did, relatively small numbers of people, may have been due to the decision of two or three Catholic families to move to larger centres and to the purchase of their farms by Bernese.

7. For example, immigration from the Old Canton and other German-speaking cantons resulted in an increase in the Protestant percentage of the population of the commune of Goumois (Franches-Montagnes), from 5 per cent in 1900 to 33 per cent in 1970, an increase which, in this instance, was aided by a marked absolute decline in the Catholic population of the commune (Appendix C: Table 1). This immigration was probably due, at least in part, to the fact that Goumois is situated on the French frontier and includes a number of federal government officials and their families in its population.

8. In the commune of Moutier, for example, Catholics accounted for 44 per cent of the Swiss population in 1970, compared to only 31 per cent in 1930 (Appendix C: Table 1). Even so, it can still be said that, in general, the religious map of the former Bernese Jura in 1985 represents a situation which is remarkably similar to that which prevailed 435 years earlier, in 1550.

9. These events will be discussed in more detail in Chapter 7.

10. The comments in this chapter, and the data provided, have focused solely upon *Swiss citizens* residing in the former Bernese Jura. The substantial numbers of foreign workers (primarily, though not exclusively, Catholics from such countries as Italy, Spain, and Portugal) who live and work in a number of towns and cities in the region have not been included in the discussion. This is because these 'guestworkers'—even those who have been granted permanent residence in Switzerland—are not permitted to vote in Swiss elections.

6

The Political Development of Canton Berne and the Swiss Confederation

The Swiss cantons regard themselves as having been there before the Confederation, and as having created the Confederation by a voluntary act. . .

CHRISTOPHER HUGHES (1975)

Up until now, we have examined the region known as the Bernese Jura from a number of geographic viewpoints. The physical geography, human geography, economic geography, the geography of language, and the geography of religion of the region have all been discussed in order to set the stage for the development of certain theories concerning Jura separatism. We cannot, however, disregard the larger political units with which the Bernese Jura was associated. Because we are particularly concerned with geographical determinants of Jura separatism, we must also be prepared to come to some conclusions regarding the degree to which geographical factors have played a part in the formation of both Canton Berne and present-day Switzerland.

The Role of Berne in Swiss History

No observer can study the history of Switzerland without being impressed by the major role played by the city and state of Berne from the fourteenth century onwards. The Bernese are, of course, aware of this role and are proud of it. We have already noted (in Chapter 5) the active role played, historically, by Berne and its allies such as Biel, in the affairs of the South Jura. We also noted that this role predated the Reformation by over two centuries. It also predated the Bernese assumption, in 1815, of sovereignty over the former bishopric of Basle, by five centuries.

Nor can the observer study historical and present-day maps of Switzerland without being impressed by the size of Canton Berne as it existed prior to the formal establishment of the new Canton Jura in 1979, and the way it has dominated—and, even now still largely dominates—the map of west-central Switzerland (Fig. 29). Between 1815 and 1978, Berne was the second largest Swiss canton in terms of area (behind the sprawling, thinly populated Canton Graubünden) and, with almost a million inhabitants in 1970 (Table 6), the second largest in population, behind Canton Zurich. Describing Canton Berne as it existed prior to the establishment of Canton Jura, Hughes (op. cit.) makes the following comments: 'Berne is a big, rather rich, and disproportionally rural canton. It includes all types of the Swiss scenery north of the

Alps, reaching from the snow-clad peaks of the Bernese Oberland, through the
Mittelland and the Seeland, to a chunk of the Juras, protruding thence into
France.' Even *after* the establishment of Canton Jura, the remaining portion
of Canton Berne, with a population of approximately 916,000, at the time of
the 1970 census, remains the second most populous Swiss canton after Zurich.
Even if (and this is, of course, a hotly debated issue) the South Jura, too, were
eventually to choose to detach itself from the Old Canton as the North Jura has
done, the remaining portion of Canton Berne, which had approximately

Table 6.   *Population and Land Area of Swiss Cantons Prior to Establishment of Canton Jura in 1979* [a]

Canton	Date of entry to Confederation	Land area (km²)	Population, 1970
Zurich	1351	1,730	1,107,788
Berne	1353	6,880	983,305
Lucerne	1332	1,490	289,641
Uri	1291	1,070	34,091
Schwyz	1291	910	92,072
Obwalden ⎫ Unterwalden	1291	490	24,509
Nidwalden ⎭		275	25,634
Glarus	1352	685	38,155
Zug	1352	240	67,996
Fribourg	1481	1,670	180,309
Solothurn	1481	790	224,133
Baselstadt ⎫	1501	37	234,945
Baselland ⎭		430	204,889
Schaffhausen	1501	300	72,854
Appenzell Inner Rhodes ⎫	1513	240	13,124
Appenzell Outer Rhodes ⎭		170	49,023
St Gallen	1803	2,010	384,475
Graubünden	1803	7,110	162,086
Aargau	1803	1,400	433,284
Thurgau	1803	1,010	182,835
Ticino	1803	2,810	245,458
Vaud	1803	3,210	511,851
Valais	1815	5,235	206,563
Neuchâtel	1815	800	169,173
Geneva	1815	280	331,599
Switzerland		41,272	6,269,783

[a] Following the establishment of Canton Jura, data for Canton Jura and the revised
Canton Berne (based on 1980 population figures) are as follows: *Canton Jura:* land area
836 km², population 64,800; *Canton Berne:* land area 6,044 km², population 916,035.

Source: Swiss Federal Bureau of Statistics.

857,000 inhabitants in 1970, would *still* easily be the second largest Swiss canton in terms of population (Table 6).

In area, too, Berne retains its position as the second largest canton (after Graubünden), in spite of the establishment of Canton Jura. If, subsequently, the South Jura were to detach itself from Berne, the latter would, even then, merely be reduced in total area to the approximate size of Canton Valais (Fig. 29). The Valais, however, is far less densely populated than Berne (Table 6), and far less influential in the affairs of Switzerland.

We have already noted that the medieval town of Berne and its modern counterpart were, and are, situated in the Mittelland, or Swiss Plateau. This is the region in which the vast majority of Swiss live and have always lived. In sharp contrast, the Bernese Jura occupies a region which differs markedly from the Mittelland in its physical features. We have noted that its mountain ridges lie at right-angles to the normal line of approach from the Mittelland (including Berne) and, as we have also noted, it occupies a remote, north-western, peripheral position in relationship to the Mittelland itself. Moreover, it can only be penetrated by means of a very limited number of winding, easily defended gorges or mountain passes.

Within that part of the Holy Roman Empire which was destined to become modern Switzerland, a number of ecclesiastical and feudal rulers enjoyed a high degree of local autonomy during the period beginning around the year

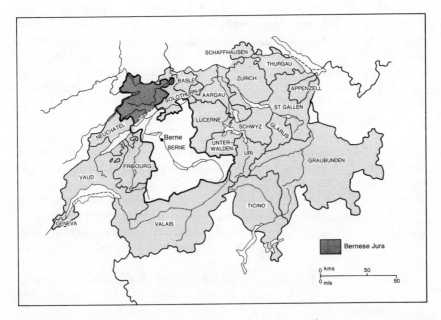

Fig. 29. Switzerland: 1815–1978, showing Canton Berne in Relation to the other Swiss Cantons.

1,000. Ecclesiastical rulers, such as the bishops of Basle were, almost without exception, also temporal, feudal rulers (i.e., princes). In spite of their local authority, the ecclesiastical authorities, including the bishops of Basle gave, in turn, their ultimate allegiance to the Holy Roman Empire.

The Origins of the Swiss Confederation

From about 1230 onwards, the St Gotthard Pass, situated in the present-day Canton of Uri, in the Alps to the south of Zurich, became increasingly important as a trade route between the trading and commercial centres of the German portion of the Empire, on the one hand, and those of northern Italy, on the other. It was thus quite natural that the powerful Habsburgs[1] (the nominal protectors of the Uri region at the end of the thirteenth century, who had also become Dukes of Austria) should begin to show an increasing interest in controlling both Uri and the St Gotthard trade route more directly.

The political history of the region at this period is only sketchily known. It does appear, however, that a tradition of local autonomy, freedom, and independence existed, particularly in Uri, but to a lesser extent also in Schwyz and Unterwalden. This resulted in the historic Oath of Rütli, which, it is believed, was sworn by men who met secretly (hence, some have suggested, the word 'confederates', which survives in the word 'Confederation') in the meadow of Rütli (in Uri), at the end of the thirteenth, or in the early years of the fourteenth century. Popular tradition holds that the confederates met at Rütli in 1291. Whether this is true or not, the agreement reached at Rütli appears to have been incorporated, either in 1315 or subsequently, into a document known as the *Bundesbrief*.[2] In the *Bundesbrief*, while pledging vague sentiments of continuing allegiance to the Emperor, the three forest cantons expressed hostility towards the Habsburgs and entered into a formal alliance for the defence of their common interests. These three states formed the nucleus of the subsequent Swiss Confederation.[3]

The geographical location of the three *Bundesbrief* states in relation to the remainder of present-day Switzerland, and to the Bernese Jura in particular, is significant. The founding cantons constituted what Deutsch (op. cit.) and other observers have called a 'pass state'. Uri, Schwyz, and Unterwalden occupied a position of great strategic significance where a vital medieval, north–south trade route from Germany to Italy (the St Gotthard Pass) opened on to the well-populated Mittelland. By contrast, the bishopric of Basle, lying to the north-west, was some distance from the major trade routes of the period (Fig. 30).

In 1330 an anti-Habsburg faction seized control of Lucerne, and formed a defensive alliance with Uri, Schwyz, and Unterwalden. In 1351 a pact was signed between Zurich, Lucerne, and the forest cantons which, among other things defined a wider geographic area (including substantial areas of the Mittelland) as being within the signatory states' sphere of influence. The

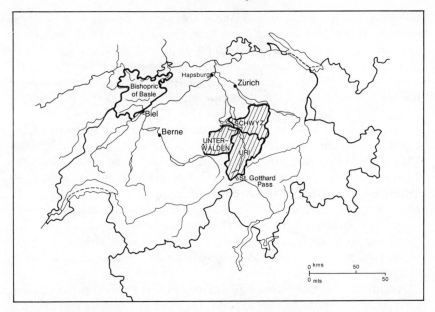

Fig. 30. Switzerland, showing the Geographical Relationship between the Bishopric of Basle and the 'Three Cantons'.
Note. Present-day cantonal boundaries are shown for the 'Three cantons'.

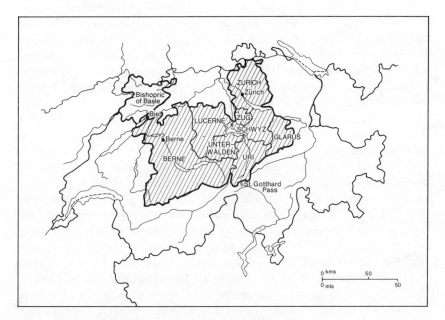

Fig. 31. 'The Confederation of the Eight States', 1353.
Note. Present-day cantonal boundaries are shown for the 'Eight States'.

following year (1352), Zug and Glarus also signed alliances with the forest cantons. In 1353 the town of Berne formed an alliance with the seven confederate states.[4] The subsequent 'Confederation of the Eight States' (Uri, Schwyz, Unterwalden, Lucerne, Zurich, Zug, Glarus, and Berne) consisted of a number of exclusively German-speaking cantons occupying that portion of the Mittelland lying to the north, north-west and north-east of, and controlling access to, the strategic St Gotthard Pass (Fig. 31).

Through a common military effort the Confederates defeated the Habsburgs, who attempted to subjugate them, at Sempach in 1386 and at Näfels in 1388. In 1415 confederate troops occupied the Aargau, and in 1460 the Thurgau. These lay to the north and north-east, respectively, of the Confederation, and both were subsequently administered as subject territories. In 1454, in the Burgundian War (1474–7), the Confederates helped France to eliminate Charles the Bold and his Duchy of Burgundy as a political force, as a result of their victories at Grandson and Morat (German: Murten). All these events took place in the Mittelland region; none directly affected the bishopric of Basle.

A significant event took place in 1481. After an extremely heated discussion, the confederate states agreed to admit the states of Solothurn and Fribourg into the Confederation. Although, as was mentioned in Chapter 4, language appears to have been of relatively little significance anywhere in Europe in the Middle Ages, the addition of Fribourg is, nevertheless, of interest because it meant that the hitherto exclusively German-speaking Confederation (whose members were, of course, distinguished from the Confederation's German-speaking subject territories, such as the Aargau, which were called 'common dominions') included, for the first time, a region of the west-central Mittelland which was inhabited, in part, by French-speaking peoples.

From 1438 onwards, the Habsburgs occupied the imperial throne. Following a series of battles, the Confederates defeated the Emperor and his Swabian League of German principalities and states during the fifteenth century. The Treaty of Basle in 1499 finally severed the Confederation's links with the German Empire.

In 1501 the towns of Basle and Schaffhausen joined the Swiss Confederation, and in 1513, Appenzell. The Confederation then numbered thirteen states. After the Battle of Marignano in 1515, at which they were defeated by the King of France, the confederate states, while permitting the Bernese and Fribourgeois to conquer and administer the French-speaking region of Vaud in 1536, did not admit any new territories to the Confederation with full rights until 1803, i.e. almost three centuries later.

The Reformation,[5] in the early sixteenth century, had a profound effect on the Confederation. It may appear surprising, to the observer, that the latter survived the various pressures caused by such a major religious upheaval. It did survive, however, in spite of the fact that some of its member-states became Protestant and others remained Catholic, and in spite of the fact that the

Reformation engendered intense bitterness and a series of civil wars. For-
tunately, certain member-states of the Confederation preached calm and
moderation.

The Period from 1648 to 1815

In 1648, at the close of the Thirty Years War, the Confederation's independence of the Empire was *legally* recognized by the Treaty of Westphalia. At this
juncture, the Swiss confederative structure consisted of three types of territories, namely the Thirteen Cantons or member-states, the Permanent
Allies[6] and the Subject Territories. The Thirteen Cantons (which were linked
by a complicated system of treaties and agreements) occupied the central
portion of the Mittelland and the northern Alps. Its member-states met
regularly in a *tagsatzung* (diet), composed of two representatives from each
canton (Martin, op. cit.).

After 1735 the bishopric of Basle was no longer considered, by the Catholic
states of the Swiss Confederation, to be an ally.[7] Moreover, when the Confederation signed an alliance with pre-Revolutionary France in 1777, the then
prince-bishop's territory, as a whole, was not included in this pact. Significantly, however, both Biel and the southern (Protestant) districts of the Jura
remained loosely linked (through their earlier military assistance pacts) with
the state of Berne.

In 1791, following the beginnings of the French Revolution, a French army
occupied the northerly (Catholic) portion of the bishopric of Basle. It is
significant that the French delayed attacking the southern districts of the
bishopric because of the latter's military alliance with Berne and other Confederates. It was not until December 1797, in fact, that a French army
occupied the valleys of the South Jura as part of a wider campaign of conquest.
They captured Biel (an early ally, as we have seen, of Berne) in February 1798,
and entered Berne, a key stronghold of the Thirteen Cantons, the following
month. The greater part of the remaining area of present-day Switzerland was
conquered by French armies in 1798 and 1799.

Interestingly, however, the conquering French made a distinction between
the northern and southern districts of the bishopric, treating them differently.
After a brief period as the puppet Rauracian Republic, the North Jura became
a French department. In sharp contrast, from 1799 to 1813, the South Jura
(i.e., the districts of Courtelary, Moutier, and La Neuveville) and the town of
Biel became, together with a number of other regions of modern Switzerland,
regions of the puppet Helvetic Republic.[8] As Napoleon's strength weakened,
Austrian troops occupied both the bishopric of Basle and the city of Biel
toward the end of 1813. In May 1814 the Swiss diet ordered the occupation of
the bishopric of Basle by Swiss troops (Bessire, op. cit.). This was a historic
event, since it represented—for the first time in history—an extension of Swiss
military power to the bishopric of Basle *as a whole*.[9] Soon afterwards, the Paris

treaty of 30 May 1814 detached the whole of the bishopric (including the Ajoie) from French rule.[10]

Following the final defeat of Napoleon at Waterloo and his permanent exile to St Helena, the Swiss Confederation sent more than twenty delegates to the Congress of Vienna in 1815. Three delegates represented the people of the bishopric of Basle (i.e. the Jurassians). Another delegate represented the town of Biel, and yet another the bishopric of Basle. As Martin (op. cit.) has succinctly put it: 'None of these men agreed about anything.' Linguistic factors seem to have mattered little at this time, though religious factors were important. In any event, the Swiss frontiers which were established at this time were, for better or worse, those of present-day Switzerland. Of greatest significance to this study is that the bishopric of Basle was given to a reluctant Berne to compensate it for the loss of the Vaud and Aargau territories, both of which became fully fledged cantons. The Swiss Confederation, as it emerged in 1815, is depicted in Fig. 29.

The Period from 1815 to the Present Day

At the Congress of Vienna the Great Powers formally recognized the neutrality of Switzerland, which, consisted henceforth of an enlarged confederation of cantons. A balance of power among these cantons (which was due in part to the relatively weaker position of Berne, as a result of its loss of Vaud and the Aargau), allowed the Confederation to achieve a state of relative harmony and tranquility for some years. The *Sonderbundskrieg* or Swiss Civil War of 1847 (in which seven Catholic cantons were defeated by twelve Protestant cantons after a short struggle), led to a new constitution in 1848. A two-chamber system of government[11] gave a high degree of recognition to linguistic and religious minority groups. This 1848 constitution was revised in 1874. The 1848 and 1874 constitutions struck a compromise between traditional federalism and the centralized form of government which had been the objective of the reformers. Single, unified 'Swiss' systems for customs, postal administration, currency, and weights and measures were established. Foreign policy became the responsibility of the central authority, but sovereignty was, in effect, divided between the central authority and the cantons.

To all intents and purposes, the Swiss constitution of 1874, with some minor revisions, is the one which exists today. It has survived the internal tensions caused by two World Wars. In spite of present-day strains and stresses, many of which are caused by the increasingly rapid rate of change in the world, the Swiss constitution continues to work reasonably well in the 1980s. In only one region of Switzerland—the Bernese Jura—have the Swiss Constitution and the Swiss system of government seemed, at first glance, to have been insufficient to deal with internal stresses and strains. Only in this same region has this insufficiency resulted, in modern times, in such un-Swiss phenomena as exploding bombs, damaged war memorials, arson directed at farmhouses, and street battles in which riot police have used tear-gas against demonstrators.

Summary and Conclusions

Certain geographical facts of interest emerge from a study of the history of the Swiss Confederation. Firstly, the original Swiss Confederation developed originally in certain Alpine valleys at the northern entrance to the geographically strategic St Gotthard Pass (Fig. 30). Subsequently, it expanded outwards from that region, in a north-westerly, northerly, and north-easterly direction to include a number of German-speaking Mittelland districts (Fig. 31).

The bishopric of Basle, as a political unit, was situated some considerable distance to the north-west of the original Confederation. Consisting primarily of relatively high mountain ranges, it was physically distinct from the Mittelland, and was geographically peripheral to it. Because its ridges ran at right-angles to the traveller who approached the region from Berne or Biel, it could be penetrated (via gorge or pass) only with difficulty. Consequently missionaries, and armies from Berne and Biel, exerted their greatest influence and power in those districts which lay *closest* to Berne and Biel. By contrast, the northern portion of the bishopric (consisting primarily of the districts of Porrentruy, Delémont, and Franches-Montagnes) was geographically more remote from the Mittelland and could only be reached from the Mittelland after several days journey from Berne, either across the ridges of the Jura mountain range, or via its few north–south gorges.

The peripheral geographical location of the Bernese Jura to both the Swiss Confederation as a whole, and to Berne in particular, has already been emphasized on a number of occasions. Although Berne was able to develop strong military and religious ties with that part of the Bernese Jura which lay geographically closest to it, it was only in 1815 that the entire region became an *official part* of Canton Berne. Expressing this another way, the North Jura was only joined to Canton Berne *for the first time* in 1815, after a hitherto *completely separate existence*.

Our examination of Swiss history in this chapter suggests that simple distance from Berne (both 'as the crow flies', and in terms of medieval and modern travel time), may also have been a determining factor in Jura separatism. It is possible that the greater the distance of a Jurassian village from Berne, the greater its sense of alienation from Berne, and we shall consider this possibility at greater length in Chapter 8.

During the nineteenth and twentieth centuries, relationships between the government of Canton Berne on the one hand, and between the French-speaking people of its newly acquired Jura territory on the other, were exacerbated on a number of occasions prior to the development of the present-day Jura problem. These earlier Jurassian separatist movements will be discussed in the next chapter.

Notes

1. In 1218 the Uri protectorship was awarded by the Holy Roman Emperor to the noble (and, at that time, apparently loyal and unassuming) family of Habsburg. In the absence of strong rule from the Holy Roman Emperor, however, the Habsburgs rapidly became the most powerful family between the Alps, Rhine, and Jura. As they grew more powerful, their loyalty to the Emperor diminished.

2. Some authorities question the alleged date, the actual occurrence of the Oath of Rütli, and the authenticity of the *Bundesbrief*. (The latter document, which purports to be the Rütli manuscript, was rediscovered in the archives of Canton Schwyz in 1758.) No one, however, would question the fact that, in its phraseology (e.g., 'we shall not retain or accept a foreign or mercenary judge'), the Rütli Oath is, as Hughes (op. cit.) puts it '... a declaration of independence, unilateral and illegal like all such declarations worthy of their name.' Few Swiss or non-Swiss historians, if any, would question that it accurately represented the feelings of the majority of the people or Uri, Unterwalden, Schyz, and Unterwalden at that time.

3. The official name of Switzerland is *Confoederatio Helvetica* (i.e. 'Swiss Federation' or 'Confederation'). The second part of the name derives from the Celtic tribe, the Helvetii (or Helvetians) to whom reference was made in Chapter 2.

4. The confederate towns and districts were originally known as *orte* (plural of the German-Swiss word *ort*, meaning 'place', 'locality', or 'region'). The term 'canton' only came into use in 1789.

The inhabitants of the Confederation enjoyed civil rights 500 years before the French Revolution, since its citizens elected the authorities and decided all important matters. In the *Landsgemeinde* or cantonal folk parliament (which has survived today in a few Swiss cantons), each citizen was entitled to express his views at an open-air meeting. On occasions when the states of the confederation made joint military conquests, common dominions (such as the Aargau and Thurgau) were set up, being alternatively ruled by a deputation from a single member-state.

5. The effects of the Reformation (which, in Switzerland, can be said to date from the activities of Zwingli, the religious reformer, in Zurich in 1519, and Calvin in Geneva soon afterwards), on the bishopric of Basle (the future Bernese Jura) were discussed in Chapter 5.

6. The most important Permanent Allies of the thirteen confederate states (in terms of the power they exercised), were the growing, German-speaking town in Biel at the foot of the Jura, and the prince-abbot of St Gallen. The so-called Subject Territories of the Confederation primarily included the present-day cantons of Ticino, Thurgau, and much of the Aargau. Those confederate member-states which possessed governing rights over a subject territory sent representatives to a special diet, which exercised rights of sovereignty and decided all matters (except those involving religion), by majority vote.

7. During the period from 1648 to 1790 the individual states which comprised the Thirteen Cantons, their Permanent Allies, and their Subject Territories occasionally fought among themselves, and often engaged in foreign, military, and diplomatic adventures. In spite of such individual involvements and crises (such as civil wars and insurrections) which served to disunite rather than unify, the loosely knit Swiss Confederation survived until the end of the eighteenth century.

8. The Helvetic Republic had certain features which are appealing to most of us living in the twentieth century. For example, it proclaimed the equality of Swiss citizens in law. The Republic is also of interest in that it introduced certain laws and enunciated certain principles which, while familiar to us today, were new in 1799. For example, its government proclaimed the principle of the equality of languages and freedom of belief and speech. It suppressed internal trade barriers, it instituted a unified system of weights and measures and reformed civil and penal law. In addition, it authorized mixed marriages, abolished torture, and improved the judicial system. Finally, it made progress in education and public works, and abolished all feudal obligations of a personal (i.e. non-fiscal) nature (Hughes, op. cit.).

9. In April and May 1814 the Allies, having restored the Bourbons, began drawing up the future frontiers of France. This was of great significance to the Swiss because they shared frontiers with the latter power. The Confederate diet, however, neglected to send a representative to the Congress being held in Paris, even though the diet's Federal Chief-of-Staff, Colonel Firsler, had prepared an 'optimum Swiss frontiers' report for the diet which, interestingly, excluded the Ajoie

region of the Porrentruy district (including Porrentruy) from the proposed Confederation. It was proposed that this latter region would become a part of France.

10. Subsequently, on 12 September 1814, Neuchâtel, the Valais, and Geneva were officially received into the Confederation as cantons. For the first time in the history of the Confederation, therefore, three new cantons, two of which (Neuchâtel and Geneva) were entirely, and one of which (the Valais) was predominantly French-speaking, were added to an association of states which had hitherto (with the exception of Canton Fribourg) been exclusively German-speaking. In addition, as indicated elsewhere, the French-speaking territory of Vaud (a former Bernese dependency), also became a canton.

11. The Swiss Parliament (or Federal Assembly) consists of two equal chambers, a senate (or Council of States) to which each canton sends two representatives, for a total of forty-six representatives since Canton Jura became Switzerland's twenty-third canton in 1979, and a popular chamber (or National Council) to which 200 representatives are elected on a proportional basis. The two chambers jointly elect seven representatives to a governing cabinet (or Federal Council). The Swiss Presidency rotates among members of the Federal Council on an annual basis.

7

The Development of the Jura Separatist Movement

> The will that creates a people is always in agreement with the individual
> will, but can develop only in persons who want to retain, share and
> participate in their homeland, language, state, or whatever else unites
> them.
>
> HERMANN WEILENMANN (1966)

Separatism in the Bernese Jura in its various nineteenth-century forms and in
its more recent manifestations has, as was mentioned in Chapter 1, attracted
the attention of a number of writers. Historians such as Prongué (op. cit.),
Amweg (op. cit.), and Bessire (op. cit.) have discussed the various Jurassian
separatist movements in the course of more extensive studies of Jurassian
history. Sociologists such as Bassand and Fragnière (op. cit.), Heneka (op.
cit.), Mayer (op. cit.), and Windisch and Willener (op. cit.) have examined it
as a social phenomenon. Political scientists, including Hughes (op. cit.) have
discussed the Jura problem in terms of the workings of the Swiss political
system.

Spokesmen for the various political movements of the Bernese Jura have
also published their thoughts and opinions extensively. In particular, the Jura
separatist movement, the *Rassemblement jurassien* (RJ), published a large number of books and pamphlets prior to the establishment of Canton Jura in 1979,
and has continued to publish extensively since that time. Among these RJ
publications have been a large number of books and pamphlets by Béguelin
(for example, 1968, 1972, 1980, 1982), Schaffter (for example, 1965, 1967,
1968), Fell (op. cit.), Huguelet (op. cit.), and Wilhelm (op. cit.). Other
separatists who, singly or with colleagues, have written on the subject include
Charpilloz (op. cit.), Crevoisier (op. cit.), Girard (op. cit.), and Moser (op.
cit.). Anti-separatists who have published books and booklets include Aubry
(op. cit.) and Flückiger (op. cit.). In addition, non-Jurassian Swiss and a
number of foreign journalists have found Jura separatism, and the emotions it
has aroused, to be newsworthy on a number of occasions since World War II.

As mentioned in Chapter 1, to the best of the writer's knowledge, however,
neither the development of earlier Jurassian separatist movements nor Jurassian separatism in its present-day form have been examined from the viewpoint of the geographer.

In 1815, prominent Jurassians varied widely in their views with respect to
the political future of the former bishopric of Basle. There were certainly some
Jurassians who wanted the region to become a separate canton. However,
they, like many others who held a variety of differing views, were to be

Table 7. *Jura Separatist Movements: 1815 to Present Day*

Movement	Dates	Issues	Objectives of movement
1	1826–31	(1) Liberal concepts vs. Bernese authoritarianism (2) Historic unity of Jura	New canton or regional autonomy within Canton Berne
2	1834–6	(1) Bernese anti-Catholic legislation (2) Bernese authoritarianism (3) Historic unity of Jura	(1) New canton (2) Union with France
3	1839–46	(1) Legal system dispute (2) Bernese authoritarianism	New canton
4	1867–78	Bernese discrimination against Catholic Jurassians	New canton
5	1910–18	(1) Germanization threat (2) French-Swiss and German-Swiss wartime rift	New canton
6	1947–78	Moeckli affair	(1) New canton
(Phase 1)			(2) Autonomy within Canton Berne
(Phase 2)	1979 to present	Historic unity of Jura	Union of Canton Jura and South Jura

Source: adapted from Bassand and Fragnière (op. cit.).

disappointed when the region was awarded to Berne.[1] Thus, in 1815, the Canton of Berne's boundaries were extended to take in not only the town of Biel with which it had a good many characteristics in common (such as its Mittelland location, its German language, and its Protestant tradition), but also the former bishopric of Basle, a peripheral mountainous region in the extreme north-west of the Swiss Confederation, which subsequently became known as the 'Bernese Jura'. As we have noted, the most distant districts of this region were Catholic, and had no historic links with Berne whatsoever. As a result of the Act of Union in 1815, therefore, the boundaries of Canton Berne, for the first time in its history, extended all the way from the High Alps to the French Frontier.

There appears to have been some recognition by the Bernese government, even at this early juncture, that Berne would be dealing with a region whose people differed significantly from those of the Old Canton. In any event, certain concessions to the people of the Bernese Jura were made at the outset. Among other things, the Act of Union guaranteed the people of the predominantly Catholic districts of the North Jura that they would be allowed to practise their traditional faith. On the other hand, Article 10 of the Act guaranteed the population of the predominantly Protestant districts of the South Jura that they would be ruled by the same laws as were the Protestant inhabitants of Canton Berne. Thus, the prevailing Protestant religion of the South Jura was also formally recognized.

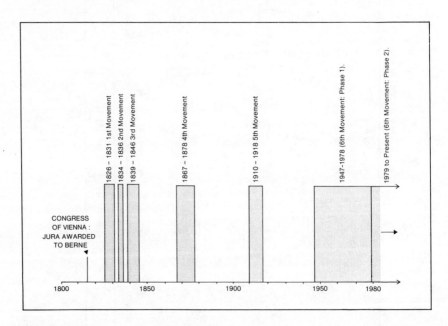

Fig. 32. The Six Jurassian Separatist Movements.

Nevertheless, a number of separatist movements subsequently appeared in the Bernese Jura during the following century and a half. These are shown on a time-scale in Fig. 32, and are summarized in Table 7. Each will be discussed in turn and, in each instance, certain geographical aspects of the movement will be examined.[2]

The First Jurassian Separatist Movement: 1826–1831

During the 1820s a number of Jurassian intellectuals, especially in Porrentruy in the extreme north-west of the Bernese Jura, were influenced by liberal political ideas which were affecting Europe. Some of these intellectuals (of whom Xavier Stockmar was the best known) favoured the separation of the Bernese Jura from Berne and the establishment of a new canton (Fig. 32 and Table 7). However, when the German-speaking regions of Canton Berne joined with anti-clerical Jurassians in a popular uprising, the patrician rulers of Berne abdicated and liberals of both language groups joined together to draft a new constitution.

In 1831, the citizens of the canton adopted, by popular referendum, a cantonal constitution which guaranteed civil rights to the population. It established representative democracy, though suffrage was still restricted by property qualifications. The new constitution also recognized French as the second official language of the canton, and stipulated that in French-speaking areas all official documents must be published in both German and French. For the first time, two French-speaking Jurassians were elected members of the Executive Council of Canton Berne. The new liberal government of the Bernese state thus clearly recognized the simple geographical fact that one region of the state—the Bernese Jura—spoke a separate language (French), and endeavoured to reflect this in its day-to-day administration. This linguistic recognition of the 'French fact' in the Bernese Jura was, in retrospect, a remarkably farsighted act, given the times. Because of this, most Jurassians of the period felt that they were being allowed to participate fully in the government of Canton Berne, and separatist feeling waned for a brief period.

The Second Jurassian Separatist Movement: 1834–1836

Unfortunately, however, the anti-clerical zeal of the new liberal government led to a serious power struggle involving the Catholic Church. In 1834 the government of Berne (which included some anti-clerical Jurassians), together with the governments of six other liberal Swiss cantons, adopted a declaration which proposed to nationalize the Catholic Church, 'democratize' its organization and subordinate it to the state. This was a clear violation of the religious guarantees given, in the 1815 Act of Union, to the Catholic population of the North Jura by the Bernese government of the time. The 1834 declaration by Berne and the other liberal cantons was condemned by the

Pope, and unrest and dissatisfaction followed in the North Jura (Fig. 32 and Table 7).

In 1836, 8,000 Catholic Jurassians from the northern districts of the region petitioned the cantonal government not to ratify the agreement. However, the Bernese legislature disregarded the petition and voted in favour of ratification. As a result, the population of several towns in the North Jura clamoured loudly for separation and rose in open rebellion. Some of these Jurassian separatists favoured the establishment of a separate canton, while some favoured union with France. In response, the Bernese government deposed three prefects who tried to mediate in the dispute, and ordered the military occupation of the Catholic districts of the North. The Jurassian rebels thereupon asked for the help of France, in the latter's capacity as one of the guarantor powers of the Treaty of 1815. The French reacted sharply, sent an ultimatum to Berne and threatened war. The Bernese government backed down, rescinded the ratification of the offending principles, and agreed to negotiate the dispute with the Papal authorities. As a result, peace and order were restored, and the second Jura separatist movement dissolved.

It is suggested that the occurrences of 1834–6 reveal two significant facts with geographical implications. Firstly, the considerable geographic distance (with its resultant implications in terms of early nineteenth-century travel time) which separated the city of Berne (the heart of the canton) from the remote northern districts of the Bernese Jura which bordered France, clearly reflected itself in sharp religious differences and regional attitudes which contrasted sharply with those of Berne. Secondly, there appears to have been no significant outcry against the anti-clerical policy of the Bernese government in the southern, predominantly Protestant areas of the Bernese Jura. This emphasizes the significance of the religious divide which crossed the Jura from west to east, separating populations with important differences in philosophy and attitude (the Catholic North Jura and the Protestant South Jura) on any occasion when religious feelings were aroused.

The Third Jurassian Separatist Movement: 1839–1846

Only a few years later, in 1839, the Bernese Jura was thrown into turmoil once again (Fig. 32 and Table 7). The cause of the unrest on this occasion was the legal system which prevailed in the region. French rule in the former bishopric during the early years of the nineteenth century had resulted in the establishment in the area of the *Code Napoléon*, the French Civil Law. The provisions of this code were clear and logical. In 1815 the Jurassians resisted its proposed replacement by the ancient local laws (which were cumbersome), or by the equally antiquated Bernese legal system. Due to this resistance only *some* Bernese statutes were declared applicable for the whole region. Others were declared applicable only in the South, while parts of the French code were allowed to remain in force in the North. The result was legal confusion.

In 1839 a parliamentary delegation from the Bernese Jura demanded unanimously, in the Bernese legislature, that the entire *Code Napoléon* be restored to the whole of the Bernese Jura. The Bernese legislature refused this demand, and this led to renewed separatist agitation in the North Jura. Berne took sharply repressive measures against the Jurassian leaders, accusing them of treason. Xavier Stockmar, the most outstanding Jurassian politician of the era, who had served as a member of the Executive Council of the government of the canton, was leader of the radical movement. Stockmar was forced to flee to France, while other Jurassian leaders were jailed.

In 1846 a new radical popular movement overturned the liberal government. Stockmar was allowed to return from exile, took a seat in the new radical government, and played a major role in drafting the new constitution of Canton Berne in 1846. This constitution included a number of important laws. One of these confirmed the earlier recognition of both French and German as the fully equal, official languages of the canton. Another law permitted the Bernese Jura to retain the *Code Napoléon*. (The latter remained valid in the Jura until the whole of Switzerland adopted a unified modern code in 1912.) In addition, some longstanding tax inequities were settled, and an unwritten rule was established that two of the nine seats on the Executive Council of the canton would be *permanently reserved* for Jurassians. In addition, another un-written rule was established by which the Bernese Jura was subsequently, with rare exceptions, assigned one of Canton Berne's two seats in the Council of States, or Swiss senate.

As a result of the acceptance of this new constitution the third Jurassian separatist movement ended, and the period which followed, from 1846 to 1867, was one of relative political stability both for the Bernese Jura and for Canton Berne. There were sharp political swings in cantonal politics from radical to conservative majorities, and back again. The Bernese Jura, however, partici-pated fully in Bernese affairs, with similar political trends occurring both in the region and in the Old Canton.

The geographical significance of the third Jurassian separatist movement, and of the means of its solution is that, in the new Bernese constitution of 1846, the cantonal government confirmed its earlier constitution of 1831, which implicitly recognized that the canton consisted of *two regions* which differed significantly from each other, i.e. the French-speaking Bernese Jura and the German-speaking Old Canton.

The Fourth Jurassian Separatist Movement: 1867–1878

In 1864 Pope Pius IX published a syllabus castigating all liberal ideas and political programmes as fundamental errors. A number of liberals who dis-agreed with the Pope's views took up the challenge. The result was a major struggle (the *Kulturkampf*) between Church and State, which was particularly bitter in Germany and in a number of Swiss cantons, including Berne. In

Canton Berne, a number of anti-clericals, both from the Old Canton and the Bernese Jura, introduced legislation which reduced the number of legal holidays in the Catholic northern Jura from seventeen to six, and prohibited all members of religious orders from teaching in public schools. In 1867 unrest began to develop once again in that area of the canton which was almost exclusively Catholic, i.e. the North Jura. The fourth Jurassian separatist movement had begun (Fig. 32 and Table 7).

In 1869 the Vatican Council proclaimed the dogma of Papal Infallibility, whereupon a number of dissenters defected from the Catholic Church in certain areas of Switzerland, and established a new denomination which became known as the Old Catholics. The situation worsened when, in 1873, Canton Berne and four other cantons in the Catholic diocese of Basle ordered Bishop Lachat of Basle not to announce the new dogma of Infallibility in the churches. The bishop disregarded this order, and excommunicated those priests who held Old Catholic views. The five cantons thereupon declared the bishop deposed, withdrew their state recognition from the diocese, and recognized the Swiss 'National Bishopric' of Old Catholics. Canton Berne, in addition, ordered all Catholic priests to stop all communication with the deposed bishop. Sixty-nine priests in the North Jura disregarded the order. These were deposed by the cantonal government, and were threatened with jail if they continued to officiate. The Bernese government further reduced the seventy-four Roman Catholic parishes to twenty-eight; all these latter parishes were handed over to the Old Catholic clergy. In 1874, the legislature of Canton Berne enacted a law requiring all clergy to be elected by the populations of their respective parishes. Furthermore, their eligibility was to be determined by a state exam, with the cantonal government reserving the right to confirm the results of the elections.

A popular referendum was then held on the issue in the canton. The new law was accepted by a majority of the people of the canton as a whole. In the predominantly Catholic areas of the North Jura, however, the negative votes ran in a 3:1 ratio. In the predominantly Protestant regions of the South Jura (which, by this time, it will be recalled, were experiencing substantial immigration from the Protestant Old Canton), 95 per cent of those participating voted 'Yes'. As might have been expected, the Catholic communities of the North Jura actively resisted the new anti-Catholic law and supported their clergy. As a result, the government of Canton Berne ordered a military occupation of the North, and ruthlessly expelled the deposed priests from the canton. As these events developed, a number of Jurassian leaders, primarily from the North Jura, proposed the creation of a separate canton in the Bernese Jura.

At this point, the federal government of Switzerland intervened, declaring the expulsion of the priests from their native canton unconstitutional. The federal government, in addition, forced Berne (and Geneva, where similar incidents occurred) to rescind the expulsions. The expelled Catholic priests

1. The southern exit of the gorges de Moutier, as viewed from the town of Moutier.

2. St-Imier, a watch-manufacturing centre and predominantly anti-separatist, pro-Bernese, stronghold in the valley of the Suze (vallon de St-Imier), in the district of Courtelary, South Jura.

3. Delémont, the capital of the district of the same name, the largest town in the Bernese Jura, and the seat of government of Canton Jura. A view facing west. The *Rue du 23 Juin* (named after the date of the 1974 referendum) is decorated for a fête. The Jurassian flag (right foreground) is prominently displayed on both sides of the street.

4. Porrentruy, the capital of the district of Porrentruy ('the Ajoie') in the north-west corner of Canton Jura. The Château de Porrentruy (or Bishop's Palace), which from 1528 to 1792 served as the residence of the prince-bishops of Basle (the titular rulers of the whole of the Bernese Jura), can be seen on the hill.

5. The village of Moron, a German-speaking, Anabaptist settlement in the commune of Châtelat, South Jura. The German-language school is to the left of the picture. The Anabaptist meeting-house (place of worship) is to the right.

6. A 'Free Jura' sign at the southern outskirts of the village of Les Bois. This commune lies just inside the cantonal boundary in the south-western corner of Canton Jura.

7. The 'free commune' of Vellerat, situated on a mountainside overlooking the northern end of the gorges de Moutier to the east, and the Delémont basin to the north.

8. St-Ursanne, in the valley of the Doubs, near the French frontier (district of Porrentruy, Canton Jura).

were allowed to return to their parishes in 1875. Their pulpits, however, continued to be occupied by Old Catholic priests. Moreover, the government of Berne passed a law which threatened to jail any individual who was not recognized by the canton and who performed, in any Bernese community, a religious function not recognized by the canton. The law also specifically prohibited religious processions outside church buildings.

These measures clearly represented an attempt by the government of Canton Berne to replace the Roman Catholic Church with the Old Catholic Church. The attempt failed, however. Old Catholic priests preached to empty churches, while at the same time Catholic priests officiated in woods and barns. The struggle, especially between 1873 and 1878, caused great bitterness between the government of Canton Berne and the peoples of the North Jura. Eventually a face-saving compromise permitted Canton Berne to end its struggle with the Catholic Church. As a result of the compromise, the Vatican agreed to recognize the law of Canton Berne, which required that priests be elected by their parishioners. In return, the canton granted amnesty to all priests, who were promptly reinstated by their parishioners. Old Catholic priests, with two exceptions, disappeared from the North Jura, and the fourth Jurassian separatist movement, to all intents and purposes, came to an end.

It is suggested that the events occurring between 1867 and 1878 are highly significant from the geographical viewpoint, because they indicate that a more extensive rift than hitherto was beginning to develop among the inhabitants of two subregions *within* the Jura when certain issues (religious issues for the most part) were involved. The rift did not divide one social or economic class of Jurassian from another. Rather, it could be delineated geographically. It divided the predominantly Catholic northern part of the region from the predominantly Protestant southern part. The referendum of 1874 on the clerical election issue (cited earlier), was particularly significant in that, as we saw, the two regions were almost diametrically opposed to each other in voting behaviour, with the South Jura (stiffened in its anti-Catholic traditions by a significant infusion of Bernese Protestants), siding with its immediate neighbour to the south, the Old Canton.

From about 1878, a new period of relatively amicable and calm relations began between the Bernese Jura and Canton Berne. This situation was eased further when, in 1893, a new cantonal constitution granted the Catholic Church equal status with the Protestant and Old Catholic Churches. All three Churches were recognized as official bodies, with the privilege of collecting tithes from adherents through the agency of the state's tax administration. Unfortunately for all parties, and in spite of further subsequent concessions,[3] the hostile feelings aroused in the northern, Catholic districts by Bernese religious policy during the *Kulturkampf* crisis lingered in the memories of their inhabitants for many years, and find an echo in present-day Jura separatism. Geographically speaking, this phenomenon is, as has already been indicated, present in much greater strength in the North Jura than the South Jura, and it is difficult for an outside observer who has studied Jurassian history not to conclude that the religious factor was an important determinant of the 1974 vote, by a large majority of the people of the North Jura, in favour of the establishment of a new canton.

The Fifth Jurassian Separatist Movement: 1910–1918

The period from 1900 to 1914 marked the first occasion on which language became a more important cause of friction between the Bernese Jura and Canton Berne than religion (Fig. 7 and Table 32). In 1902, certain cantonal officials announced that the Bernese Jura was to be germanized.[4] This, not unnaturally, aroused misgivings amongst almost all French-speaking inhabitants of the Bernese Jura. The latter's concerns with respect to their language and culture had already heightened by the heavy late nineteenth- and twentieth-century immigration of German-speaking Bernese, especially in the South Jura, and by the rapid increase in the number of German-language schools, even in the North Jura.

From about 1910 onwards, Germany began to engage in active pan-German propaganda, which raised concern among many French-speaking Swiss. In addition (as noted in Chapter 4), the German-Swiss cultural organization *Deutchschweitzerischer Sprachverein* was also extremely active during this period. In 1913 the geological branch of the Swiss federal government announced that it planned to change the official names of the eastern Jurassian communes of La Scheulte and Elay to their German equivalents, Schelten and Seehof, respectively.[5] This federal government announcement was regarded by French-speaking Jurassians as advance notice of a plan by German-speaking Swiss in general, and by the government of Canton Berne in particular, to germanize the Jura as intensively as possible.

In 1913, too, it was learned that Anabaptists in Germany were providing financial aid to Anabaptist schools in the Bernese Jura. A wave of hostility towards all German-language schools (both Anabaptist and non-Anabaptist) swept through the French-speaking inhabitants of the region. By 1914, therefore, it would not be an exaggeration to say that the actual or supposed threat of germanization united a majority of French-speaking Jurassians—whether from the North or the South, and whether Catholic or Protestant—in what Mayer (op. cit.) has called 'a defensive stance'. In this concern French-speaking Jurassians of both faiths, from Porrentruy in the north to the northern outskirts of Biel in the south, represented a solid geographic bloc of concerned French-speaking Jurassians.

We earlier noted that World War I had the effect of intensifying feelings of mutual suspicion between French-speaking and German-speaking Swiss. Speaking generally, many German-speaking Swiss were sympathetic to the German cause, while the great majority of French-speaking Swiss, including the French-speaking inhabitants of the Bernese Jura, sympathized with

France and the Allies. It will be recalled from Chapter 4 that, even as early as the latter years of the nineteenth century, French-speaking Jurassians began to demand that the German-language schools in the Bernese Jura be closed.[6] The demands grew in intensity as the twentieth century progressed. However, after 1918, the defeat of Germany by the Allies (leading to a decline in the Jurassian fear of a Pan-German threat), a decrease in Bernese immigration to most Jurassian communes, the gradual decline in enrolment in the remaining German-language schools, and the closing of the majority of the latter over a period of some years led to a period in which a relatively smooth relationship prevailed between Jurassians and the cantonal government.

To the observer who studies the geographical significance of Jura separatism, the so-called fifth Jurassian separatist movement is of particular interest because, as noted earlier, not only was it the first Jurassian movement in which the main issue was one of language and culture, but also because it extended to the *whole* of the Jura. While concerns were, perhaps, stronger in the North Jura (where they fed upon old suspicions of Berne), many Jurassians in southern districts (some of whom had, unwillingly become members of a linguistic minority group in their own native villages because of the heavy influx of Bernese) shared the concerns of their northern fellow-Jurassians. Jurassian separatist leaders, from both the North and South Jura, and from Biel, reminded their audiences of the long history of the bishopric of Basle as a political unit, and of the important literary tradition of the French-speaking Jura. They further emphasized the fact that a number of the region's leading French-language writers and poets had been born in its southern valleys.

On this occasion it would appear, therefore, that despite the religious division between the North and South Jura, and despite the heavy German-speaking, Bernese immigration to the southern Jura districts especially, (immigration which tended to stiffen both the Protestantism and the pro-Bernese sentiments of these districts), there nevertheless existed at least a degree of Jurassian regional feeling among the inhabitants of the Bernese Jura *as a whole* during the early twentieth century. This was based, in part, on historic ties to a bishopric which, although fragmented into various subregions, had survived in at least nominal form for 800 years. It was also based, in part, on a pride in the French culture of the entire region, and of the literature which this culture had produced.

The Sixth Jurassian Separatist Movement. Phase One: 1947 to 1978

Until the 1940s, Jurassian separatist movements tended to be short-lived. The longest-lived of these movements (that of 1867–78) lasted, to all intents and purposes, no more than ten years. The sixth Jura separatist movement which began with the Moeckli affair in 1947, can be considered to consist of two phases, the first of which ended with the establishment of Canton Jura in 1979 (Fig. 32 and Table 7).

The Moeckli affair has been discussed in detail by a number of observers of the Jurassian scene; a brief account only will be given here. In September 1947 the members of the legislature of Canton Berne rejected the Bernese government's nomination of M. Georges Moeckli,[7] a French-speaking Jurassian and a Social Democrat, as the canton's Director of Public Works and Railways, on the ground that the office was too important to be filled by a francophone member of the Council. (Moeckli was already a member of the Executive Council of the canton, and had even served as president of the canton some years earlier.) Eight days later, a motion to reconsider the earlier motion failed by a margin of two votes.

The people of the Jura were angered by these developments. A *Comité de Moutier* (Committee of Moutier) was formed almost immediately, and demanded recognition of the rights of the people of the Bernese Jura as guaranteed by the 1815 Act of Union. Some members of the committee merely wished to express mild concern at the slight to French-speaking Jurassians; some sought a degree of autonomy for the French-speaking Bernese Jura within Canton Berne (though no Swiss precedent for such a step existed), and others sought a completely separate new canton.

Two months later, primarily because the Committee of Moutier did not appear to be accomplishing a great deal, the political movement known as the *Mouvement Séparatiste Jurassien* (Jurassian Separatist Movement or MSJ) was established to work for a completely independent Canton Jura within the Swiss Confederation.[8] Subsequently, MSJ's supporters participated in separatist political activities as individual members of *established* political parties, since the MSJ did not consider itself to be a political party in the traditional sense.

In response to Jurassian concerns, the Bernese government eventually made some concessions. In 1950 the Constitution of Canton Berne was amended so as to distinguish between the inhabitants of the Old Canton and those of the Bernese Jura. In addition, a red and white flag (featuring the episcopal crozier of the former bishopric of Basle) was recognized as the official symbol of the region. The Bernese Jura was *officially* guaranteed two ministerial seats on the Cantonal Council, and the archives of the bishopric of Basle were ordered to be returned, to Porrentruy, from Berne.

While the concessions made by the cantonal government satisfied many of the inhabitants of the South Jura, they did not satisfy many of those living in northern districts of the region. In September 1952 the MSJ changed its name to the *Rassemblement jurassien* (RJ), and began to intensify its campaign for a new canton. The Committee of Moutier ceased to exist in the autumn of 1952. Subsequently, in November 1952, anti-separatist Jurassians living predominantly, though not exclusively, in the traditionally pro-Bernese South established the *Union des patriotes jurassiens* (UPJ). This political group later renamed itself the *Force démocratique* (FD).

In 1957 the RJ launched a popular initiative (a device permitted by the

Table 8.   *Bernese Jura: Results of Poll of 5 July 1959, by District (initiative to hold a Jura referendum)*

District	% 'Yes' vote (in favour of referendum)	% 'No' vote (opposed to referendum)
Courtelary	24	76
Delémont	72	28
Franches-Montagnes	76	24
Moutier	34	66
La Neuveville	35	65
Porrentruy	66	34
Total: 6 French-speaking districts	49	51
Laufen	27	73
Total: 7 districts of Bernese Jura	48	52
Old Canton (excluding Jura)	11	89
Total: Canton Berne	22	78

Swiss political system) to organize a consultative vote which would enable the people of the Jura to decide if they wanted to become a new Swiss Canton.[9] The RJ collected more than sufficient signatures to submit the initiative to the people. In the 1959 poll which followed, the initiative was rejected by the population of the canton as a whole.[10] Moreover, the Bernese Jura itself rejected the initiative by 16,355 votes to 15,159 (a 52:48 per cent majority), with even the French-speaking districts, as a whole, voting 'No', by 14,905 votes to 14,626. In the three French-speaking northern districts of Delémont, Franches-Montagnes, and Porrentruy, however, the initiative was approved by majorities of 72 per cent, 76 per cent, and 66 per cent respectively (Table 8). Voting data by communes in the 1959 poll is provided in Appendix C: Table 2.

The RJ intensified its activities following the 1959 initiative, establishing separatist organizations for young people, for women, and for Jura citizens living outside the Jura. It was also strongly represented at the annual European *Conférences des minorités ethniques de langue française*, in which various French-speaking minority groups (such as those in Belgium, the Val d'Aosta in north-western Italy, and Québec) participate.

In the 1960s certain Jurassians who held extremely anti-Bernese views, but who were officially disowned by the RJ, formed the *Front de libération jurassien* (FLJ), or Jurassian Liberation Front. During the years which followed, the

FLJ was held responsible for certain attacks on railways, Swiss army instal-
lations, and isolated Anabaptist farms in the Bernese Jura. A group of pro-
separatist youths, who were official RJ supporters, and who named themselves
Les béliers ('the Rams', or 'Battering-Rams'), demonstrated on a number of
occasions against the Bernese authorities.[11] In 1967 the government of Canton
Berne established a commission of enquiry (known as *la Commission de 24*) to
investigate all aspects of the Jura problem, which had, by this time, aroused
the concern of the whole of Switzerland. The Commission of 24 made its report
to the Bernese government in March 1968.

Events moved quickly. In 1968, even before the publication of the report of
the Commission of 24 in November of that year, the Bernese government
decided that the electorate of the Bernese Jura should itself determine its own
political future, and requested that the federal authorities suggest the names of
respected individuals to serve as advisers with respect to the referendum. The
Bernese government's proposal was accepted, in 1970, by a large majority in a
cantonal vote which modified the cantonal constitution, so that henceforth it
granted the right of self-determination to all regions of the canton.

In 1969, in the meantime, a third political movement was founded in the
Bernese Jura, in addition to the RJ and FD. It was named *le Mouvement pour
l'unité du Jura* (The Movement for the Unity of the Jura, or MUF), and was also
known as *la Troisième Force* (The Third Force). The Third Force aimed at
re-establishing a dialogue between separatists and anti-separatists to prevent
a political division of the Bernese Jura. It did proclaim, however, that it sought
a solution which would guarantee the region a substantial degree of autonomy
within Canton Berne, even though, as we noted earlier, the Swiss Constitution
did not permit this.

The RJ, while supporting the concept of a referendum, stated that it would
not participate unless only the following individuals were allowed to vote:

(1) Traditional citizens of the Bernese Jura (i.e., individuals who were
    born, or whose ancestors had been born, in a Jurassian commune), who
    were living in the Bernese Jura at the time of the referendum.[12]
(2) Members of families of Swiss origin who, while not possessing Jura
    citizenship, had nevertheless lived in the Bernese Jura for 90 years or
    more at the time of the referendum (i.e. from 1884 or earlier).
(3) Individuals living in other Swiss cantons, but who had been born in a
    Jurassian commune, or who had Jurassian ancestors who left the Jura
    less than 90 years ago.

These demands reflected the RJ's belief that the second- and third-
generation descendents of Bernese settlers in the Bernese Jura—even if they
had become French-speaking—were usually pro-Bernese and would vote in
favour of Bernese interests and against a separate Canton Jura. However, the
federal government and the government of the canton, citing Article 43 of the

Swiss Constitution (which states that Swiss citizens are allowed to vote in their community of residence and nowhere else), refused to accept the RJ's criteria.

In view of the impasse, in 1972 the Executive Council of Canton Berne proposed autonomous status for the Bernese Jura within Canton Berne. While some Jurassians reacted favourably to this proposal, the RJ refused to consider it and established a 'shadow government'. In September 1973, however, after further reflection, and to the surprise of all other political groups, the RJ asked the cantonal government to organize a referendum as quickly as possible, and recommended to its followers that they vote 'Yes'. The FD asked its followers to vote 'No', and the Third Force (MUJ) recommended casting blank votes.

In the referendum supervised by the cantonal government and held on 23 June 1974, the separatists won with 36,802 votes in favour of the establishment of a new Swiss canton (Canton Jura) in the seven districts of the Bernese Jura as a whole. 34,057 'No' votes were cast, and there were 1,726 votes supporting the MUJ. As indicated in Table 13, a high percentage (over 90 per cent) of those eligible to vote did so. A summary of the votes cast in the June 1974 referendum is provided in Table 9. The voting pattern, by commune, is summarized in Appendix C: Table 2.

Figure 33 depicts the 1974 voting pattern for the Bernese Jura as a whole. It lists, by name, the two French-speaking communes of the North Jura (Asuel and Roche d'Or) which voted against a new canton, and another (Bonfol) in which the vote was evenly divided.[13] It further indicates the nine communes of the Moutier district of the South Jura which voted decisively for a new canton, and also an additional eight communes (including, interestingly, German-speaking Schelten) in the South Jura, in which more than 40 per cent of the voters favoured the establishment of a new canton.

Table 9. *Bernese Jura: Results of Referendum of 23 June 1974, by District ('Do you wish to form a new canton?')*

District	% 'Yes' vote	% 'No' vote
Courtelary	23	77
Delémont	79	21
Franches-Montagnes	77	23
Moutier	43	57
La Neuveville	34	66
Porrentruy	68	32
Total: 6 French-speaking districts	54	46
Laufen	26	74
Total: 7 districts of Bernese Jura	52	48

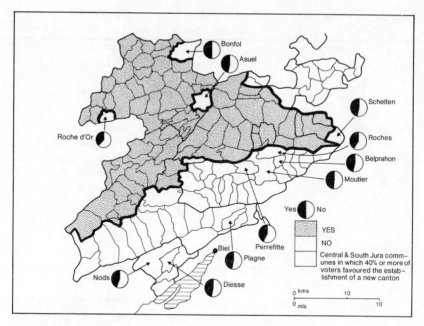

Fig. 33. The Bernese Jura: Voting Patterns in the 1974 Referendum.

Further referendums were held on 16 March and 14 September 1975, in accordance with the agreed referendum procedure, in order to give, firstly, the inhabitants of the three southern districts and, subsequently, certain communes situated on the frontier between the North and South Jura an opportunity to reconsider their earlier votes, in view of the results of the June 1974

Table 10. *Bernese Jura: a Comparison of the Results of the 1959 Poll, 1974 Referendum, and 1975 Plebiscite*

	% of voters in favour of forming/joining a new canton		
District	1959 poll	1974 referendum	1975 plebiscite
Courtelary	24	23	23
Delémont	72	79	*
Franches-Montagnes	76	77	*
Moutier	34	43	44
La Neuveville	35	34	34
Porrentruy	66	68	*
Laufen	27	26	6

* Indicates no 1975 plebiscite held.

referendum. (These communes all, in actual fact, reconfirmed their earlier 'No' votes). Table 10 compares the percentage of 'Yes' votes for each district for 1959, 1974, and 1975 where applicable. (Appendix C: Table 2 summarizes the results, by district and commune, of the 1975 plebiscites).

As a result of these subsequent plebiscites, the boundaries of the new Canton Jura were delimited as outlined in Fig. 34. In total, 82 communes became a part of the new Canton Jura; whereas the remaining 62 (including 12 Laufen communes) voted in favour of remaining a part of Canton Berne.[14]

The Constituent Assembly of the new canton met for the first time at Delémont (chosen to become the capital of Canton Jura) on 20 April 1976. The constitution of the new canton appeared in 1977 and, on the whole, was received favourably by most outside observers. Facilitated by a tripartite committee (consisting of representatives of Canton Jura, Canton Berne, and the Swiss federal government), the transfer of powers of the government of Canton Jura on 1 January 1979 was relatively smooth.

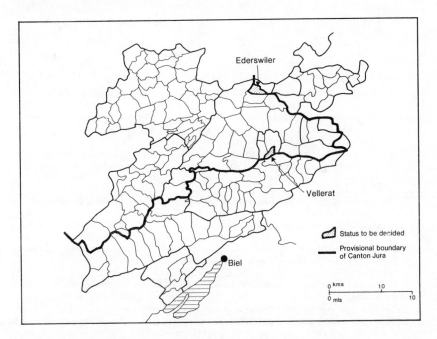

Fig. 34. The Bernese Jura: Provisional Boundary of New Canton, 1979.

Visitors to the former Bernese Jura are usually left in no doubt as to the political affiliations of the inhabitants of any given area. In Canton Jura, the Jurassian flag and/or coat of arms are proudly displayed. In the South Jura (sometimes known as the 'new' Bernese Jura) the Bernese coat of arms is prominent. As one moves northward from the South Jura, crosses the border and enters Canton Jura, *Jura Libre* (Free Jura) slogans are painted on walls, buildings and bridges (Plate 6). In some areas the new boundary between the cantons of Jura and Berne separates villages which have, historically, enjoyed close relationships.

The Sixth Jurassian Separatist Movement. Phase Two: 1979 to the Present Day

Unfortunately for Switzerland, and as Chapter 9 outlines, the lines of division between separatist Jurassians and pro-Bernese Jurassians have hardened since 1979. The RJ has made it clear that it will not rest until the South Jura is reunited with the North Jura in a unified Canton Jura. For this reason, the sixth Jurassian separatist movement can be viewed as consisting of two phases. Phase one, which extended from 1947 to 1978, can be considered to have ended with the establishment of an 'incomplete' Canton Jura in 1979. The separatist movement in existence at the time of writing (1985) can thus be considered to be a second phase of the sixth Jurassian separatist movement.

Notes

1. The original Act of Union between the bishopric of Basle and the canton of Berne, by which the former territory became known, for the first time, as the Bernese Jura, is to be found in the canton's Official Archives. The Document of Union, which is dated 14–23 November 1815, was signed by the mayors of Porrentruy, Delémont, Courtelary, and the former mayor of Crémines, together with individuals representing other areas of the Bernese Jura. Its signatories appear to have been reasonably representative of all districts of the region.

2. The writer, in chronologically listing the various Jurassian separatist movements since 1815, has made extensive reference to an article by Mayer in *Social Research*, Vol. 4, Winter 1968, pp. 707–41. The geographical interpretation of these events, however, and the conclusions reached are the author's.

3. The last remnants of religious friction were removed when, in 1917, the cantonal law prohibiting processions was rescinded by popular vote and when, in 1921, Canton Berne resumed contractual relations with the diocese of Basle.

4. The policies of certain Bernese government officials at this time (i.e. the turn of the century) seem to have been based partly on a belief that German was the 'language of the future', and partly on a desire to simplify the daily administration of the canton.

5. The resultant outcry in French-speaking Jurassians circles tended to mask the fact that these two sparsely populated mountain communities, which lay on the border of German-speaking Canton Solothurn (Figs. 21 and 22), had been, it appears from records, at least partially—if not predominantly—German-speaking for at least two centuries.

6. It will be recalled from Chapter 4 that some German schools were indeed closed as early as the last decade of the nineteenth and first decade of the twentieth century, but a number of others remained.

7. Like many present-day French-speaking Jurassians, including many separatists, his surname indicates German-Swiss immigrant ancestors.

8. The first president of the MSJ (the subsequent *Rassemblement jurassien*) was the aged Daniel Charpilloz, a southern Protestant who had been an active Jurassian leader during the 1910–18 crisis.

9. The question which would have been asked of the voters if the initiative had carried would have been: 'Do you wish the (Bernese) Jura to become a sovereign canton of the (Swiss) Confederation?'

10. At the time of this referendum, only adult *male* Swiss citizens were permitted to vote.

11. The Rams' activities included an 'invasion' of the Federal Parliament of Switzerland during the 1968 presidential installation ceremony, occupations of the Swiss embassies in Paris and Brussels, and the occupation of the Belgian embassy in Berne.

12. The concept of Swiss 'citizenship' will be discussed in more detail in a subsequent chapter.

13. The 'No' votes and the 50:50 vote in the French-speaking North Jura communes of Roche d'Or, Asuel, and Bonfol respectively (Appendix C: Table 2) were due to the personal influence of powerful local families, according to local informants. The number of voters involved was particularly small in Roche d'Or and Asuel. Ederswiler and Roggenberg (the other North Jura communes which voted against the establishment of a new canton) are, of course, German-speaking.

14. For technical reasons the status of Ederswiler (one of the German-speaking communes on the northern language frontier which—as indicated in the previous footnote—voted 'No') and Vellerat (a French-speaking, Catholic hilltop commune to the north-west of the gorges de Moutier, which voted 'Yes') had yet to be decided in 1985 (Fig. 34). This situation will be discussed in more detail in Chapter 11.

8

Jura Separatism: Some Geographical Theories

Swiss democracy may be cumbersome and tedious and it is certainly not perfect, but it is worthy of the name. And on the whole the way in which the people have voted over the years on federal, cantonal and community issues has shown an astonishing maturity.

NORMAN CROSSLAND (1979)

Before reaching any conclusions about Jura separation and about geographical factors which may have contributed to the existence of this phenomenon, it is important that we take note of the basic arguments put forward by opposing political factions in the Bernese Jura.

Basic Political Viewpoints

Expressed in simple terms, Jurassian separatists, as represented by the *Rassemblement jurassien*, argue that historically the Bernese Jura should be considered a political entity because of its existence as the bishopric of Basle for almost 900 years. Separatists further point out that six districts of the Bernese Jura have always been predominantly French-speaking, and that there is a distinctive Jurassian, French-language literary and cultural tradition. However, it is argued, the region is constantly being threatened by germanization.[1]

It will also be recalled, from Chapter 7, that the RJ reasons that the descendants of the Bernese immigrants to the Bernese Jura are still 'Bernese' rather than 'Jurassians' at heart, and constitute a 'fifth column' which votes against the best interests of the region. These Bernese are particularly numerous in the South Jura which, argue the separatists, explains why the South Jura voted against the establishment of Canton Jura. These thoughts have been expressed on many occasions, and most recently by such separatist politicians and writers as Schaffter (op. cit.), Béguelin (opp. citt.), Charpilloz (op. cit.), Fell (op. cit.), and others.

In sharp contrast to the arguments of the RJ, the pro-Bernese Jurassians of the *Force démocratique*, represented by writers such as Aubry (op. cit.), Fluckiger (op. cit.), and Gasser (1978), argue, firstly, that the Jurassians of the North Jura are different in many ways from those of the South Jura, and that the two peoples have little in common. Specifically, it is emphasized that there is an obvious religious difference between the North Jura and South Jura, the North Jura being predominantly Catholic and the South Jura being predominantly Protestant.

Some anti-separatists also counter the francophone propaganda of the RJ by emphasizing the fact that there was originally a dialectal difference between the French spoken in the North Jura, as opposed to that spoken in a part of the South Jura. This difference, as was mentioned previously, was based on the difference between the langue d'oïl of the North Jura and the Francoprovençal variant of the langue d'oc spoken in the south-western part of the South Jura. It is further claimed, by the anti-separatists, that there are differences in personalities and lifestyles within the region. The northerners, it is argued, have a 'Dionysian' culture, in that they are lively, emotional, and outgoing. In contrast, the southerners are said to have an 'Apollonian' culture, in that they are more reserved, thoughtful, and hard-working.

The anti-separatists point out that even observers who confess to separatist sympathies, such as Windisch and Willener (op. cit.), acknowledge the difference between the personalities and lifestyles of the northerners and southerners. The southerners, these anti-separatist writers claim, personify Weber's 'Protestant ethic' (Weber, op. cit.). Anti-separatists also state that the germanization threat is a 'red herring'. On the contrary, they point out that the percentage of German-speakers in the six French districts of the Bernese Jura is steadly declining (Table 4). Moreover, say the anti-separatists, the attachment of the majority of the southern Jurassians to Berne has been born of centuries of friendship and military alliances which pre-date the Reformation. It is a friendship, say the anti-separatists, of which the people of the South Jura have every reason to be proud.

As for the views of the middle-of-the-road Third Force, it will be recalled that its spokespersons, at the time of the 1974 referendum, felt it vital that the Jura not be split up, since it had been a distinctive political entity (as the bishopric of Basle) for centuries.[2] The Third Force (which had supporters in both the North and South Jura) advocated the seeking of a modest degree of autonomy within the framework of Canton Berne.[3] It recommended that its supporters cast blank ballots in the 1974 referendum.[4]

Possible Geographical Causes of Jura Separatism

In earlier chapters of this book the region known between 1815 and 1978 as the Bernese Jura was examined from a number of geographic viewpoints in order to identify certain geographic factors which appeared to be possible causes of Jura separatism. It is now appropriate to discuss each of these factors in turn:

The Geography of Language

The resentment caused by the massive Bernese immigration into the Bernese Jura during the latter part of the nineteenth and the early part of the twentieth century, the Schelten–Seehof crisis, the uproar caused by the revelation of Pan-German support for German cultural activities, of German Anabaptist support for Anabaptist schools in the Bernese Jura, and the Moeckli Affair in 1947, all suggest that the language issue has been, and remains, important to many Jurassians. Fears that the French language, occupying an area which, as we have seen, protrudes eastwards into German-speaking Switzerland, is threatened by German, still appear to be widespread among at least some sections of the population of the former Bernese Jura, including separatists in the South Jura, the majority of whose communes have, as we have seen, elected to remain a part of Canton Berne.

Members of the RJ claim that the single most important concern of their movement has been to preserve their language and culture (situated, as it has been, in a powerful and influential Swiss canton which is predominantly German-speaking), by establishing a new canton to include the *entire* French-speaking portion of the Bernese Jura. Members of the RJ further point out, as justification for their fears that German-Swiss are 'anti-Jurassian', that in the six predominantly French-speaking districts, not a single Jurassian commune with a German-speaking majority voted in favour of establishing a new Canton Jura either in the 1959 initiative, or in the referendum of 1974 (Table 11). Moreover, it is pointed out that every commune in the Bernese Jura's seventh (and German-speaking) district of Laufen voted against joining the new canton.

This would suggest that French-speaking Jurassians and predominantly French-speaking communes were predisposed to vote for a new canton in 1974, whereas German-speaking Jurassians and predominantly German-speaking communes were predisposed to vote against the establishment of a new canton. In order to test this argument, the following theory was developed:

> (1) The higher the percentage of Swiss citizens in a commune whose first language is French, the higher the (1974 percentage) vote in favour of (the establishment of) the new Canton Jura.

The Geography of Religion

Observers of the political scene in the Bernese Jura have remarked that, on a number of occasions during the past 150 years, disputes between the people of the Bernese Jura and the government of Canton Berne have involved predominantly religious issues. It was noted, in Chapter 7, that these disputes have, at times, been so acute that the Bernese government has had to resort to the armed occupation of certain areas of the Bernese Jura. Furthermore we have noted that, because the opposition to Bernese rule has, traditionally, been particularly intense in the northern, predominantly Catholic districts of the region, and because a number of Jurassian separatist movements in the past have been related to religious issues, many observers have suggested that 'Catholicism is separatism'. These observers claim that, in spite of the claims of many members of the RJ that the basic issue is a linguistic one, it is only the predominantly Catholic communes which have, traditionally, favoured separatism. By contrast, it is suggested that communes which are predominantly Protestant have traditionally wished to maintain their close links with Canton Berne, and have voted against the establishment of a new canton.

Table 11. *Bernese Jura: Voting Patterns of Communes with German-speaking Majorities in French-speaking Districts, 1959 and 1974*

District	Commune	% German-speakers		% 'No' vote	
		1959[a]	1974[b]	1959	1974
Delémont	Ederswiler	95	96	67	55
	Rebévelier	63	82	62	65
	Roggenburg	97	95	68	76
Moutier	Châtelat	65	64	89	84
	Schelten	98	98	67	58
	Seehof	97	91	100	85

[a] 1960 census figures.
[b] 1970 census figures.

As was suggested earlier, there appears to be a great deal of solid evidence to support this contention. Even the most cursory comparison of a religious map of the Bernese Jura and a map showing the distribution of the 'Yes' vote in the 1974 referendum (Figs. 28 and 33 respectively), suggests a remarkable degree of coincidence between the two 'patterns'. A more detailed examination of the 1974 referendum data reveals, in fact, that not a single electoral subdivision which recorded a Protestant majority in the 1970 census voted in favour of the establishment of a new canton.

Following the initiative of 1959 (in which, it will be recalled, the pro-Jurassian vote of 15,159 was outweighed by the pro-Bernese vote of 16,355), Mayer (op. cit.) conducted a regression analysis which involved the six predominantly French-speaking districts. Using 1950 census figures and the 1959 referendum data, Mayer found that religious preference explained 67 per cent of the variation between the 'Yes' votes in the various electoral subdivisions.[5] The 'Catholicism is separatism' theory appears to be strengthened still further when, on examining the individual data for each commune, we note that those nine communes in the district of Moutier which (unlike the other, remaining communes of Moutier) voted for the establishment of a new canton in 1959, were predominantly Catholic.

In spite of this impressive evidence of a strong relationship between religion and political preference with respect to Jura separatism, members of the RJ argue, firstly, that there are significant numbers of Protestant southerners

Table 12. *Bernese Jura: Citizenship of Resident Swiss Citizens, 1970*

District	% citizens of Bernese Jura	% citizens of Old Canton	% citizens of A German-Swiss canton[a]
Courtelary	35	41	50
Delémont	64	17	30
Franches-Montagnes	75	13	19
Moutier	42	37	50
La Neuveville	35	34	51
Porrentruy	73	14	21
Total: 6 French-speaking districts	54	27	37
Laufen	51	12	47
Total: Bernese Jura	54	25	38[b]

[a] Includes Old Canton but not German-speaking Laufen District of Bernese Jura.
[b] Percentages do not always total 100 because Swiss citizens whose ancestors came from Canton Ticino, Romansh areas of Canton Graubünden, and other countries are not included.

Source: Swiss Federal Bureau of Statistics.

(some of whose families can trace back their Jurassian roots for centuries) who are separatists.[6] The RJ has also pointed out that significant numbers of northerners (who, of course, are predominantly Catholic) are opposed to separatism.[7] These statements are correct though they do not, of course, refute the 'Catholicism is separatism' argument.

Members of the RJ argue further, however, that religious preference cannot be the most significant determinant of separatism. If this were the case, they reason, why did the Catholic, but German-speaking, population of the Bernese Jura district of Laufen, in the extreme north-eastern corner of the region, vote *against* a new canton in both 1959 and 1974? Surely, they argue, language is just as important a determining factor as religion in Jura separatism, if not more important? In order to test the 'Catholicism is separatism' argument, the following theory was developed:

(2) The higher the percentage of Swiss citizens in a commune who are Catholics, the higher the 1974 vote in favour of the new Canton Jura.

The Geography of Citizenship

The citizenship of a Swiss involves his relationship with that commune *in which his ancestors resided* during the early and middle years of the nineteenth century,

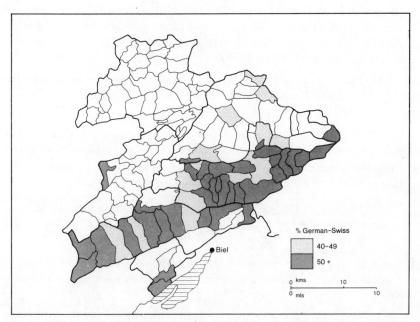

Fig. 35. French-speaking Districts of the Bernese Jura: Communes in which Citizens of German-Swiss Cantons Account for more than 40% of Resident Swiss Citizens, 1970.

when the Swiss federal authorities first began to record census data on a regular basis.

As indicated in Chapter 7, prior to the 1974 referendum the RJ demanded that those residents of the Jura whose ancestors had not lived in the region for 90 years (i.e. the vast majority of the descendants of Bernese immigrants to the Jura) *not* be allowed to vote. It will be recalled that the RJ argued that, because of family tradition, descendants of immigrants from the Old Canton (and, to a lesser extent, of immigrants from other German-Swiss cantons) would almost automatically vote in favour of Berne. In this sense, the RJ still argues that the descendants of the Bernese and other German-Swiss immigrants, who are particularly numerous in the South Jura, constitute a fifth column which is opposed to the best interests of the 'real' Jurassians (Table 12).

The RJ further argues that the South Jura voted against the establishment of a new Canton Jura in 1974 not because of its Protestant traditions but because so many of the people of the South Jura were of *Bernese origin*. (Figure 35 indicates those communes of the Bernese Jura in which German-Swiss citizens accounted for 40–49 per cent of all Swiss residents in 1970, together with those in which the proportion exceeded 50 per cent.) There would seem to be some evidence in support of the RJ's argument. For example, 78 per cent of the inhabitants of the commune of La Ferrière, in the extreme south-west of the southern district of Courtelary, were citizens of German-Swiss communes at the time of the census of 1970 (Appendix C: Table 2). In 1974 the commune registered an 85 per cent vote against a new canton (Appendix C: Table 2).

In order to test the relationship between an individual's citizenship and his voting behaviour, three theories were developed. Firstly, the RJ's 'Bernese fifth column' theory was stated as follows:

(3) The higher the percentage of Swiss citizens in a commune who are Bernese citizens, the lower the 1974 vote in favour of the new Canton Jura.

It was also decided to examine the degree to which the presence, in the Bernese Jura, of Swiss who themselves come from (or whose ancestors came from) German-speaking cantons *other* than the Old Canton of Berne, might influence voting behaviour.[8] This resulted in the following theory:

(4) The higher the percentage of Swiss citizens in a commune who are citizens of a German-Swiss canton other than the Old Canton, the lower the 1974 vote in favour of the new Canton Jura.

It was next decided to examine the apparent combined influence of *all* citizens of German-Swiss background on voting behaviour, by means of the following theory:

(5) The higher the percentage of Swiss citizens in a commune who are citizens of *any* German-Swiss canton (including the Old Canton) the lower the 1974 vote in favour of the new Canton Jura.

Theories (3), (4), and (5) all suggest the existence of so-called 'inverse' (or reverse) relationships; in other words, the *higher* the percentage of 'non-Jurassians' in a commune, the *lower* the 'Yes' vote. The implication of the claims of the RJ relating to the origins of Jurassians (i.e. 'the reverse side of the coin') is that Jurassian citizens are more 'patriotic' than non-Jurassian citizens—or at least those of the latter who come from, or whose ancestors come from German-Swiss cantons, and especially the Old Canton. These claims were examined by developing, and then testing, a number of other theories.

Firstly, it was considered possible that an individual from a family which had lived in its native Jurassian commune for many generations would have been more likely to vote for a Jurassian canton in the 1974 referendum, giving rise to the following theory.[9]

(6) The higher the percentage of communal citizens resident in a commune, the higher the 1974 vote in favour of the new Canton Jura.

It was also considered possible that a communal resident who was a citizen of a nearby commune within the *same district* would also have a high degree of emotional attachment to the Bernese Jura—an attitude which would affect his or her voting behaviour. The latter theory was tested by means of the following theory:

(7) The higher the percentage of district citizens (including communal citizens) resident in a commune, the higher the 1974 vote in favour of the new Canton Jura.

Finally, it was decided to check the theory that individuals who were citizens of *any Jurassian commune* would be likely to vote for a new canton. (Figure 36 indicates those Jurassian communes in which Jurassian citizens constituted 40–9 per cent of Swiss residents in 1970, together with those in which Jurassian citizens exceeded 50 per cent of the total.) The following theory was propounded:

(8) The higher the percentage of Jurassian citizens (including communal and district citizens) in a commune, the higher the 1974 vote in favour of the new Canton Jura.

The Geography of Economic Health

We noted in Chapter 3 that the RJ claimed, on a number of occasions, that the Bernese Jura had suffered economically as a result of its association with Canton Berne. It was therefore decided, in addition, to investigate the degree to which the 'economic health' of a commune appeared to be associated with

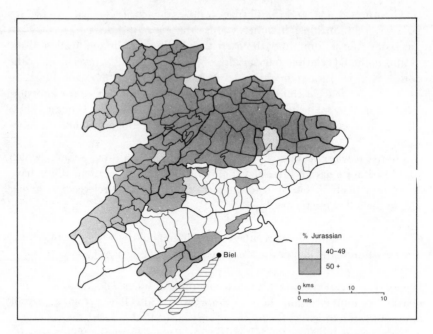

Fig. 36. French-speaking Districts of the Bernese Jura: Communes in which Citizens of the Bernese Jura Account for more than 40% of Resident Swiss Citizens, 1970.

its voting behaviour, by testing the following theory, which suggested the existence of an inverse relationship:

(9) The lower the economic index of a commune, the higher the 1974 vote in favour of the new Canton Jura.

Population movements to and from an area are also related to its economic health, as a general rule. We have already noted that one of the strongest and most emotional arguments used by the RJ in its campaign for a new canton was that, for many years, the Bernese Jura had been losing many of its native sons and daughters, and, especially, large numbers of its young people. The RJ reasoned that emigration had occurred primarily because the economy of the Bernese Jura had been neglected by the Bernese authorities.

A rather similar population exodus has unquestionably been occurring in many parts of rural Switzerland for hundreds of years. However, it will be recalled that the RJ argued prior to the 1974 referendum that, in the case of the Bernese Jura, the exodus became a 'population haemorrhage' towards the end of the nineteenth century, and that this haemorrhage continued up until the 1970s. The RJ argued that this population drain not only greatly weakened both the economy and overall vitality of the Bernese Jura, but was also one cause of the reduction of the region's percentage of the population of Canton Berne as a whole.[10]

There is no doubt that the population drain in question was substantial. Census figures indicate that the populations of some rural communes reached their peak as early as 1870, and have declined precipitously since then. During the century prior to the 1974 referendum, thousands of young Jurassians left their native communes, never to return on a permanent basis. In the early days of the Industrial Revolution, as we have seen, many individuals simply moved from rural communes to larger centres of population in the Bernese Jura. In subsequent decades, however, there was an increasing tendency for migrants to move a greater distance, to Biel, to towns and cities elsewhere in French-speaking Switzerland, to France, and to the United States.

Even after World War I, census figures indicate that the exodus from rural communes in the Bernese Jura continued unchecked. Between 1920 and 1960, for example, 60 per cent of the communes of the six French-speaking districts of the region experienced population decreases. In some communes this decrease exceeded 33 per cent. It was also pointed out, in Chapter 2, that approximately two-thirds of the communes experiencing a population loss were situated in the North Jura.

In the years leading up to the 1974 referendum, the RJ consistently argued that a new cantonal government which was independent of Berne would make the people of the Bernese Jura 'masters in their own house', and would arrest the population drain by establishing more light industries in the region and by encouraging tourism. In this way, it argued, the necessary jobs would be provided for young Jurassians.

It would seem logical to expect that, in communities where job opportunities do not exist and young people are forced to leave to find employment elsewhere, dissatisfaction with authority will increase. It could be further argued that such dissatisfaction might lead those individuals who remain in the commune to vote in favour of the establishment of a new canton, the government of which might arrest out-migration. This theory was phrased as follows:

(10) The greater the percentage population loss in a commune between 1960 and 1973, the higher the 1974 vote in favour of the new Canton Jura.

It was, alternatively, reasoned that the memories of human beings are limited in many ways, and that *more recent* population changes (say, those which occurred during the three years prior to the 1974 referendum) were likely to have had a greater impact on Jurassian attitudes toward outside authority than longer-term trends. The following modified theory relating to depopulation was thus also developed:

(11) The higher the percentage population loss in a commune between 1970 and 1973, the higher the 1974 vote in favour of the new Canton Jura.

It was also decided to investigate the voting behaviour of those communes of the Bernese Jura in which a relatively high percentage of the working population was still engaged in *agriculture*. On the one hand, those employed in agriculture often work longer hours and for lower wages than those employed in other types of work and, therefore, might conceivably be dissatisfied with the economic and political status quo.

On the other hand, it was recognized that, in most countries, farmers and those living in rural areas are considered to be conservative in their attitudes and behaviour, including their voting behaviour. It was further recognized that Bernese immigrants settled many farms originally occupied by Jurassians, and that this might 'muddy' the data. Nevertheless, the possibility that those living in agricultural communes might, for economic or other reasons, be *more* separatist in their politics than individuals living in urban communes was considered to be worth investigation, and Theory No. 12 was therefore developed:

(12) The higher the percentage of the working force of a commune employed in agriculture, the higher the 1974 vote in favour of the new Canton Jura.

Distance from Berne

It will be recalled that in Chapters 4 and 5 we discussed the degree to which the *geographical distance* from Berne, the Mittelland city which has played such a major role in Swiss history, of various communes of the Bernese Jura might have affected their respective linguistic and religious characters and possibly, in addition, their attitudes toward the cantonal government. A quick glance at religious and linguistic maps is sufficient, for example, to tell us that the Catholic districts of the Bernese Jura, as a group, are situated further from Berne than are the Protestant districts. Moreover, speaking generally, as one moves northwards and westwards from Biel, and increasingly further away still from Berne, the language of the majority of the population changes, rather abruptly, from German to French. Speaking generally, too, the more distant Jurassian communes appear to be more separatist in feeling than those situated closer to Berne.

While recognizing that the original causes of a phenomenon may, more recently, have become blurred by other factors, it was nevertheless considered desirable to examine the data to determine whether or not there appeared to be an association of this kind today. The following theory was therefore formulated:

(13) The greater the travel distance between the commune and the city of Berne, the higher the 1974 vote in favour of the new Canton Jura.

Altitude Above Berne

Reference was made, in earlier chapters, to the height of the Jura mountain chain, and the altitude of many Jurassian communities in comparison with those of the Swiss Mittelland. While consideration was being given to the distance factor it was, therefore, also considered possible that, distance being equal, the higher the altitude of a settlement, the more remote it would be in terms of travel time.

It will be recalled that, in the 1959 initiative, certain high-altitude Protestant communes in the South Jura (such as Diesse and Nods in the district of La Neuveville) actually voted *in favour* of a referendum for a new canton (Appendix C: Table 2). In the 1974 referendum, though cut off from the North Jura by other communes which were clearly strongly pro-Bernese, these latter two communes still recorded pro-separatist votes of 46 per cent and 42 per cent respectively (Fig. 33 and Appendix C: Table 2). The question thus arises as to whether or not the remoteness of an individual's mountain village *vis-à-vis* Berne might make him or her feel more distant from Berne, and somewhat alienated in his or her attitudes toward Berne. The following theory was therefore developed to test this:

(14) The higher the altitude of a commune compared to the city of Berne, the higher the 1974 vote in favour of the new Canton Jura.

In summary, in considering the causes of the Jura problem in Chapters 3 to 7, it was reasoned that a number of geographical factors might be related, in some way, to the phenomenon of Jura separatism, as expressed in the percentage of the 1974 referendum votes cast, in each commune of the Bernese Jura, in favour of the establishment of a new canton. These geographical factors, listed in the order in which they have been discussed in this chapter, are as follows:

(1) The percentage of French-speaking Swiss citizens in a given commune, based on the 1970 census.

(2) The percentage of Swiss citizens in a commune who were Catholics.

(3) The percentage of citizens of the Old Canton of Berne in a commune (an inverse relationship).

(4) The percentage of citizens of other German-Swiss cantons in a commune (an inverse relationship).

(5) The percentage of total German-Swiss (including Old Canton) citizens in a commune (an inverse relationship).

(6) The percentage of citizens of a Jurassian commune living in that same commune.

(7) The percentage of Jurassian district (including communal) citizens living in a commune in that same district.

(8) The percentage of Jurassian (including communal and district) citizens living in a given Jurassian commune.

(9) The economic status (i.e. level of prosperity) of a commune (an inverse relationship).

(10) The communal percentage population increase or decline in the thirteen-year period between the 1960 census and 1973, i.e. the year prior to the 1974 referendum. (An inverse relationship might exist between the degree of population decrease and the strength of the separatist vote.)

(11) The communal percentage population increase or decline in the three-year period (1970–3) immediately preceding the 1974 referendum.

(12) The percentage of the population of a commune employed in agriculture.

(13) The distance between a commune (via the normal road or rail route followed by travellers) and Berne.

(14) The altitude of the commune compared to that of Berne.

Measuring Jura Separatism

After careful consideration, the author concluded that the most meaningful available measure of the relative strength or weakness of the phenomenon known as Jura separatism was the Jurassian voter response to the referendum conducted by the Bernese Government on 23 June 1974. In this referendum all adult male and female[11] Swiss citizens who were residents of the seven districts of the Bernese Jura were asked this question: 'Do you wish to form a new canton?' It will be recalled, from Chapter 7, that in all seven districts of the Bernese Jura, 36,802 votes were cast in favour of the establishment of a new canton (52 per cent of the total). In the six predominantly French-speaking

Table 13. *Bernese Jura: Registered Voters vs. Participation in Referendum of June 1974, by Districts*

District	Registered voters	Actual voters	% participation
Courtelary	15,187	13,673	90
Delémont	15,725	14,548	93
Franches-Montagnes	5,046	4,717	93
Moutier	18,366	16,804	91
La Neuveville	3,178	2,749	87
Porrentruy	15,615	14,608	94
Total: 6 districts	73,117	67,099	92
Laufen	7,666	5,608	73
Total: 7 districts	80,783	72,707	90

districts, as a group, 54 per cent of the voters voted 'Yes'. In the South Jura district of Courtelary and in the German-speaking district of Laufen, however, only 23 per cent and 26 per cent of the voters, respectively, favoured the establishment of a new canton.

It is suggested that the number and percentage of 'Yes' responses to the question in any given area provide us, as observers, with a satisfactory measure of the strength of Jura separatism in that area in 1974. This is more particularly the case because participation in the referendum reached high levels. (As indicated earlier, 90 per cent of those eligible to vote did so.) In the six French-speaking districts of the Bernese Jura, the vote ranged from 87 per cent of the electorate in La Neuveville to 94 per cent in Porrentruy. Even in the German-speaking district of Laufen, 73 per cent of the eligible voters participated. Table 13 provides details of voting participation in the various districts of the Bernese Jura, while Appendix C: Table 2 provide similar information on an electoral subdistrict basis.

As we have noted, a majority of the residents of the six predominantly French-speaking districts of the Bernese Jura (namely Porrentruy, Franches-Montagnes, Delémont, Moutier, Courtelary, and La Neuveville) voted, *as a whole* and by a 54:46 majority, in favour of the establishment of the new Canton Jura in June 1974 (Table 9). However, the percentage of 'Yes' votes varied greatly, not only between districts, but also between communes within the same district. This was true in both the North and South Jura. The percentage of 'Yes' votes in each commune was therefore considered to be the so-called dependent variable (i.e., the index of the strength of Jura separatism in that commune) in the analyses which followed, and which will be described in the next chapter.

Notes

1. Prior to the early 1960s the RJ stressed the historic unity of the Jura rather than its Frenchness, so as not to offend inhabitants of the German-speaking Laufen district. However, after the 1959 poll, when Laufen registered a 73 per cent anti-separatist vote, the RJ concentrated its energies on obtaining a Canton Jura composed of the six French-speaking districts only, and stressed the latter's francophone character. (See also Chapter 4, n. 1.)

2. In this respect, the Third Force was in agreement with the RJ.

3. As pointed out in Chapter 7, this type of autonomy has never existed in Switzerland, and its establishment would have required a number of constitutional changes.

4 It will be recalled from Chapter 7 that, in the event, the Third Force only attracted a small percentage of the total ballots cast.

5. It will be recalled that only Swiss males were permitted to vote at the time of the 1959 referendum. Mayer (op. cit.) found that the linguistic factor added another 5·5 per cent, so that combined religious and linguistic factors accounted for 72·5 per cent of the variation in 1959 'Yes' votes. Henecka (op. cit.) claims similar findings to Mayer's.

6. These include the secretary-general of the RJ himself. Roland Béguelin is a Protestant who was born in Tramelan, in the southern district of Courtelary, although he now lives and works in the predominantly Catholic town of Delémont, the capital of the new canton. At the time of writing the secretary-treasurer of *Unité-jurassienne*, the South Jura separatist organization, is Alain Charpilloz, a Protestant from Malleray, and a nephew of the famous Jurassian separatist leader, Daniel Charpilloz.

7. A leading anti-separatist leader, Mme Geneviève Aubry, is a northern Catholic by birth, although she has now lived in the South Jura for a number of years. Many such examples of Protestant separatists and Catholic pro-Bernese could be cited.

8. Naturally, many of these individuals who are of Bernese and other German-Swiss background, but whose families have now lived in the Bernese Jura for some generations, speak French only. Nevertheless, as indicated earlier, the RJ argues that, in the South Jura in particular, they would still tend to have a traditional family affection for all things Bernese and that their loyalty would be to Berne and/or German Switzerland rather than to the Bernese Jura.

9. Today, in fact, one finds only a very limited number of communes in the Bernese Jura where a clear majority of residents are also citizens of that same commune. Among them is the commune of Plagne in the southern district of Courtelary. Fifty-seven per cent of its population consisted of *citizens* of Plagne at the time of the 1970 census. Ninety-four per cent of Plagne's population was Protestant in 1970. Interestingly, Plagne registered a majority vote in favour of calling a Jura referendum in the 1959 poll, and 46 per cent of its voters favoured a new Canton Jura in the 1974 referendum (Fig. 33 and Appendix C: Table 2).

10. In 1850 the Bernese Jura accounted for 17 per cent of the total population of Canton Berne, and this rose to close to 19 per cent in 1880, due to heavy immigration from the Old Canton. By 1970, however, the region only accounted for 14 per cent of the population of the canton.

11. It was noted, in Chapter 7, that the 1974 referendum differed from the 1959 initiative in that adult *women* had the right to vote in 1974.

9

Jura Separatism: Some Geographical Findings

The principle of Swiss democracy is, in fact, to be communal before being
cantonal, and to be cantonal before being federal.

ANDRÉ SIEGFRIED (1956)

This chapter will describe how the various geographical theories discussed in
Chapter 8 were investigated by means of a research study. This study consisted of a number of statistical analyses. While analyses were conducted for
the seven districts of the Bernese Jura as an overall entity (as well as for a
number of individual areas of the region), our comments to be made in this
chapter will focus primarily on the six French-speaking districts of the region.
This is because, as noted earlier, the German-speaking Laufen district, which
voted heavily against joining the new canton (Table 9) and which subsequently voted to remain in Canton Berne, is not coveted by the RJ or its
sympathizers.

The Geography of Language

It will be recalled that our first theory suggested the following: 'The higher the
percentage of Swiss citizens in a commune whose first language is French, the
higher the (1974 percentage) vote in favour of (the establishment of) the new
Canton Jura.' A simple regression analysis suggested that, in the six predominantly French-speaking districts of the Bernese Jura, approximately 26
per cent of the variation between the various electoral subdistricts in the
separatist ('Yes') vote in the referendum of 23 June 1974 appeared to be
associated with (or explained by) variations in the percentages of French-
speaking citizens living in those subdistricts (Table 14).

It would appear from these data that in 1974 Jura separatism was associated
with an individual's French mother-tongue to only a moderate degree in the
French-speaking Bernese Jura as a whole. In view of the concerns expressed by
the RJ with respect to the purported threat to the French language, a substantially stronger association (indicating that a great many more French-
speaking Jurassians were concerned about the menace of germanization),
might have been expected.

The relationship between French-speakers and Jurassian separatist feeling
may well have been much stronger in earlier years, when Bernese and other
German-Swiss immigrants to the Bernese Jura could be differentiated from
native Jurassians not only by their place of origin but also by their German
speech. However, the great majority of present-day descendants of Bernese

Table 14. *Bernese Jura Referendum of 23 June 1974: Percentage of Variation in Separatist ('Yes') Vote Explained by Various Factors in Six Predominantly French-speaking Districts (122 communes)*

Factor	R^2 value	Degree of significance
French language	0·25819	0·001
Catholicism	0·76636	0·0001
Bernese citizenship	0·63609	0·0001
Citizenship of other German-Swiss cantons	0·07079	0·01
Total German-Swiss citizenship	0·58285	0·0001
Communal citizenship	0·35005	0·001
District citizenship	0·50366	0)0005
Jura citizenship	0·65724	0·0001
Economic status	0·02956	0·05
13-year population change	0·00068	*
Recent (3-year) population change	0·04093	0·05
'Agriculturalness'	0·00001	*
Distance from Berne	0·25051	0·001
Altitude above Berne	0·09874	0·01

* Indicates that the degree of significance falls below 0·25.

immigrants to the Bernese Jura are French-speaking. There has also been over a century of intermarriage between immigrant Bernese and natives, which would have been facilitated in the South Jura, particularly, because of a common Protestant religion. These factors mean that many present-day, French-speaking, South Jurassian families proudly display Bernese emblems inside and outside their homes, and see no inconsistency in this.

We must be more cautious when we examine data for smaller groupings of subdistricts because of their limited numbers of observations (Appendix C: Table 3). Nevertheless it appears that the French language is more closely related to separatism in the North Jura (0·26518) than in the South Jura (0·18984).[1] A good deal of the higher North Jura R^2 value may be explained by the fact that it included the district of Delémont (0·74849). Delémont's score, in turn, is at least partly explained by the fact that its French-speaking communes contrast sharply with its three strongly German-speaking sub-districts (Ederswiler, Rebévelier, and Roggenburg) which voted over-whelmingly for Berne. One further interesting finding, however, was the extremely low R^2 value (0·09629) for the Porrentruy district of the North Jura. It may be that the inhabitants of this district, which protrudes into France, felt so secure in their French culture that language was not a political issue to them.

In the South Jura, the apparently strong association between the French language and separatist feeling (0·82667) for the small district of La Neuve-ville (five subdistricts) is of interest. This district included such extremes as the subdistrict/commune of Prêles (in which only 60 per cent of the population spoke French as its first language and which only registered a 26 per cent separatist vote), and the subdistrict/commune of Diesse, which was 91 per cent French-speaking, and which registered a considerably higher 39 per cent 'Yes' vote.[2]

The Geography of Religion

It will be recalled that our second theory stated: 'The higher the percentage of Swiss citizens in a commune who are Catholics, the higher the vote in favour of the new Canton Jura.' Table 14 provides strong evidence to support the 'Catholicism is separatism' theory since, in the French-speaking districts as a group, it can be seen that approximately 77 per cent (0·76636) of the variation in the 'Yes' vote was explained by the variation in the percentages of Swiss citizens in these subdistricts who were Catholic. It will be recalled, from Chapter 8, that an earlier regression analysis by Mayer (op. cit.), using 1950 census data and 1959 poll figures, also provided evidence of a strong relationship between Catholicism and Jura separatist feeling, with Mayer finding that approximately 67 per cent of the variation was explained by the religious factor.

The apparent increase in importance (from 67 to 77 per cent) of the religious factor between 1959 and 1974 may be due, firstly, to the increasing polarization of political attitudes which took place during that time. Old religious suspicions appear to have been fanned to a white heat between the popular initiative of 1959 and the referendum of 1974. Secondly, the higher 1974 figure may also be due to the fact that women (who may sometimes be more conservative in their religious views than men, and who were not allowed to vote in 1959), participated in the 1974 referendum. In any event, Catholicism appeared, in 1974, to have become associated with separatism, and Protestantism with anti-separatism to an even greater degree than hitherto.

Once again, caution must be exercised in examining the religious variable in smaller groupings of subdistricts (Appendix C: Table 3). Nevertheless, there is some evidence of the existence of certain interesting religious–political patterns. To begin with, the religious factor appears to be extremely important in the South Jura (0·80369), but far less important in the North Jura (0·18378). Within the South Jura, the high scores for the districts of Moutier (0·91699) and, to a lesser extent, the smaller district of La Neuveville (0·68369), appear to have caused the South Jura to register such a high Catholic–separatist association, since the value for Courtelary (0·06011) was quite low.[2]

Although traditionally considered to be a South Jura district, Moutier can more precisely be described as a central region which included, prior to 1979, nine predominantly Catholic communes which were strongly separatist in sympathy. Seven of these communes lie to the north of the gorges de Moutier.

The remaining two communes (Lajoux and Les Genevez) lie in the extreme north-western corner of the district where there was a weakening of Protestant influences which, as we saw earlier, had advanced to the gorges de Moutier, the gorges du Pichou, and to the headwaters of the Sorne and Trame rivers. We noted that, beyond these points, the supply lines of Bernese armies became dangerously attenuated, and Protestant influences were unable to take firm root. The Moutier district thus included, within its boundaries prior to 1979, communes which were often geographically separated for each other by mountains and gorges, which contrasted sharply with each other in their respective religious traditions, and which appear to have regarded each other with a good deal of suspicion (Fig. 26).

The Geography of Citizenship

With respect to citizenship, it will be recalled that the first of our three theories was stated as follows: 'The higher the percentage of Swiss citizens in a commune who are Bernese citizens, the lower the vote in favour of the new Canton Jura.' This theory suggests the existence of a strong inverse relationship between a 'Yes' vote and Old Canton citizenship; in other words, a high percentage of Bernese in a commune should have resulted in a low 'Yes' vote. It would appear, from Table 14, that 64 per cent (0·63609) of the variation in the separatist vote in the six 'French' districts was associated with the presence of individuals who were citizens of the Old Canton of Berne. The relationship was, as anticipated, inverse. This figure supports our theory, and suggests that the RJ has strong grounds for suggesting that Jurassians of Bernese origin are, by and large, anti-separatist in their political views. Appendix C: Table 3 indicates that Bernese citizenship–anti-separatist association was particularly strong in the South Jura (0·59026) where, as we are aware, the Bernese settled in greater numbers, compared to the North Jura (0·14724). Within the South Jura, the Bernese citizenship association with anti-separatist sentiment appeared to be the strongest in the south-central 'hinge' district of Moutier (0·74000).

We noted in Chapter 2, and subsequently, however, that immigrants also moved to the Bernese Jura from German-Swiss cantons other than Berne during the latter part of the nineteenth century and during the twentieth century. It will be recalled that it was thus decided, in Chapter 8, to investigate whether there was any evidence to suggest how German-Swiss of non-Bernese origins might have voted in 1974.

Table 14 suggests that, in the six French districts of the Bernese Jura as a whole, approximately 7 per cent (0·07079) of the variation in the separatist vote was associated with non-Bernese, but German-Swiss, citizenship, on an inverse basis.

In the six French-speaking districts *as a whole* the influence, on the referéndum vote, of German-Swiss immigration from areas of Switzerland other than the Old Canton appears, therefore, to have been slight. However, a moderately high score was recorded in Franches-Montagnes (0·32104), and a high value (0·76690) was recorded in La Neuveville, where 17 per cent of the Swiss citizens of the district were of German-Swiss, but non-Bernese, origin at the time of the 1970 census. Many of these were elderly German-Swiss, referred to earlier (Chapter 3, n. 8), who lived in the lakeside resort commune of La Neuveville. Logic would suggest that they would seem unlikely, as a group, to have voted separatist. The figure for the Bernese Jura as a whole was 0·16019. (Appendix C: Table 3.)

In the German-speaking district of Laufen, a substantial number of Swiss citizens (approximately 35 per cent of the total at the time of the 1970 census) had come from—or had ancestors who came from—German-Swiss cantons other than the Old Canton. (Bernese, in fact, only accounted for 12 per cent of the total Swiss population of the district.) The fact that the non-Bernese German-Swiss were living in a completely German-Swiss district may have encouraged them to vote against what they may have perceived as a purely French-Swiss separatist movement. The heavy Laufen anti-separatist vote clearly influenced the higher R^2 figure (0·16019) for this variable for the Bernese Jura as a whole, compared to the six French-speaking districts only (0·07079).

It will be recalled that in addition to other analyses, it was also decided to make an effort to measure the *overall* effect of the presence of *all* voters of German-Swiss background (including Bernese) on voting patterns in the 1974 referendum by testing the validity of the following theory: 'The higher the percentage of Swiss citizens in a commune who are citizens of any German-Swiss canton (including the Old Canton), the lower the vote in favour of the new Canton Jura.' The results of this regression, too, are listed in Table 14. Fifty-eight per cent (0·58285) of the variation in the separatist vote in the six French-speaking districts of the Bernese Jura appears to have been inversely associated with the variation in the percentage of German-Swiss (i.e. Bernese and non-Bernese) voters. This value was significant at the 0·0001 level.

The R^2 value for the Bernese Jura as a whole was 0·55456 (Appendix C: Table 3). The R^2 value for the North Jura (0·12726) was much lower than that for the South Jura (0·48692), and in one northern district (Porrentruy) the R^2 value was only 0·08934. Porrentruy had one of the lowest percentages (21 per cent) of residents of German-Swiss origin in the region in 1970, however.[2] It may well be that only when the percentage of German-Swiss (including Bernese) immigrants exceeds a certain critical point does the native population become hostile and resentful, thus provoking a counter-reaction from the non-natives. Moreover, other things being equal, it may be that in the Swiss context, the smaller the percentage of German-speaking immigrants to a French-speaking area, the more likely they are to be assimilated and/or to conform to prevailing political attitudes of the host community over two or three generations. These R^2 values (as was the case with the values relating to the specifically Bernese 'fifth' column theory), however, provide strong support for the argument of the RJ that the descendants of German-Swiss immigrants, as an overall group, are opposed to Jura separatist aspirations.

The reverse side of the Bernese and German-Swiss fifth column argument is that Jurassian citizens would tend to vote for a new canton. It will be recalled that our first theory relating to Jurassian citizenship focused on Jurassians who still lived in the commune of their ancestors, and was expressed as follows: 'The higher the percentage of communal citizens resident in a commune, the higher the vote in favour of the new Canton Jura.' It was suggested, in effect, that an individual whose family had lived in a community for many generations, and who was therefore a citizen of that same commune, might conceivably have developed a strong emotional attachment to his or her native settlement. It was further considered possible that such native Jurassians might feel some resentment toward individuals of Bernese and/or German-Swiss background, and that this might cause them to vote for an independent Jurassian canton free of Bernese influences.

The results of this particular simple regression indicated that communal citizenship appeared to account for 35 per cent of the variation in the 1974 'Yes' vote in the six predominantly French-speaking districts (Table 14). The relationship was positive (i.e., the higher the percentage of communal citizens, the higher the separatist vote tended to be). This suggests a moderately strong association between residence in one's ancestral commune and Jura separatism in the French-speaking Bernese Jura. However, a more detailed examination of figures for the two Juras indicates only a $0 \cdot 07846$ R^2 value for the North Jura, but a relatively high value ($0 \cdot 42376$) for the South Jura where, as we have seen, a larger number of German-Swiss settled, and where both native Jurassians and immigrants may have been more likely to have become more conscious of their origins, and more polarized in their attitudes towards Berne. The R^2 values were particularly high in the southern districts of Moutier ($0 \cdot 52906$) and La Neuveville ($0 \cdot 59006$). The figure for the Bernese Jura as a whole was $0 \cdot 23627$.[2] (Appendix C: Table 3.)

As was the case with the factor of language, the relationship being investigated may well have been stronger in earlier years. However, intermarriage, especially in the South Jura (where, as we have noted, in a number of communes the original inhabitants and their descendants became a minority in their own 'ancestral' village), has probably resulted in at least some instances where, at the present time, an individual may be a citizen of the commune in which he lives because one of his male line great-grandfathers was a native Jurassian. However, his other great-grandfathers may all have been of Bernese origin, and he may therefore have inherited a strongly pro-Bernese family tradition in spite of his official Jurassian citizenship. Another possible reason why the R^2 figure was not higher still may be that at least some individuals who have remained, to this day, in the commune of their remote ancestors may be less ambitious, more content with the status quo and less resentful of newcomers than an observer might expect.

If residence in the commune of one's ancestors is related in some way to separatist feeling, it could be argued that citizens of one particular Jurassian commune who resided in another, but nearby, commune in 1974 would, similarly, have an emotional attachment to the district, and would tend to share the same separatist sympathies as were held by citizens of that commune. This theory was, it will be recalled, stated as follows: 'The higher the percentage of district citizens (including communal citizens) resident in a commune, the higher the vote in favour of the new Canton Jura.' Table 14 suggests that loyalty to one's native district did, in fact, appear to be quite strong in the Bernese Jura, and did appear to influence attitudes towards Berne. Fifty per cent (0·50366) of the variation in the 1974 'Yes' vote was explained by the variation in the percentage of 'district citizens' in that commune. The relationship was, as we would expect, positive.

However, a closer examination of the data once again indicates important differences between the North and South Juras. In the North Jura the R^2 value was only 0·09836, while in the South Jura it was 0·43109. In the Moutier district the figure was 0·54296, and in La Neuveville 0·55658. The figure for the Bernese Jura as a whole was 0·42488 (Appendix C: Table 3). Irrespective of the group of subdistricts examined, we would logically expect the R^2 values of these regressions to be greater than those relating only to communal citizens—as, indeed, they were. This is because the latter regressions took account not only of the village natives of the earlier regression, but also of the natives of nearby villages in the same district who, it appears, would often hold similar attitudes to the village natives.

It will be recalled that our next theory represented an effort to establish whether or not the previously-discussed concepts of communal and district 'patriotism' extended to feelings, held by a citizen of *any* Jurassian commune who still resided in the Bernese Jura, regarding the region as a whole: 'The higher the percentage of Jurassian citizens (including communal and district citizens resident in a commune), the higher the vote in favour of the new Canton Jura.' The results of these regression analyses were quite spectacular. Table 14 suggests that 66 per cent (0·65724) of the variations in the 'Yes' vote appeared to be associated with variations in the numbers of Swiss who were Jurassian citizens in the six French districts. This value was positive, and was significant at the 0·0001 level.

Clearly, the regression values resulting from the testing of our various 'citizenship theories' provide strong evidence to suggest that the origin of a present-day Jurassian, as evidenced by his citizenship, has an important influence on his attitude to Jurassian separatism. The figures emerging from the regression analyses suggest that, as a general rule and all other things being equal, individuals in the French-speaking districts of the Bernese Jura tended to vote separatist in 1974 if they held Jurassian citizenship.

In sharp contrast, as a general rule and other things being equal, the regression figures suggest that Swiss residents of the French-speaking districts of the Bernese Jura voted anti-separatist in 1974 if they held Bernese or other German-Swiss citizenship. It will be recalled that 58 per cent of the variation in the 'Yes' votes were explained by this variable.

It is clear from the figures, however, that an individual's origin (as indicated by his citizenship) has been a much more divisive factor in South Jura (which received the greater number of Bernese and other German-Swiss immigrants) than in the North Jura.[2] This is probably because, as suggested earlier, the original citizens of the South Jura (or those who are of predominantly Jurassian background) have felt more threatened by the massive German-Swiss (predominantly Bernese), influx during the 125 years leading up to the 1974 referendum, than have their fellow Jurassians in the North Jura. In turn, the German-Swiss of the South Jura (and those exclusively or predominantly descended from them), sensing and reacting to this hostility, have sought, perhaps, to feel more secure by stressing their ties to Berne in particular, and to German-speaking Switzerland in general.

The Geography of Economic Health

It was suggested, earlier in this work, that individuals living in a commune which was economically depressed might regard this situation as being the fault of the government of the canton of Berne. Certainly, as we have seen, the RJ has repeatedly suggested that this is the case. It was further hypothesized that such resentment might lead to an individual voting separatist, i.e., that there was an inverse relationship between economic well-being and separation. The following theory was therefore tested: 'The lower the economic index of a commune, the higher the vote in favour of the new Canton Jura.' However, only in La Neuveville was there evidence of a strong relationship, and only in Franches-Montagnes was there evidence of a moderate relationship.[2] Although La Neuveville is a small district in area, we have already noted that it includes communes with widely differing characteristics, and its overall R^2 value reflects this to some degree. For example, the rather remote, high-altitude subdistrict of Diesse had an economic index of only 57 per cent of the cantonal average, while the lower-altitude, lakeside subdistrict of La Neuveville had an index of 104 per cent. Diesse registered a separatist vote of 46 per cent, whereas La Neuveville's was only 33 per cent (Fig. 33).

It will be recalled that a number of observers of the political situation in the Jura have suggested that Jura separatist feeling may have increased in the post-World War II period because of the steady haemorrhage of the population of many communities in the Bernese Jura; this haemorrhage has been due, in part, to the economic crises which have been experienced by the region. Once again, we have seen that the RJ blamed the Bernese administration for this situation. The following theory endeavoured to develop the latter theme further, arguing that a steady, continual year-by-year population drain over a thirteen-year period (extending from the census of 1960 to the year immediately preceding the 1974 referendum) would exacerbate Jurassian separatist feelings still further: 'The greater the percentage population loss in a commune between 1960 and 1973, the higher the vote in favour of the new Canton Jura.' This theory would appear to be an eminently reasonable one and, because of this, the results of this particular simple regression analysis came as a considerable surprise to the author. The data provided no evidence of the existence of *any* association between depopulation in the 1960–73 period, on the one hand, and Jura separatist sympathies on the other (Table 14), except in the district of La Neuveville.[2]

Before discussing these findings, our second depopulation theory will be discussed: 'The higher the population loss in a commune between 1970 and 1973, the higher the vote in favour of the new Canton Jura.' In this variant of the previous theory, it will be recalled, it was reasoned that human beings, in some respects, have short memories. This being the case, it was argued, their political viewpoint may tend to be coloured almost entirely by *more recent* experiences. For this reason, it was suggested, the effects of depopulation during a more recent three-year period (i.e., from the census of 1970 to 1973, the year preceding the 1974 referendum) were likely to have a greater influence than would a longer thirteen-year population trend. However once again, surprisingly, the simple regression analysis gave no indication of any association between recent depopulation and a 'Yes' vote for a new canton (Table 14), except in this case, in the district of Franches-Montagnes.[2]

One possible explanation of these surprising findings may be that individuals who seek employment, but do not find it in their home commune, eventually 'vote with their feet', by leaving their village to obtain employment elsewhere. In this way, it could be argued, those whose dissatisfaction is greatest remove themselves from the communal voting list. It could be further argued that those who remain in the commune are more satisfied with the status quo, and less likely to vote against Bernese authority. In Franches-Montagnes, however, where eleven of the seventeen communes lost population during the three-year period being studied, the population haemorrhage may have exceeded what were locally regarded as 'acceptable' limits, and thus caused the higher 'haemorrhage–separatist' score.

In Chapter 8, it will be recalled, it was decided that the question of whether or not the more agricultural communes of the Bernese Jura were more separatist than others should be investigated: 'The higher the percentage of the working force of a commune employed in agriculture, the higher the vote in favour of the new Canton Jura.' Table 14 indicates that no relationship whatsoever seemed to exist between such a characteristic and Jura separatism in the Bernese Jura as a whole in 1974. The same general pattern also held for both the northern and southern regions. Only in the district of La Neuveville (0·63376), with its sharp communal contrasts, was there some evidence to suggest a possible relationship between agriculturalism and separatism. There was also some evidence of the existence of relationships—though somewhat weaker ones—in Franches-Montagnes, in Delémont, and in Courtelary.[2]

Distance from Berne

It will be recalled that, in earlier chapters, it was theorized that if Bernese influences declined as distance (in terms of road and rail routes) from the city of Berne increased, the more distant communes would tend to be more separatist in feeling. The reason would be that remote communes would have less contact with Berne, and would consequently be more likely to feel neglected and alienated. The following statement was used to test this theory: 'The greater the travel distance between the commune and the city of Berne, the higher the vote in favour of the new Canton Jura.' This *does* appear to be the case for the six French-speaking districts of the Bernese Jura as a whole (Table 14). They recorded an R^2 value of 0·25051 (significant at the 0·001 level), suggesting the existence of a moderately strong relationship. No such relationship appeared to exist *within* most districts or groupings, however.[2]

Altitude in Relation to Berne

Finally, it will be recalled from Chapter 8, an attempt was made to differentiate between ground travel routes and altitude. The theory being tested was that, before modern means of transportation were available, a one-mile journey to a village situated 'on a mountain top' would take an individual longer than a similar journey over level ground. It was further hypothesized that the inhabitants of a remote mountain village might consequently develop stronger-than-average feelings of suspicion and distrust toward Berne, a powerful Mittelland city.

In the event, the analysis provided no strong evidence of any such association. Less than 10 per cent of the 'Yes' vote variation in the six French-speaking districts was explained by this factor. Only in the district of La Neuveville, with its high-altitude communes overlooking the lower-altitude town of La Neuveville on the shore of the Lac de Bienne (German: Bielersee), was there some faint evidence of a relationship of this kind (0·15106).[2] Even here, however, the coefficient of determination must be regarded with caution because of the limited number of observations and the influence of other geographical factors, already noted. Recent population movements and the greater availability of cars may, in fact, have eliminated any relationship between altitude and separatism which may have existed during some periods of the nineteenth century.

The research results discussed in this chapter will be discussed in more detail in Chapter 10. An attempt will also be made to reach certain conclusions as to their interrelationships. In the course of this discussion, reference will be made, in addition, to the results of further analyses conducted by the writer.

Notes

1. More detailed statistical breakdowns are provided in Appendix C: Table 3.
2. See Appendix C: Tables 1 and 2.
3. For a detailed explanation of Swiss communal citizenship, see Appendix A, p. 171, paragraphs 2–6.
4. See Appendix C: Table 1.

10

Jura Separatism: Geographical Interrelationships

> Confederation is primarily concerned with enabling (the Swiss) to
> maintain and enjoy their various peculiarities.
>
> GEORGE SOLOVEYTCHIK (1954)

In examining the geography of the Bernese Jura and its effects on the
phenomenon of Jura separatism, the writer believes it useful to differentiate
between certain geographical influences which appear to have prevailed, and
contributed toward the development of a Jurassian identity, during *earlier*
periods in the history of the region (extending from the end of the Roman
Empire to the Treaty of Vienna in 1815), on the one hand, and similar
influences prevailing in more recent times (i.e. since 1815) on the other.

Geographical Influences in Past Times

While we can attempt to measure the strengths of various geographical
influences on Jura separatism in modern times, it is clearly impossible for us to
project ourselves into the past. Nevertheless, the writer believes it possible to
make certain assumptions about the Bernese Jura in times past—assumptions
which, it is suggested, are intuitively reasonable ones.

In the first place, ever since human settlement began in the area which is
now Switzerland, the Jura chain has existed, approximately, in its present
physical form. More specifically, it has consisted of a high mountain range,
consisting of a number of parallel ridges, running in a south-westerly to
north-easterly direction. It is difficult of access from any direction except, to
some degree, from the Belfort Gap where the Ajoie protrudes into France. It
was, in times past, particularly inaccessible to those approaching it from the
Swiss Mittelland because its ridges run at right-angles to the normal approach
route from Berne and other Swiss towns and cities.

As we have already seen, since the break-up of the Roman Empire the Jura
mountain range west of Laufen appears to have been occupied by people
speaking a Romance language (French), while those lower-lying areas to the
north (in Alsace) and south (across the Mittelland) have been occupied by
German-speaking peoples. The people of the Jura mountains west of Laufen
have thus formed a French-language, eastward-pointing promontory flanked
by German-speakers. Speaking generally, then, in this part of Switzerland
French-speaking people have occupied the high ground (i.e., the Jura chain's
ridges and valleys) whereas German-speakers have occupied the low ground.
German-Swiss have, in fact, never been able to penetrate, successfully, the

Jura range to the west of the Laufen district, or the gorges du Taubenloch to the north of Biel.[1] Nor have they been able to advance beyond the northern shores of the Bielersee, to settle the slopes of the Montagne de Diesse to the north of this lake.

While we cannot *prove* that it was the physical geography of the Bernese Jura which influenced its human geography, and specifically enabled it to remain a French-speaking promontory for the past fifteen hundred years, nevertheless the similarity between the topography–drainage map of the region, on the one hand, and its linguistic map, on the other, is so striking that it seems unlikely to be coincidental. Since the beginnings of a formal education system and of widespread literacy in the mid-nineteenth century, language has been 'institutionalized' in Switzerland, despite the temporary exception of German schools in the Bernese Jura, and the French culture of the latter region has become a *raison d'être* for Jura separatism.[2]

We also noted, in an earlier chapter, that the entire Bernese Jura lies at the extreme north-west periphery both of Canton Berne and of present-day Switzerland. We have seen that it did not play any significant role in the development of the Swiss Confederation, and we have noted that the canton of Berne was unenthusiastic when awarded this relatively remote region in 1815. The dimension of distance may well have contributed, especially in the North Jura, to a feeling of remoteness and alienation from Switzerland in general and from the government of Canton Berne in particular.

The topography of the Bernese Jura, while serving to discourage penetration by outsiders, has also discouraged contacts between the peoples of the region themselves. This has resulted in the development of somewhat different subcultures in the various valleys of the French-speaking districts of the Bernese Jura. The beginnings of these subcultures existed, it can be argued, in Celtic times, with different tribes (the Sequani, Rauraci, and Helvetii) each occupying separate areas of the region. Various subcultures were also evident in the thirteenth and fourteenth centuries, long *before* the Reformation added a further (i.e. religious) dimension to Jurassian politics. We have noted that the valleys of the South Jura (those closest to the Mittelland) developed close ties of both friendship and commerce with Biel and Berne, and cemented these with military alliances. By contrast, the valleys of the North Jura, which were more distant from Biel and Berne, maintained closer links with successive prince-bishops of Basle, the titular rulers of the entire region.

During the Reformation and the two centuries which followed, the Protestant armies of the Bernese and their allies of the southern valleys of the bishopric, like a massive series of waves moving in a north-westerly direction, were able to enter the South Jura via the gorges du Taubenloch, were able to cross the col de Pierre-Pertuis, were able to move westward along the longitudinal river valleys to the western and eastern headwaters of the Sorne and Trame, and eastward up the Chaluet valley and the Grandval (east of Moutier) to the Solothurn border. Proceeding further, they were able to establish themselves as far north as the natural east–west barriers of the Montagne de Moutier and Mont Raimeux (Fig. 26). To the north of these mountain ridges, which could be penetrated only via the easily defended gorges du Pichoux and gorges de Moutier, lay less friendly territory, which was geographically closer to successive prince-bishops' seat of power (originally Basle and subsequently Porrentruy). This northern area of the Bernese Jura was thus much more easily held for Catholicism.

The Treaty of Aarberg in 1711 officially acknowledged the geographic 'facts of life' in the Bernese Jura by confirming the east–west Montagne de Moutier–Mont Raimeux barrier ridge as the frontier between Protestantism and Catholicism in the region, with the gorges du Pichoux and gorges de Moutier, and the western headwater regions of the Sorne and Trame tributaries of the Birse, forming a kind of no man's land between the two religiously differentiated subregions. As Weigandt (op. cit.) has put it, the Treaty 'territorialized' religion in Switzerland, with Protestants and Catholics being awarded formal control over specific areas in both the Bernese Jura and elsewhere. While the Reformation—whose limits, as we have just suggested, were themselves determined by geographical factors—unquestionably accentuated the differences between northern and southern Jurassians, it is important for us to remind ouselves, once again, that the South Jura had strong ties to Biel and Berne *before* Protestants came into existence.

Figure 37 represents an effort to depict, in the form of a diagram, the geographical influences which, it is suggested, have served in past times to

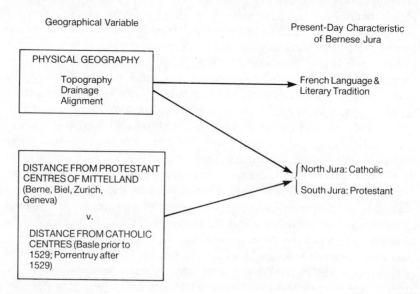

Fig. 37. Past Geographical Determinants of Jura Separatism (six French-speaking Districts).

bring into existence the phenomenon of Jura separatism. These geographical influences (topography–drainage–alignment in the case of language, and the first, together with the geographical distance dimension, i.e., distance from Berne and other Mittelland Protestant centres vs. distance from Basle and subsequently Porrentruy, in the case of religion) have become blurred by other geographical factors, with which they have themselves interacted, in more recent times. Nevertheless, it is suggested that we should regard them as extremely important, in that they have caused the Bernese Jura, in more modern times, to be unified in terms of its language, but divided in its territorialized religious beliefs.

Present-day Geographical Influences

While we are obliged to use what is, it is hoped, intelligent judgement with respect to the influence of geographical variables on the history of the Bernese Jura and in the development of Jura separatism in earlier times, we are on somewhat surer ground when dealing with the twentieth century. In the comments which follow, we shall focus primarily on the six French-speaking districts, since, as we have noted on previous occasions, these constitute the core of the region which Jurassian separatists seek as their 'ideal' canton.[3] Some general conclusions follow.

The Geography of Language and Jura Separatism

It will be recalled that variations in the degree to which French was spoken seemed to have a moderate influence (26 per cent) on the 1974 separatist vote in the six French-speaking districts of the Bernese Jura (Table 14). The French language seemed to be much more strongly associated with separatist feeling in the district of Delémont (which contained, at the time, three German-speaking communes), in the North Jura. In this district 75 per cent of the variation in the separatist vote seems to have been associated with variations in the degree to which French was spoken. The only southern exception was La Neuveville, where the language factor appears to have accounted for 83 per cent of the variance, and where German-Swiss retirees in La Neuveville itself are likely to have caused the separatist vote in this town to be much lower than in certain other subdistricts.

While the apparent association between French-speakers and Jura separatism may seem surprisingly low to the reader, we should not allow ourselves to conclude that the geography of language is unimportant. The statistics *do* indicate that language is a moderately important ingredient in the Jura situation. The French language, in fact, appears to be *a necessary condition* for Jurassian separatist feelings to emerge in a community. The 'No' votes of the German-speaking district of Laufen, and of the various isolated German-speaking communities within the Bernese Jura, suggest that this may be so.

Not a single German-language community in the Bernese Jura voted 'Yes' in 1974. However, the French language is clearly *not* a *sufficient* condition for Jura separatism, as the 1974 'No' votes of the southern, French-speaking valleys of the Bernese Jura demonstrated.

The Geography of Religion and Jura Separatism

Religion does appear, at least on the surface, to be the most important single factor influencing Jura separatism, with 77 per cent of the variance in the 'Yes' vote being explained by the variance in the percentage of Catholics in the various subdistricts of the French-speaking Bernese Jura. However, there appears to be an important difference between the North Jura, where the Catholicism–separatism relationship appeared to be weak, and the South Jura. Within the latter region, there appeared to be an extremely strong relationship (92 per cent) between Catholicism and separatism. (We have already noted the existence of a clearly-defined religious divide *within* the Moutier district.)

Like the French language, however, Catholicism—while it may be a *necessary* condition for Jura separatism in that not a single non-Catholic commune voted 'Yes' in 1974—is *not* a *sufficient* condition. The 'No' votes of every commune of the Catholic Laufen district support this contention. We shall subsequently investigate the degree to which Catholicism (or religion) may be related, in some way, to other variables.

The Geography of Citizenship and Jura Separatism

It will be recalled from Chapter 9 that statistical analysis provides us with strong evidence to support separatist claims that Jurassians of Bernese origin and, to a lesser degree, other German-Swiss, tend to be pro-Bernese. The majority of Bernese immigrants to the Bernese Jura clearly brought with them, to their new homes, a deep and abiding affection for, and loyalty to, Berne. The political structure of the times encouraged this, since the Bernese Jura was a *part* of Canton Berne from 1815 onwards. By contrast, it seems reasonable to assume that a Bernese moving to, say, Vaud after 1815 would recognize that he and his family were moving in a different 'state' (canton) and would adjust his attitudes accordingly. While first-generation Bernese immigrants to Vaud would probably always remain Bernese at heart, their children would usually become loyal Vaudois. Second-generation Bernese in the Bernese Jura, however, appear to have regarded themselves as Bernese who still lived within the boundaries of Canton Berne.

In sharp contrast to Jurassians whose ancestral roots are in the Old Canton or elsewhere in German Switzerland, it appears from the data obtained in the study that Jurassians of Jurassian origin tend to be separatists. Many of their ancestors, especially in the South Jura, would probably have felt overwhelmed by the Bernese newcomers. As we have seen, they often became a minority or near minority in their own native village. The defensive stances of both groups seem to have been passed down to their descendants, in many instances. The personal observations of the writer, and the regression analysis data to some degree, suggest that a substantial number of French-speaking, Protestant southerners are separatists. These latter, however, appear to consist primarily of individuals who consider themselves to be descendants of the *original, non*-Bernese inhabitants of the South Jura (see Chapter 8, n. 9).

Economic Geography and Jura Separatism

We earlier noted that economic factors do not appear to play a significant role in causing separatism in the region as a whole, even though the writer originally suspected that this would have been the case. The northern and southern regions, in this instance, appear to be similar. We speculated earlier that those individuals still living in economically deprived regions may often be more conservative in attitudes and more fatalistic about economic poverty than we might previously have imagined. However, we cannot dismiss all economic factors as being insignificant in *any* area of the Bernese Jura. There is some indication, in fact, that economic conditions, including depopulation, have exacerbated separatist feelings in the largely rural district of Franches-Montagnes, as well as in the district of La Neuveville (whose subdistricts, with the exception of La Neuveville itself, are high-altitude, agricultural, subject to depopulation, of low economic status, and with one exception, overwhelmingly French-speaking). There may be some critical point of depopulation which triggers separatist feeling.

Spatial Geography and Jura Separatism

In the French-speaking Bernese Jura as a whole, 25 per cent of the variance in the 'Yes' vote seemed to be accounted for by increasing distance from the city of Berne. Thus it does appear, to a degree, that the greater the distance from Berne, the greater the alienation from Berne. This pattern held true only for the region *as a whole*, however, and did not show up to any extent in individual districts. Altitude did not, however, seem to be a particularly important factor in Jura separatism, with the partial exception of the upland communes in the district of La Neuveville.

The Most Important Single Geographical Determinants of Jura Separatism

The most important individual geographical determinants of Jura separatism, for each of the regional groupings in the French-speaking region of the Bernese Jura, are listed in Table 15.

Table 15.   *Most Important Single Geographical Determinants of Jura Separatism*

Grouping	Most important variable	R^2 value
1. All six French-speaking districts	Catholicism	0·76636
2. North Jura	French language	0·26518
3. South Jura	Catholicism	0·80369
4. Courtelary	German-Swiss origin (inverse)	0·45850
5. Delémont	French language	0·74849
6. Franches-Montagnes	Recent depopulation	0·39248
7. Moutier	Catholicism	0·91699
8. La Neuveville	Economic status	0·91653
9. Porrentruy	Jurassian origin	0·32735

These figures suggest that we should be cautious in making sweeping statements to the effect that there is one single determinant of Jurassian separatism in the French-speaking Bernese Jura. While, in the region as a whole, Catholicism *is* pin-pointed as the single most important factor associated with separatism, it scores as highly as it does in the six-district region and in the South Jura largely because of its very strong apparent association with separatism in the Moutier district, which is sharply divided on a religious basis and which accounted for 60 per cent of all research observations in the South Jura. In fact, the figures in Table A suggest that the more important single determinant of separatism differs according to the district being examined. In the Courtelary district, for example, it appears to be the German-Swiss factor, in La Neuveville economic status. In the Moutier district, sharply divided as it is between strongly Catholic and strongly Protestant communes, it is Catholicism or, more precisely, religion. In Franches-Montagnes it is recent depopulation, in Delémont the French language, and in Porrentruy, Jurassian origin.

The Combined Effect of Geographical Variation

Table 16 indicates that, in the six French-speaking districts of the former Bernese Jura, all fourteen geographical factors, as a combined group, appear to account for 86 per cent of the variation in the separatist vote. The figures below summarize the degree to which the separatist ('Yes') vote in the six districts, and in other regional groupings, seemed to be associated with certain combinations of geographical variables. The percentages of the variance in the 'Yes' vote explained by the fourteen geographical variables tested, for various regions and districts, are shown in Table 17.

Table 16. *The Cumulative Effect of Geographical Factors on Jura Separatism (Stepwise Regressions of Independent Variables), Bernese Jura: French-speaking Districts*

Area studied with no. of observations	Independent variable(s)	Cumulative R^2 value	Degree of significance
6 French-speaking districts (122)	1. Catholicism	0·76636	0·0001
	2. +Jura citizenship[a]	0·78998	0·005
	3. +Distance from Berne	0·80284	0·01
	4. +Recent Population change	0·82470	0·005
	5. +French-speaking	0·83175	0·01
	6. +German canton citizenship	0·84207	0·01
	7. +Agriculturalness	0·84485	0·1
	8. +Other German canton citizenship	0·84738	0·1
	9. +13-Year Population change	0·84932	0·25
	10. +Altitude	0·85146	0·25
	11. +District citizenship	0·85230	*
	12. +Communal citizenship	0·85635	0·01
	13. +Economic status	0·85638	*
	14. +Bernese citizenship	*	*

[a] This table should be read as follows. The 'Catholicism factor' alone accounts for 77 per cent of the variation in the 1974 separatist vote in the 6 French-speaking districts of the Bernese Jura. If we add the 'Jura citizenship factor' to the 'Catholicism factor' the two factors account for 79 per cent of the separatist vote, and so on. Expressing this in more technical terms: if the French-speaking independent variable (FR) is regressed on Catholicism (CA) for the 6 French-speaking districts, the combined R^2 value is 0·78792, i.e., FR adds only 0·02156 to CA. This is significant at the 0·005 level.

* Indicates that the degree of significance falls below 0·25.

Table 17. *Combined Effect of All Fourteen Geographical Variables*

Grouping	% of 'Yes' vote explained
1. All six French-speaking districts	86
2. North Jura	57
3. South Jura	90
4. Courtelary	100
5. Delémont	94
6. Franches-Montagnes	100
7. Moutier	95
8. La Neuveville	100
9. Porrentruy	48
10. Laufen	99

The relatively weaker apparent relationship between separatism and our fourteen geographical variables in the North Jura is entirely due to the score for the Porrentruy district. The cause of Porrentruy's low score is not entirely clear. This district (consisting primarily, though not exclusively, of the Ajoie) recorded an overall 'Yes' vote of 68 per cent in the 1974 referendum, significantly lower than the 'Yes' votes of 79 per cent and 77 per cent for Delémont and Franches-Montagnes respectively. We earlier suggested (in Chapter 9) that the Porrentruy district may feel so secure in its French culture that it does not feel the need to be as anti-German-Swiss as do the inhabitants of other districts of the North Jura. It is also possible, moreover, that the Ajoie's geographical remoteness in Jurassian as well as Swiss terms (being cut off, as it is, from adjacent districts by yet another ridge of the Jura mountain chain, in the Les Rangiers area), has caused it to feel alienated not only from Berne but also from Delémont, the capital of the new Canton Jura.[4]

In several districts, and in the six French-speaking districts as a group, a high percentage of the 'Yes' vote appeared to be accounted for by only a few geographical variables (Table 18).

Table 18.   *Most Important Geographical Determinants of Separatism, by District*

Grouping	No. of variables	%
1. All six French-speaking districts	3	80
2. Delémont	3	82
3. Franches-Montagnes	3	84
4. Moutier	2	92
5. La Neuveville	2	99

With the exception of the Porrentruy district, the high separatism scores achieved by combinations of only a few geographical variables, and the very high scores achieved by the combination of all fourteen, are noteworthy. Reasons why the analyses do not completely explain the variances in the 'Yes' vote may include the fact that not all Swiss citizens voted in the 1974 referendum, and that some Jurassians voted for the Third Force. In addition, of those who did vote, the influence of the relatively small number of Italian and Romansh-speaking Swiss living in the region may have had some effect. We must also note the fact that the basic data used in the research study were for *all* Swiss citizens of all age-groups residing in the Bernese Jura, whereas those voting in the 1974 referendum were aged 21 or over. Finally, we must also take into account the time period (four years) which elapsed between the 1970 census and the 1974 referendum.

Interrelationships Between Independent Variables

There are clear relationships between certain of the geographical factors we have been discussing. For example, citizens of the Bernese Jura as a whole include both communal and district citizens, so that we know that all three geographical factors dealing with Jurassian origin are sequentially inter-related. Similarly, Bernese and 'Other German-Swiss' variables are included in the 'Total German-Swiss' population total and thus each, respectively, is related to the latter. In addition, Jurassian citizenship and German-Swiss citizenship clearly have an inverse relationship in terms of separatist/pro-Bernese sentiment. The 'Recent (3-year) population change' data are, of course, included in '13-year population change' data so that, once again, a relationship, albeit of a somewhat different nature, exists. Such inter-relationships are often highlighted by analyses of the type conducted by the writer, and discussed earlier.

In recognizing that fairly obvious relationships exist between various geographical factors, of the kinds described above, we must be careful not to overlook the possibility that more subtle, less obvious relationships may also exist. For example, we need to ask ourselves: 'Is there likely, in the present-day Bernese Jura, to be a relationship of some kind between citizenship and religion and, if so, what kind of relationship?' A factor analysis and subsequent Varimax rotation (described and discussed in Appendix A) were conducted in order to provide additional information in this area.[5] Caution must be taken in interpreting the results of this kind of analysis. Nevertheless, the data produced suggested the existence of at least one cluster of related geographical factors. This cluster, in turn, appeared to be closely related to the phenomenon of Jura separatism, and has been dubbed 'autochthonism' by the writer.[6] It focuses above all on the *origin* of an indiviual Jurassian's family. It also incidates that Catholicism (0·90252) is closely associated with autochthonism, but not as exclusively as are Jurassian or Bernese origin (Appendix C: Table 4).

This then suggests, in effect, that *as a general rule, and all other things being equal, if an individual Jurassian's ancestors were Jurassians, he is likely to vote separatist regardless of whether he is Catholic or Protestant.* It was earlier suggested, in fact, that a certain amount of evidence exists to support the contention that many southern separatists are Protestants of Jurassian family origin.[7] The Varimax rotation also provided some limited evidence to suggest the existence of the autochthonism factor in other area groupings which provided enough observations for meaningful results.

Other, lesser geographical clusters of factors identified were culture (which was associated with language spoken), pastoralism (which was related to agriculturalness, altitude, and economic status), and depopulation–alienation (related to depopulation and distance from Berne)[8] (Appendix C: Table 4). A simple regression analysis was next conducted to test the degree to which the leading factors identified could predict the 'Yes' vote in the 1974 referendum.[9] The autochthonism factor, used as an independent variable, was able to explain close to 61 per cent (0·60552) of the variance in the 'Yes' vote in the six French-speaking districts of the region, and 58 (0·58388) per cent of the South Jura's variance[10] (Appendix C: Table 5).

A final analysis involved a step-wise regression analysis, using the same factors discussed earlier.[11] The four clusters of geographical factors (autochthonism, culture, pastoralism and depopulation, and alienation), in combination, explained close to 72 per cent of the variance in the 1974 'Yes' vote in the six districts of the French-speaking Bernese Jura. Depopulation appeared to be a significant determinant of separatism in the North Jura, and the depopulation/alienation factor was in evidence in the South Jura.

Overall Conclusions

At the beginning of this chapter it was stated that it is important for use to distinguish between past times and the present-day situation in evaluating the influence of geographical variables on Jura separatism. There are strong indications that, in the past (Fig. 37), the physical geography of the Bernese Jura was instrumental in the region's remaining a French-language promontory. In addition, the physical geography of the region, together with the distance of its northern districts from the Protestant centres of the Mittelland, ensured that the South Jura would become Protestant while the North Jura remained Catholic; the two subregions being separated primarily by the east–west barrier of the Montagne de Moutier–Mont Raimeux ridges, and by the uplands near the eastern border of Franches-Montagnes in the west. Expressing this another way, *topography* has resulted in the existence of a French-speaking region called the Bernese Jura, and *topography* and *distance* together have caused the North Jura to remain remote from Berne in every sense of the word, while permitting the Old Canton to leave an undeniable imprint on the South Jura.

With respect to the present-day geographical determinants of Jura separatism, the overall conclusions drawn by the writer from the results of the various analyses for the six French-speaking districts of the Bernese Jura as a whole are as follows.

Geographical Determinants of Jura Separatism

(1) The geographical presence of the French language is a necessary, but not sufficient, condition for Jura separatism. It is a *sine qua non*, the importance of which, however, tends to be masked by its apparently modest statistical association with separatism.

(2) The geographical presence of the Catholic religion is also a necessary, but not sufficient, condition for Jura separatism.

(3) The geographical presence of *both* the French language *and* the Catholic religion seem to be necessary for a commune to vote separatist.

(4) The three single most important geographical determinants of present-day Jura separatism, in the six French-speaking districts *as a whole*, in order of importance, appear to be Catholicism, Jurassian citizenship, and Bernese citizenship—the latter being an inverse relationship. However, our factor analysis has revealed that these three geographical variables are themselves closely interrelated, and can be grouped together as a 'factor' which has been dubbed, by the writer, 'Autochthonism'. If this group factor is considered to be a geographical factor in its own right, it explains a not unimpressive 61 per cent of the variance in the 1974 'Yes' vote in the six French-speaking districts of the Bernese Jura.

(5) A spatial variable, namely the distance of a commune from the city of Berne, was of moderate influence on voting patterns in the 1974 referendum.

(6) Three variables alone (Catholicism, Jurassian Citizenship, and Distance from Berne) explained 80 per cent of the variance in the 1974 'Yes' vote in the six French-speaking districts. All fourteen variables explained 86 per cent of the vote.

(7) Somewhat surprisingly to the writer, the much-quoted 'population haemorrhage' did not appear to be an important determinant of Jura separatism in the former Bernese Jura as a whole, suggesting, possibly, that those most dissatisfied with the status quo 'voted with their feet' by emigrating elsewhere.

(8) The data suggested that the altitude of a commune had a minor influence on Jura separatism, but the economic prosperity of a commune, or the degree to which its labour force was engaged in agriculture did not appear to be important determinants of the phenomenon.

An effort has been made to depict these findings in Fig. 38. In interpreting the results of the various analyses conducted as part of this study, we must remind ourselves that the data for the region as a whole are heavily influenced by the data for certain large districts, such as Delémont, Moutier, and Porrentruy which, between them, account for 90 of the 122 subdistrict observations or 74 per cent of the total. The conclusions listed above, therefore, apply to the French-speaking Bernese Jura *as a whole*.

Our examination of each of the six districts (Table A) suggests that the major local (i.e. district) determinants of Jura separatism differ from one district to another. Local traditions and concerns thus appear to be of considerable significance in determining voting behaviour in the 1974 referendum. We must therefore be cautious in making sweeping assertions to

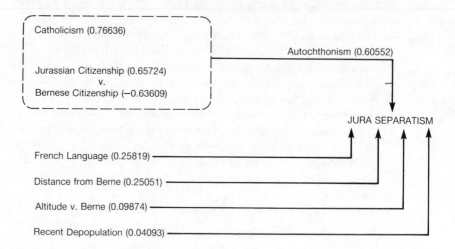

Fig. 38. Present-day Geographical Determinants of Jura Separatism (six French-speaking Districts).

the effect that any one variable is the key determinant of Jura separatism. Even within the two subregions (the North Jura and South Jura) we find evidence to suggest that separatists in *different districts* of each subregion may be motivated in different ways.

Chapters 2 to 5 of this work discussed various aspects of the geography of the Bernese Jura—all of which, it is suggested, have had an influence on Jura separatism. Chapters 6 and 7 described and discussed historical events which are related to the same phenomenon. Some of these historical events, such as the alliance of the valleys of the South Jura with Berne, occurred several centuries ago. Nevertheless, because they themselves were related to the geography of Switzerland as a whole and the Bernese Jura in particular, it has been necessary for us to take note of them. Otherwise, it would have been difficult for us to have defined Jura separatism as a phenomenon, and to have attempted to measure it by conducting various statistical analyses.

Because of the strong residual effects of certain of these geographically determined *historical* events (e.g. the spread of the Reformation), economic factors—which have often been relatively short-lived—appear to be relatively unimportant as determinants of Jura separatism in the French-speaking Bernese Jura as a whole, though they *do* appear to be important factors in two districts (Franches-Montagnes and La Neuveville). In sharp contrast, the fundamental geographical factors referred to throughout this work—topography and distance—which governed access to the region in past times, left an indelible imprint in the form of a basic—and powerful—'motive force' of present-day Jura separatism, a factor which, it is suggested, has been identified in the analyses described in this work. This factor, 'autochthonism' or 'Jurassianism' (which appears to be associated with both Catholic—in both the North and South Jura—and southern Protestant separatism), appears to be closely related to an individual's Jurassian family origin, and appears to derive a great deal of its inspiration from the historical French 'promontory culture' of the Bernese Jura.

In noting the interplay of the topography of the Bernese Jura and of the region's distance from Berne and the Mittelland, it is also important that we not only remember that the Bernese Jura is geographically remote in terms of the Mittelland, but also note that it is situated some distance away from one of the major crossroads of European history. The city of Basle, situated at the bend of the Rhine (Fig. 2), has been the focus of the interplay of ethnic, linguistic, religious, and commercial forces for many centuries. From Basle, routes led westwards through the Belfort Gap ('The Gate of Burgundy'), northwards and eastwards along the Rhine, and southwards to the Mittelland and St Gotthard Pass, and Italy. Being difficult of access, the remote Bernese Jura was often used as a region of refuge, as exemplified by the flight of Bishop Philippe de Gundelsheim to Porrentruy in 1528.

The final chapter of this work will discuss possible future developments in the Bernese Jura and their implications for the Swiss Confederation.

Notes

1. As we have seen, they did come close to a successful colonization of certain parts of the South Jura during the past 100 years, but ultimately failed.
2. We have also noted that Jurassian separatists emphasize the historic existence of the Bernese Jura as the bishopric of Basle which, no matter how illusory its unity as a political entity, nevertheless survived as a separate state for close to 800 years.
3. More detailed breakdowns are, of course, provided in Appendix C. In this connection, it is necessary to remind ourselves that the data recorded for certain Jurassian districts with large numbers of electoral subdistricts may exert a major influence on the data for that larger geographical grouping of which they are a part. (For example, the district of Porrentruy accounts for more than half the subdistricts in the North Jura, and the district of Moutier accounts for 60 per cent of all subdistricts in the South Jura.)
4. This has been reflected historically, for example, in a different mix of political party strength in the Ajoie (Porrentruy district), compared to the Delémont area. (It will be recalled that the RJ has not constituted a political party in the traditional sense.)
5. See Appendix C: Table 4.
6. From the Greek word *autochthon*: one supposed to have risen or sprung from the ground of the region he inhabits; one of the original inhabitants of the region. '*Autochthonous, autochthonal, autochthonic*: Indigenous, native, aboriginal' (Webster, 1971).
7. For example, Catholicism loads negatively (and thus Protestantism loads positively) on the autochthonism factor in the district of Courtelary.
8. See Appendix C: Table 4.
9. See Appendix C: Table 5.
10. In the seven-region area, a factor on which the French-speaking and German-Swiss variables loaded heavily (and which has been dubbed 'culture',) achieved an R^2 score of 0·10422, and in the Delémont district. Factor 2 (a factor on which agriculturalism, altitude, and economic

status loaded heavily, and which has been dubbed 'pastoralism') achieved an R^2 score of 0·10857. As was the case when the original fourteen independent variables were used as predictors, the lower authochthonism R^2 value for the North Jura appears to have been primarily due to the low R^2 value for the Porrentruy district (Appendix C: Table 5).

11. See Appendix C: Table 6.

11

The Geography of Jura Separatism: Implications

We have only won half the battle; the Jura Question is not yet resolved.

ROLAND REGUELIN (1978)[1]

As this book is being written the new Canton Jura, which came into existence on 1 January 1979, is more than six years old. The new canton occupies the northern and western portions of the former Bernese Jura (Fig. 34). It is made up of 82 communes, and as noted in Chapter 1, had a population of approximately 67,300 in 1984. It will be recalled that the greater part of the remaining portion of the former Bernese Jura (the South Jura), voted to remain part of Canton Berne. The South Jura is made up of fifty communes and had a population of approximately 59,000 in 1984 (Fig. 34).

The German-speaking Catholic district of Laufen, consisting of twelve communes in the extreme north-east of the Bernese Jura, voted against joining Canton Jura. Following a series of subsequent votes, it also rejected union with its neighbouring cantons of Baselstadt, Baselland, and Solothurn, and finally voted to remain a part of Canton Berne in September 1983. It is now, of course, physically separated from Canton Berne.

The district (including the city) of Biel (French: Bienne), which lies at the southern edge of the Bernese Jura proper and which contains a substantial French-speaking population, was not involved in the 1974 referendum and continues both as a city, and (in conjunction with a neighbouring commune), as a district of Canton Berne. The Biel district had a population of approximately 56,000 in 1984 (Fig. 34), of which the town of Biel accounts for approximately 54,000.

The supporters of the RJ and their sympathizers in the South Jura are naturally pleased that, with the approval of the people and cantons of Switzerland, the new canton has come into being. The establishment of Canton Jura was a major victory for the separatists. However, the RJ points out that the Bernese Jura *as a whole* (even when Laufen's 'No' vote was included) registered a 1974 majority vote for independence. They consequently argue that Canton Jura should include all six French-speaking districts of the region. The RJ, in other words, considers the present-day Canton Jura to be merely a first step towards the reunification of the whole of the French-speaking Bernese Jura as one political unit.

At the time of writing, the status of the communes of Ederswiler and Vellerat remains unresolved, and they thus constitute a further cause of tension between Canton Jura and Canton Berne. Because both communes were not geographically contiguous with former district boundaries, Eders-wiler must officially remain part of Canton Jura and Vellerat must officially remain part of Canton Berne, despite their votes to the contrary. Impatient at the delay in resolving the problem, and with the encouragement of the RJ, Vellerat declared itself a *commune libre* ('free commune') in August 1982, setting up roadblocks, issuing its own passports and withholding certain taxes (Plate 7). The ensuing publicity embarrassed and angered the government of Canton Berne.

There is little doubt that the government of Canton Berne would be willing to exchange Vellerat for Ederswiler. However, while insisting that Vellerat must join Canton Jura, the government of Canton Jura, strongly supported by the RJ, argues that Ederswiler should remain with Canton Jura. One of the reasons sometimes put forward in support of this argument is that Ederswiler was unfairly 'germanized' in the seventeenth century (Chapter 4, n. 16).

The anti-separatists, living predominantly in the South Jura (where they constitute, as we have seen, a majority of the population at the present time), consider that the Jura problem has now been finally settled. They strongly resent the reunification activities of the RJ and its associated political groups in the South Jura, and certain references to the South Jura in the new canton's constitution. This constitution, while considered by outside legal experts to be an excellent document in many respects, nevertheless strongly reflects the views of the RJ by stating, as one of its articles, that reunification with the South Jura is the ultimate goal of the new canton. The views of the anti-separatists of the South Jura are shared by those residents of Canton Jura (approximately 25 per cent of the latter's total population) who voted against the new Canton's establishment.

The government of Canton Berne appears willing to acknowledge that the Jura problem may not have been solved for all time. It will even, if pressed, acknowledge that parts of the South Jura may eventually choose to join Canton Jura. The Bernese government does not believe, however, that the Jura issue should be reopened for several years, because of the bitterness it has engendered. Moreover, it too, is angered by the 'reunification article' in Canton Jura's constitution.

In late 1981 a difference of opinion developed within the RJ's ranks. Certain of its leaders, including Roland Béguelin, favoured the continuation of a hard-line 'confrontational' policy with respect to 'Jura re-unification'. Accord-ingly, the RJ's sister organization, *Unité-Sud* (with headquarters at Moutier), *Jeunesse-Sud* (the southern equivalent of *Les Béliers*, based at Tavannes), and the RJ itself have all organized demonstrations in various areas of the South Jura since Canton Jura first came into existence. In addition, a separatist repre-sentative was involved in an altercation in the Swiss Federal Parliament, provoking a crisis which, in turn, eventually led to the cancellation of the formal proclamation ceremony of the new Canton scheduled for 11 May 1979. Such events, not surprisingly, have intensified the bitterness on both sides.

The more moderate separatists, many of whom hold seats in the new cantonal assembly or administrative positions in the new cantonal government, while not in any way yielding their claims on the South Jura or discontinuing all political debate of the problem, nevertheless argue that the most effective policy for the separatist movement to follow is to build Canton Jura into a successful state, which would then induce the people of the South Jura to join with the North. While there was a reconciliation between the two RJ factions in April 1972, certain philosophical differences remain.

The people of Switzerland as a whole are embarrassed by the Jura problem. The impassioned statements of some leaders of the RJ and by Roland Bégueln in particular, and the verbal and physical violence manifested on various occasions during the dispute, are considered to be distinctly 'un-Swiss'. It must not be overlooked, either, that the creation of Canton Jura has added another French-speaking canton to the Swiss Confederation, thus altering, albeit to a minor degree, the relative strengths of the French-speaking and German-speaking cantons of Switzerland in the Council of States (senate) of the Swiss Federal Assembly. This may possibly have caused concern to some German-Swiss. Nevertheless, as discussed in Chapter 1, the voters of Switzerland overwhelmingly approved, in 1978, the formation of the new canton. Presumably it was hoped that this would restore peace to the Jura. At the time of writing, this hope has not materialized.

Future Political Developments in the Bernese Jura

It takes a great deal of courage to predict future events with any confidence in a world in which the pace of change is not constant, but is accelerating. Nevertheless, it is predicted, sadly, that political unrest in the Bernese Jura will continue to cause problems for the Swiss Confederation. This is because, as we have seen, one of the parties to the present political settlement, namely the RJ and its sympathizers, regard the present settlement as only temporary. It is the RJ's hope and expectation that a combination of circumstances will eventually lead to a reunification of the North and South Jura in one French-speaking canton.

It is difficult to see how this can happen in the short-run because, as has been noted, anti-separatist feelings in the South Jura have hardened over the past few years. At the present time, the majority of the inhabitants of the South feel threatened by the Jurassians of the North and their southern sympathizers. They do not feel threatened by the Bernese; rather, they feel the latter to be their friends. Nevertheless, change may take place in the South Jura. Some changes are likely to be short-term in nature and others long-term. Each will be discussed in turn.

Short-term Developments

In the short-term, the increasing geographical mobility of the Swiss people may enable the Jurassians of the North to add some communes (communes which are border-line in terms of political sympathies) to the new canton. This is partly because substantial numbers of Catholic northerners have been settling in such mid-Jura towns as Moutier in recent years, and continue to do so. It will be recalled that the 1974 referendum result was particularly close in Moutier, with the pro-separatists obtaining 49 per cent of the vote (Appendix C: Table 2). Moreover, the same table and Fig. 33 indicate that three other communes (Belprahon, Perrefitte, and Roches) adjacent to Moutier registered 'Yes' votes of over 40 per cent of the total.[2]

In the Moutier municipal elections of December 1982 separatist sympathizers won a majority of seats on the municipal council. At the time of writing (1985) separatists also hold majorities on the South Jurassian communal councils of Sorvilier and, of course, Vellerat. At a time, within the next few years, which they judge to be appropriate, the separatists plan to take the necessary formal, constitutional steps to call for a further referendum which they hope will, at the very least, result in the addition of Moutier, and similar 'swing' communities, to Canton Jura.

Long-term Development

In the long-term, problems may arise in South Jura simply because the Jurassians of the South now constitute only a small minority of the total population of the canton. It will be recalled that the population of the *entire* former Bernese Jura, expressed as a percentage of that of Canton Berne, had been declining during the years prior to the 1974 referendum. The South Jura (i.e. the *new*, post-1974 'Bernese Jura'), with a population of 59,000 will, in fact, account for only approximately 6 per cent of the total population of the 'new' Canton Berne, with 916,000 inhabitants (Table 6). The South Jura's population is, in fact, only slightly larger than that of the urbanized city-district of Biel which, as we have noted, has 56,000 inhabitants.

Some inhabitants of the South Jura who have not, historically, been separatist may become concerned at the implications of this figure. They may feel that the views of a mere 6 per cent of Canton Berne's population will not, in future, carry much weight in the deliberations of the legislative assembly of Berne, and that decisions will therefore be made by the assembly which will not be in their (the South Jurassians') best interests.

The economic health of the South Jura is also likely to be a cause of some concern to its inhabitants. The Swiss watch industry continues to face strong competition from abroad, and the South Jura still accounts for a significant percentage of total Swiss output. Since 1975, there has been a continuing trend—in the South Jura and elsewhere—toward the closure of small, outlying establishments and a consolidation of the industry in larger establish-ments in larger population centres, including Biel.

Employment in the Swiss watch industry continued its decline of earlier years in the 1970s and 1980s, from a total of 55,539 workers in 1975, for example, to 38,150 in 1982. In this latter year, in fact, the Swiss watch industry employed fewer workers than it had done in 1880.

In contrast, the government of the new Canton Jura—which is less depen-dent on the watch industry than is the South Jura—has made ambitious plans to strengthen the economy. For example, its tourist department is actively publicizing the attractions of such packaged holiday activities as skiing, walking, riding, 'gipsy caravanning', bicycling, and fishing in the canton (though second, or 'holiday', homes owned by outsiders are not permitted). The attractions of such picturesque, Jurassian, small towns as St-Ursanne (Plate 8) are also being promoted. If the economy of Canton Jura does, indeed, appear to be increasingly healthy as the years go by, while that of the South Jura falters, at least some southerners may decide it would be in the best interests of the region to join Canton Jura.

Moreover, there has been consideration, in some Bernese circles, of the possibility of the establishment, within Canton Berne, of a bilingual region which would link the South Jura and Biel/Bienne. This possibility arouses further concern among a number of South Jurassians, since it could—at least in theory—give German equal status with French in the districts of Courte-lary, La Neuveville, and south-eastern Moutier, i.e., in those very districts in which the French language has, historically, faced the greatest threat from German-Swiss influences.

There would appear to be some ground for concern if the bilingual region plan were ever to be implemented, especially given the fact that *all* French-speakers (even including francophones living in Biel, and in Berne—the capital city of the canton—will only account for about 8 per cent of the total population of Canton Berne. Studies which have been conducted of trends in bilingual districts in other countries, such as that of Swedish-speaking com-munities in Finland (Miljan, 1976), suggest that the less widely spoken language (French) might lose ground in a bilingual region such as that proposed.

Naturally, the government of Berne recognizes that there is a danger that problems may arise with respect to the South Jura. A Bernese government department to deal exclusively with Jurassian matters, *le Sécrétariat du Conseil-exécutif pour les affaires jurassiennes* (the Executive Council Secretariat for Juras-sian Affairs), has been active for many years. The cantonal government will unquestionably take great pains not to give cause for complaint that the French-speaking population of the South Jura is being treated unfairly. For example, the South Jura enjoys the right to be consulted by the Bernese government on any issue involving the region. In addition, the communes of the South Jura have formed a *'Fédération des communes du Jura Bernois* (which for cultural reasons, also includes the francophones of Biel), to discuss matters of common concern and to protect the interests of the francophones of the region if necessary. Nevertheless, it is at least possible that an increasing number of South Jurassians may become dissatisfied with the situation. Consequently, some of them may eventually decide it would be in their best interests to join Canton Jura after all.

Another factor which must be taken into consideration by various parties to the Jura dispute is non-geographical. The younger generation of Jurassians (including some who are of Bernese origin) appear to be more radical than their parents and grandparents. This state of affairs is, of course, common in many cultures. In the Jurassian context, however, radicalism is closely assoc-iated with an impatience with the 'Old Order', which is often considered to be synonymous with the 'Bernese Order'. For this reason, and because it believes fervently in the justice of its cause, the RJ argues that 'time is on its side'. Moreover, in spite of clear reminders that there are significant differences between the northern and southern regions of the Bernese Jura and their respective peoples, a substantial number of Jurassians in both regions share the earlier (pre-referendum) views of the 'Third Force', i.e., that the region as a whole *does* have a historic and cultural claim to be considered as an entity.

Our examination of the Jura separatist movement in Chapter 8 has reminded us that, since the Reformation (when the South Jura became Prot-estant while, though not without some difficulty, retaining its French language and culture), the South Jura has formed an 'intermediate zone' between the French-speaking, Catholic inhabitants of the North Jura and by the German-speaking, Protestant Bernese of the Old Canton.

During the period since 1815 in particular, the emotions of the people of the South Jura have been pulled firstly one way and then the other, depending on whether the latest crisis involved linguistic or religious issues. If the people of the South Jura feel that their language is threatened or demeaned (as was the case in the Germanization crisis of the early twentieth century, and at the time of the Moeckli affair in 1947) many of them join forces with their fellow French-speakers of the North Jura in protest against the government of Berne, which, on such occasions, represents a German threat.

On the other hand, if a crisis develops which involves religious issues in any way, a majority of French-speaking Protestant southerners tend to side, actively or passively, with their Protestant, Bernese neighbours, even though the latter are German-speakers. This was the case, for example, in the religious crisis of 1832–34 and at the time of the *Kulturkampf* of 1868–78. Such religious crises have, as we have seen, been far more frequent than linguistic crises, even though the two most recent periods of tension (1910–18 and from 1947 to the present) have ostensibly been linguistic.

In retrospect it has appeared to many outside observers, including the writer, that an appropriate solution to the Jura problem in the late 1960s or early 1970s would have been the establishment of two new Swiss half-cantons, one representing the North Jura and the other representing the South Jura.

This solution, which was proposed by Lüthy (1972) and others, would have acknowledged the French-speaking and historical unity of the region, while recognizing the important differences which existed between the northern and southern regions of the Bernese Jura.

Moreover, there have been precedents for such a step in Swiss history. As early as 1594, the canton of Glarus split into two communities for religious reasons (though the canton was later reunited as the result of a *coup d'état*). The canton of Appenzell divided itself into a Catholic half-canton (Appenzell Inner Rhodes) and a Protestant half-canton (Appenzell Outer Rhodes) in 1597. Canton Basle divided itself into urban (Baselstadt) and rural (Baselland) half-cantons during the nineteenth century.[3]

However, it appears that it is now too late for the Lüthy solution. Canton Jura has become a full canton in the Swiss Confederation, and it is highly unlikely that it would wish to become a mere half-canton at some future date. Moreover, because of the bitterness of the post-referendum debates, many southerners would not now wish to become associated with the North Jura under any circumstances.

Nor does the establishment of two full cantons in the Bernese Jura appear to be too probable in the short term. If the South Jura ever did decide to secede from Berne, German Switzerland might be somewhat more reluctant than it was in 1978 to agree to the establishment of yet another French-language canton—even though this would still result in a total of sixteen German-Swiss cantons compared to a mere seven French-Swiss (or predominantly French-Swiss) ones.

Nevertheless, circumstances change over time and, in the opinion of this writer, some such solution—in keeping with the Swiss tradition—will probably be adopted eventually, even if this takes two or three generations. The existence of a small, but culturally vigorous region (the South Jura), within a much larger political unit (Canton Berne) whose people speak a distinctively different language appears, to the author, to be a temporary solution to the Jura problem. Even if the South Jura does not reunite with the North Jura, it seems probable to the writer that it will eventually separate from Canton Berne and become either a full canton or a half-canton.

Clearly, where a combination of circumstances has caused two groups of people possessing widely different characteristics to live together within the boundaries of a single political unit (Canton Berne in the instance being studied), tension and friction are likely to develop, even in a state such as Switzerland, which has traditionally favoured a high degree of local autonomy in its political system. In retrospect, the fatal mistake made by the Great Powers—as far as Jurassian separatists, at least, are concerned—was their decision at the Congress of Vienna to award the Bernese Jura to Berne. The creation of a 'Greater Canton Berne' discouraged immigrants from the Old Canton from adapting completely to the local culture of their new home, as they did in Canton Vaud and elsewhere in French Switzerland.

While the Jura problem, like that of Northern Ireland, is a particularly intractable one, a truly 'Swiss' solution (the establishment of, say, a new canton or half-canton) could, nevertheless and in due course, go a good way towards solving the Jura problem. Even if the South Jura became a full canton, the creation of a *seventh* Francophone canton, as indicated previously, would not greatly weaken the political power of the sixteen German-Swiss cantons, and it might be favourably received by French Switzerland. Since the South Jura would be predominantly Protestant, it would 'balance' the Catholic canton of the North Jura within the Swiss Confederation as a whole. It is thus the writer's contention that the 'Swiss model' (or, rather, a variation of it which permits two cantonal units in the North and South Jura respectively), has not yet been applied in its entirety to the former Bernese Jura.

Before concluding our study of the Bernese Jura, it may be useful for us to study, briefly, the present linguistic–religious situations in three other Swiss cantons—Fribourg, the Valais, and Graubünden. It is possible that some conclusions can be drawn with respect to the degree to which geographical factors and political problems—similar to those of the Bernese Jura—exist. An attempt can then be made to predict any future social-political developments in these cantons, developments which, in conjunction with events in the Bernese Jura itself, could conceivably affect the future political map of Switzerland.[4]

Fribourg

Canton Fribourg (Fig. 29) is a Mittelland canton which bears no topographical resemblance to the Bernese Jura. However, it *does* resemble the latter, to at least some degree, in its geography of language. Weinreich (1952), among others, has discussed the complexities of language in Canton Fribourg. McRae (op. cit.) in a thorough, meticulously researched work, has more recently evaluated the situation as it existed in the early 1980s.

Table 19 provides 1970 census data on the numbers and percentages of the population of Fribourg (German: Freiburg) who speak French and German respectively. (Figure 5 in Chapter 1 indicates the geographic distribution, in Switzerland, of French- and German-speakers respectively.) From the figures in Table 19 it can be seen that approximately 60 per cent of the population (specifically that portion living in the western part of the canton) is French-speaking and just over 30 per cent, living in the eastern part, is German-speaking.

The linguistic border between French and German Switzerland passes through the urban centre of Fribourg, the cantonal seat of government, itself. Approximately two-thirds of the city's population live in the largely French-speaking 'new town', (Fribourg) which is geographically contiguous with the French-speaking western area of the canton. The largely German-speaking 'old town' (Freiburg), containing approximately one-third of the city's population, lies to the east of the new town, adjacent to the German-speaking part of the canton and to Canton Berne, further to the east.

Table 19. *Cantons Fribourg, Valais, and Graubünden: Language Data (1980 census)*

Canton	Total population[a] (000)	Language (%)				
		French	German	Italian	Romansh	Other
Fribourg	185	61	32	3		4
Graubünden	165	1	60	13	22	4
Valais	219	60	32	5		3

[a] Population figures include both Swiss citizens and other Swiss residents.

Source: Swiss Federal Bureau of Statistics.

How successfully do the French- and German-speaking Fribourgeois co-exist? Is the separation of the Bernese Jura likely to find an echo in Canton Fribourg? A study of the facts, and informal discussions with residents of the canton suggest that this is highly unlikely. Although Canton Fribourg, like Canton Berne, contains both French and German-speaking regions, the situation is not further confounded, as it is in the Jura, by religious divisions (such as those which exist between the North Jura and the Old Canton of Berne). As was noted in Chapter 1, the Fribourgeois of both language groups, almost without exception, are Catholics (Fig. 6). Moreover, they are Catholics of a traditionally conservative persuasion. In addition, the capital city is centrally situated, and no areas of the canton have experienced abnormally severe economic or depopulation problems.

The two languages have waxed and waned in relation to each other in Canton Fribourg in the past. Unquestionably, there have been minor language frictions from time to time. Quite recently, because of concerns expressed by German-speakers, a 'language charter' was drawn up to give equal rights to both linguistic groups, and was put into effect. However, the two linguistic groups appear to live side by side, relatively contentedly, today. Political changes in the Bernese Jura are thus unlikely to have effects on the political structure of Canton Fribourg, especially since, by a fortunate geographic circumstance, as we have indicated, the two language areas 'meet' at the capital city of Fribourg. In a sense, then, both groups can feel they have a territorial stake in the seat of government.

The Valais

The Alpine canton of Valais (German: Wallis) (Fig. 29) consists, basically, of the wide valley of the Rhône and the Alpine ranges to the north and south; it thus differs significantly in its physical features from the Bernese Jura. However, like the latter, it is divided linguistically. Among others, Hughes (op. cit.) and McRae (op. cit.) have discussed the linguistic situation in the canton. Fig. 5 and Table 19 reveal that the linguistic situation in Canton Valais is rather similar to that of Canton Fribourg in at least one respect; approximately 60 per cent of the population is French-speaking and just over 30 per cent German-speaking. Moreover, as in Fribourg, the two language groups live in geographically distinct regions of the canton. The German-speakers occupy the eastern portion of Valais, namely the upper parts of the Rhône Valley and its tributary valleys as far west as, and including, the village of Salgesch. The French-speaking population occupies the lower parts of the Rhône Valley and its tributaries as far east as, and including, the town of Sierre.

To an outside observer, there might appear to be cause for linguistic friction in the Valais. This is because the Valais represents one of the few areas of Switzerland where the French–German linguistic borderline has shifted markedly during the past 130 or so years. In this instance, French has

advanced approximately 15 kilometres in an easterly direction from the neigh-
bourhood of Sion (which was predominantly German-speaking in 1850) to
include the town of Sierre.[5] The French-speaking Lower Valais would also
appear to have benefitted more, economically, from industrialization than has
the Upper Valais. An outside observer might, then, be pardoned for suspect-
ing that the German-speaking 'Wallisers' would be on the defensive, and
suspicious of, if not hostile to, French culture.

Nevertheless, there are few, if any, signs of 'linguistic warfare' in the Valais.
In this respect it resembles Canton Fribourg. The similarities between the two
cantons, moreover, extend into the field of religion. As in Fribourg, the
overwhelming majority of the people of Valais, whether French-speaking or
German-speaking, are devout Catholics (Fig. 6). This appears to lessen any
linguistic tensions which occasionally arise. Moreover, as Netting (1972) has
pointed out, German- and French-speaking villages in the Vallais have ident-
ical production systems, inheritance patterns, family organization, political
structures, and ideologies.

It is true that a cultural association was formed some years ago among the
German-speaking Wallisers, called the *Rottenbund* ('Rotten' being the German
name for the Rhône). While it purports to defend the interests of German-
speakers, and would unquestionably become more militant should the need
ever arise it is, at the present time, primarily a cultural rather than a political
organization. To all intents and purposes, the French- and German-speakers
of the Valais live side by side in relative harmony. Their tranquility seems
unlikely to be disturbed by any crises remotely resembling the Jura problem.

Graubünden

The Alpine canton of Graubünden (French: Grisons) is more similar to the
Bernese Jura than either Fribourg or the Valais (Fig. 29). To begin with, like
the Bernese Jura, its various valleys are usually separated from each other by
mountain ranges, and internal communications are difficult. There are other
similarities, too, which will be discussed later in this chapter. Weinreich (op.
cit.) and Billigmaier (1950, 1979) have written extensively on the linguistic
situation in Graubünden. McRae (op. cit.) has also examined, in detail, legal
and other aspects of the linguistic state of affairs in the canton.

Figure 5 and Table 19 provide linguistic data for Canton Graubünden. The
geography of language in this canton is more complicated than that of Cantons
Fribourg and Valais for a number of reasons. To begin with, there are three
language groups (German, Romansh, and Italian) in Graubünden rather
than two, as was the case with the other cantons. Secondly, unlike Fribourg
and Valais, Canton Graubünden includes some regions which are predominantly Protestant and others which are predominantly Catholic (Fig. 6).

There are still few signs of linguistic tension in Graubünden in spite of the
fact that the German-speaking region of the canton has been steadily increas-

ing its size at the expense of the Romansh-speaking region. The expansion of German is due mainly to the continuing growth of the tourist industry, which, as White (1974) has pointed out, attracts both German-speaking workers and German-speaking tourists, in addition to workers and tourists from other cultures. Many of the latter use German, too, as a lingua franca.

The position of Romansh is weakened further because it consists of several regional districts. There are two major dialects: the Surselvan of the Vorderrhein Valley above and below Disentis (Romansh: Mustair), and the Ladin of the Inn Valley (the Engadine). Ladin is, itself, subdivided into two subdialects (the Puter of the Upper Engadine and the Vallader of the Lower Engadine and Val Mustair). Finally, the intermediate Sutselvan and Surmeiran dialects are spoken in the Hinterrhein (Domleschg) and Oberhalbstein areas, respectively, of central Graubünden. The areas in which the various Romansh dialects are spoken (i.e. Surselvan in western Graubünden, Sutselvan and Surmeiran in Central Graubünden, and Ladin (Puter and Vallader) in eastern Graubünden) are now separated from each other by German-speaking areas.

The Romansh League (*Ligia Romontscha* in Surselvan and *Lia Rumantscha* in Ladin) a cultural organization which is located in Chur and which was established to safeguard the various dialects of Romansh, and Romansh culture in general, continues to voice Romansh concerns on a regular basis. The Romansh Foundation, (*Fundaziun Retoromana*) of Laax is also making an important contribution towards the strengthening of the Romansh language and culture in Graubünden. Increasing amounts of education materials are being produced by the Romansh League, and Romansh-language nursery schools (*scolettas* in Surselvan, *scoulinas* in Ladin) have been set up in many villages. However, there is no doubt that, in the last years of the twentieth century, Romansh faces a severe crisis. Romansh school texts have to be produced in several different versions in order to satisfy the needs of the various dialect areas, which is extremely costly. Relatively few Romansh radio and even fewer Romansh television programmes are broadcast. Certain tourist-oriented communes, as White (op. cit.) has pointed out, continue to be more and more germanized. Moreover, substantial numbers of Romansh-speakers continue to leave Canton Graubünden for better job opportunities elsewhere in Switzerland, thus further weakening the language in its home areas.

In spite of these threats to Romansh culture, to date no political problem exists in the Canton Graubünden which even remotely resembles in severity that which has existed in the Jura region of Canton Berne. This seems to be primarily due to the fact that because of cross-cutting religious and language patterns, religious differences in Graubünden counteract rather than exacerbate linguistic divisions.[7] To quote just one example, each linguistic group in Graubünden (including even, to a limited extent, the Italian-speaking group) is divided into both Protestant and Catholic subgroups. On some issues, therefore, German, Italian, and Romansh-speaking Protestants, united in a common Protestant cause, will oppose a loose grouping of German, Italian, and Romansh-speaking Catholics in Graubünden. On such occasions, a common religion will unite different language groups.

Nevertheless it would be true to say that there is increasing concern about the survival of Romansh among Romansh-speaking intellectuals. As we have seen, the pressures on Romansh are growing, the total number of Romansh-speakers (both in Graubünden and elsewhere) is small, and its survival is unquestionably threatened. As earlier noted, Romansh-speaking communities are, increasingly, becoming geographically isolated from each other by communities which have been Germanized in the recent or distant past. In 1970 the Romansh-speaking region comprised only 86 of Graubünden's 220 communes, compared to 113 in 1888 and 100 in 1950 (McRae, op. cit.).

As in the case of the Bernese Jura, the major language of government of Graubünden is German. Like the Bernese Jura, Graubünden is situated on the periphery of the Swiss Confederation. This may well have added to the feelings of alienation on the part of at least some of the canton's inhabitants. Finally, a significant number of Romansh-speaking communities, like their French-speaking countertparts in such Jurassian districts as Franches-Montagnes, are economically deprived, are predominantly agricultural, and have experienced severe depopulation.

As McRae (op. cit.) has pointed out, '. . . around 1980 . . . concern (for Romansh) began to take on a new note of urgency. The *Ligia Romontscha*, in a carefully worded appeal to the Federal Council for increased grants for linguistic and cultural support, referred to the 'growing menace' that threatened the language and to the necessity of 'Draconian measures' to preserve it.'

Jean-Jacques Furer (Gion Giachen Furer), a Romansh-language activist who, interestingly, is a Jurassian by background, expresses the views of a number of present-day Romansh-speaking intellectuals (Furer, 1982):

It is thus necessary to determine Romansh territory, and then guarantee its integrity by introducing or reintroducing Romansh there as the sole official language, just as German is the sole official language in the Oberland and French in the Pays d'Enhaut. Romansh territory must include all the communes which one can consider traditionally Romansh, that is to say all those which remained Romansh-speaking up to the end of the last century.

The political tradition of Graubünden has been such that Romansh-speakers have seldom acted aggressively to protect their language. Even today, in the mid-1980s, such opinions as those expressed by officials of the *Ligia Romontscha* and by Furer are not held by the great majority of Romansh-speakers in Graubünden. If the position of Romansh weakens still further, it will be interesting to see whether or not the present ambivalent attitude of the majority of Romansh-speakers toward their language will change.

If Romansh-speakers in general were to become as concerned as are Romansh intellectuals about the future of their language, and began to demand the establishment of a 'Romansh region' they would, in all probability, receive a sympathetic hearing from the Swiss federal authorities. There are at least three reasons why this is likely to be the case. Firstly, 'the cadaver of Romansh' (*Ligia Romontscha* 1980) would be, as McRae (op. cit.) puts it, 'a permanent indictment against Switzerland'. Secondly, the creation of a new Canton Jura constitutes a post-Napoleonic Swiss precedent; it has shattered any attitudes (which may have previously existed among some segments of the Swiss population), that the Swiss Confederation and the precise number of its member cantons must for ever remain unchanged. Thirdly, a substantial amount of goodwill towards the Romansh language exists among the population of Switzerland as a whole, for a number of historical and political reasons. It should not be forgotten that, in 1938, 92 per cent of the people of Switzerland voted in favour of the establishment of Romansh as Switzerland's fourth 'national'[8] language. The writer believes it probable that, if Romansh-speakers as a group became increasingly concerned about the future of the language, and more militant in demanding increased territorial protection for Romansh, the Swiss nation will pay heed.

Wider Implications of the Swiss Experience

The particular combination of geographical and other factors which, over the course of several centuries, has resulted in the Swiss federal form of government, does not exist anywhere else in the world. However, this does not mean that the model itself cannot serve as a useful guide to other countries which are confronted with various types of separatism. For a number of reasons, including the development of separatist movements in their own countries, writers in a number of European states have paid attention to federal forms of government in recent years. In Britain, for example, Banks (1971), Bogdanor (1979), and others have examined the factors which eventually caused the Labour government of James Callaghan to propose a form of devolution in the United Kingdom.

Switzerland, it can be argued, is the 'ideal state' in many respects from the viewpoints of autonomy-minded individuals in other countries. This is because it has a 700-year-old history of respecting the traditions, languages, and religions of local communities. All but the most extreme Jurassian separatists, in fact, quote the 'Swiss tradition' to support their political aspirations and argue that, in fighting for the 'Jurassian heritage', they are 'better' Swiss than are the anti-separatists.

The Swiss approach of permitting high degrees of local autonomy within a loose federal framework, or some modification of it, could conceivably be considered in—and could even be applied in—other countries with distinctive regional cultural traditions. Certainly, some regions of Europe which have separatist movements share certain geographical features with the Bernese Jura. Brittany and Wales are examples. Like the Bernese Jura, they are peripheral to their respective states' seats of government, are economically depressed, and have relatively poor internal and external communications. All these characteristics, ironically, have enabled them—albeit imperfectly—to preserve the languages and cultures which provide their respective devolutionist movements with a powerful *raison d'être*. As in the Bernese Jura, too, over the past century or so large numbers of outsiders, who possess equal voting rights with the natives, have settled in areas of Brittany and Wales in which the traditional language was previously dominant, increasing local feelings of resentment.

Devolutionists in both Brittany and Wales have, like supporters of the RJ, argued that on key issues vital to the future of their languages and cultures (such as the granting of devolution in the case of Wales) they are constantly being out-voted by immigrants and/or by anglicized Welsh or 'frenchified' Bretons who are often antagonistic to the traditional language and culture, and whose primary loyalty is to the larger political unit (Britain or France).

What is so often lacking, it seems to this writer, is a willingness, on the part of governments of many states confronted with so-called separatist movements, to consider the Swiss federal–cantonal–communal model of government—or some variant of it—as a possible improvement on their own. Hand in hand with this there must be a willingness, while an indigenous language is still widely spoken and vigorous, to recognize it as *an integral part of the cultural heritage of the state as a whole*, and to grant it official support. (It could be argued, for example, that the Welsh language is as much a part of the wider, 'British' heritage as is a historic castle in Sussex which is assiduously protected by the National Trust, or an animal, bird, fish, or plant once widespread in the British Isles, but now facing extinction.)

We have noted that official linguistic support of the type cited was indeed granted—albeit grudgingly at times—to French in the Bernese Jura in the nineteenth and twentieth centuries, and to French in the Canadian province of Québec as long ago as the mid-nineteenth century. More recently, certain provincial government legislation has helped strengthen the French language in Québec, the only one of Canada's ten provinces in which French-speaking Canadians constitute the majority of the population, and they are able to feel thoroughly at home.

The legislation referred to has been particularly significant in Montreal, the largest city in Québec and often described as the 'second-largest French-speaking city in the world'. In spite of this reputation, the French-speakers of Montreal, prior to the legislation to which reference has been made, were in danger of being overwhelmed linguistically by a large influx of non-French immigrants from the British Isles, northern and southern Europe, Asia, Africa, and Latin America. In the 1960s and early 1970s an estimated 95 per cent of the latter chose to learn English rather than French, and to send their children to English-speaking schools. This situation has now changed significantly. Many Quebec 'anglos' are now assiduously learning French and/or sending their children to bilingual schools. Montreal is considered, by some experts, to be more 'French' than it has been at any time during the past 150 years. Interestingly, this has heightened its appeal to many English-Canadian and foreign tourists.

By contrast, and ironically, similar legislation has not occurred at all in the French province of Brittany, where the native Breton language is seriously threatened by French, yet receives practically no effective support from Paris. The situation has only recently begun to change in the case of the Welsh language in Wales, and only at a time when the language has been seriously weakened.

When a 'language area' (such as that of Romansh, Breton, or Welsh) has become seriously eroded by the arrival, over a period of a century or so, of large numbers of immigrants, even if generous official support is given to the historic language of the region along the lines suggested by Furer (op. cit.) in the case of Graubünden, there is no danger that the language of the 'wider state' (German in the case of Canton Graubünden, French in Brittany, and English in Wales) will be threatened in this bilingual age. In the opinion of the writer such support of the historic language in a given region, in an age when it has become fashionable even for fourth-generation Americans to cultivate their ethnic roots, would not be unreasonable.

Concluding Remarks

This work has endeavoured to examine the Jura problem from the viewpoint of the geographer. It concludes that two geographical variables (the *physical geography* of the Bernese Jura and *distance*) were fundamental, during the period of approximately nineteen centuries following the birth of Christ, in developing a distinctive identity for the region which became the Bernese Jura in 1815, and in thus setting the stage for the appearance of the phenomenon called Jura separatism (Fig. 37).

We saw, firstly, how the Bernese Jura's rugged topography, its drainage, and the alignment of its ridges made the region difficult of access, and thus enabled it to remain French in culture. We saw, secondly and subsequently, how the physical geography of the region interacted with the relative distances of the North and South Juras from Basle/Porrentruy and Berne respectively, to ensure that the South Jura became Protestant while the North Jura remained Catholic.

With respect to present-day separatism in the Bernese Jura, the findings of the study described in this book suggest that an attachment to the French language *and* Catholicism are *each necessary but not sufficient* conditions for separatism in the region. (Only when *both* conditions were present did a Jurassian community vote separatist in the 1974 referendum.) The study, in addition, found evidence that Jura separatism's origins and motive power were strongly associated with a group of interrelated variables which was dubbed autochthonism, and which suggested the existence of a strong attachment to the Bernese Jura on the part of those present-day residents (both Catholics and Protestants) whose ancestors were also Jurassian. (In sharp contrast, *anti*-separatist feeling in the Bernese Jura appeared to be closely associated with an individual's *Bernese* family origin.)

A commune's distance from Berne, even today, also appears to explain the phenomenon of separatism to a moderate degree, and there is some indication that the altitude of a community exerts a minor influence. The greatest surprise of the study, to the writer, was the finding that economic variables, in spite of Jurassian separatist arguments, appear to have only a minimal association with separatist feeling, except in communities in which economic conditions and depopulation are *particularly* severe.

These findings, it will be recalled, apply to the six French-speaking districts of the Bernese Jura as a whole. Within individual Jurassian districts, other geographical factors (such as the French language in Delémont) appear to be the single most important influence on separatism. The old saw that 'predictions are dangerous, particularly those which involve the future' applies with particular force to the Jura. If the South Jura as a whole eventually decided, for various reasons, that it was unhappy within the confines of Canton Berne (a most unlikely eventuality in the immediate future), the most logical development might seem to involve the traditionally Swiss solution of establishing a canton or half-canton of the South Jura. However, in view of the possibility (mentioned earlier in this chapter) that a number of communes of the South Jura may gradually be added to Canton Jura on a piecemeal basis, the territory of the South Jura might be reduced to a size where it could not logically be considered—by the people of Switzerland as a whole—as a potential new canton. The future of the South Jura therefore remains clouded in doubt as this book is being written.

Switzerland, despite some faults, is a country which is remarkably democratic and extraordinarily effectively governed when compared to most other modern states. In its treatment of minority languages alone (such as its giving Romansh the status of a fourth national language) Switzerland sets an example to the world. As McRae puts it in his admirable study of the relationships between the four Swiss language communities (McRae, op. cit.):

> . . . our . . . analysis of the Swiss language situation indicates that Switzerland really does deserve its reputation . . . as a highly successful example of linguistic co-existence. But the analysis also suggests very strongly that this success has been built upon an intricate combination of historical, structural, attitudinal, and institutional factors skilfully and patiently woven into a reinforcing pattern by human effort and statesmanship.

A Swiss-type solution might, at the very least, be examined by the governments of other states which are confronted by so-called separatist movements. Such an examination might not only ascertain what geographical, and other, characteristics their particular separatist movements might share with, say, Jura separatism. A result of a greater understanding of (and, even, perhaps a greater resultant sympathy for) such movements—might also suggest, to these governments, a range of alternative optional solutions to their respective 'separatist problems'. As also indicated, however, what is usually lacking, unfortunately, is a willingness on the part of such governments even to consider such an approach.

Notes

1. Quoted by Keith Richardson (1978).
2. It is interesting to note that each of these communes was at least 70 per cent Protestant in 1970. See also Chapter 8, n. 9.
3. See Chapter 1, n. 2.
4. There are other, smaller, regional frictions in Switzerland in addition to those listed in this chapter. For example, some of the inhabitants of a small area of Canton Zug say they would like to join Canton Zurich, and two separate areas of the Aargau have expressed a desire to join Baselland and Zurich respectively. These are considered to be relatively minor problems, however. In contrast, as noted at the beginning of this chapter, the Laufen district of the former Bernese Jura eventually decided, in 1983, to remain a part of Canton Berne—despite the warm overtures of neighbouring cantons.
5. In total, six formerly German-speaking communes in this area became French-speaking between 1860 and 1900.
6. Because of this, the *Ligia Romontscha* is now promoting the use, in schools of *Rumantsch Grischun*, an artificial composite Romansh which contains elements of all the leading Romansh dialects. It is hoped that *Rumantsch Grischun* can be used as a common educational medium throughout the Romansh area in order to reduce the prohibitive costs of producing as many as five different sets of text materials. It is also hoped that it can be used as a *Romansh Hochdeutch*, or common means of communication between all dialect areas, while still permitting each community to continue to use its local, spoken dialect for everyday purposes. It should be noted, however, that earlier, nineteenth-century attempts to develop a standardized Romansh language foundered because of regional jealousies and suspicions.
7. It will be recalled that Wiegandt (op. cit.) differentiates between overlapping characteristics (characteristics such as a group's language, religion, and economic situation), which are superimposed upon each other and thus accentuate a people's feelings of being different from other groups, and 'cross-cutting' characteristics, or zig-zag loyalties (Henecka, op. cit.) which cut across each other, and tend to weaken such feelings.
8. Switzerland has four 'national' languages: German, French, Italian, and Romansh. Because the latter is spoken by less than 1 per cent of Swiss citizens, however, it is not an 'official' language, i.e. it is not used in the Swiss Federal Assembly and official documents are not necessarily translated into Romansh. Nevertheless Romansh *does* enjoy a certain status in Switzerland and many official publications *do* appear in Romansh versions.

APPENDIX A

DETAILS OF THE RESEARCH STUDY

This work is based, in part, on a research study conducted in connection with the writer's 1981 D.Phil. thesis at Oxford University. Subsequently, during the period 1982–4, the writer paid three additional visits to the Jura and to Berne, in order to revise and update his data in the light of subsequent developments both in the Jura and in Switzerland as a whole.

Preliminary Research

Prior to the inception of his D.Phil. study, the writer paid two visits to the Bernese Jura and became reasonably familiar with the region and its inhabitants. Subsequently, during the course of the study itself, the writer made five additional visits to the Bernese Jura, and spent a total of approximately seven months conducting field research there. The longest period spent in the region at any one time was just over three months; the shortest period was three weeks. During the course of the field research, the writer visited each of the 145 communes (local administrative units) of the region. Some of these communes were visited five or six times in all.

An additional period of time—approximately a month in all—was spent in Berne,[1] consulting books and documents (published in French, German, and English), studying maps and charts in the Swiss Federal Library, and obtaining data from the Swiss Federal Bureau of Statistics and the government of Canton Berne. In addition, discussions were held with officials of the federal government of Switzerland and the government of Canton Berne.

In the Bernese Jura itself, and prior to developing a set of hypotheses, the writer conducted a number of formal interviews with Jurassian political figures of all viewpoints, with local government officials, and with local businessmen and women. In addition, a large number of informal discussions were held with Jurassians in all walks of life and all political shades of opinion in each of the 145 communes, and elsewhere in Switzerland. All formal interviews and informal discussions in the Bernese Jura were conducted in French, the language of the greater part of the region. In Berne, interviews and discussions with Bernese officials with responsibility for the Bernese Jura were also conducted in French, while other interviews and discussions in Berne were conducted in French and English.

Following careful consideration, the writer decided that a logical starting-point of the study would be to select what appeared to be the strongest single piece of evidence of the presence of Jurassian separatist feeling in the region, and then to relate this 'dependent variable' to various other measurable regional phenomena which appeared to be related to Jurassian separatism in some way.

The Study Itself

Choice of the Dependent Variable

A number of pieces of evidence of Jurassian separatism (e.g., the degree to which Jurassian and Bernese flags and signs were displayed in a commune, personal opinions expressed by local inhabitants, etc.) were evaluated on the basis of whether or not each of them would constitute a meaningful dependent variable. Each of them was considered useful as an *indication* of the intensity of Jurassian separatist feeling, but none were considered to be sufficiently precise for the purposes of the planned study.

The distribution of questionnaires to a selected cross-section of inhabitants of the region was also considered. This was rejected, after careful consideration, on two grounds. Firstly, the intensity—and sometimes bitterness of political feeling in certain communes meant that the distribution of questionnaires by an outsider would have been met by, at best, suspicion and, at worst, hostility, thus affecting both the amount and accuracy of information provided in completed questionnaire forms. Secondly, given the circumstances, there appeared to be a real danger that an insufficient number of completed questionnaires would be returned to the researcher over what was considered to be an acceptable period of time.

The writer also considered, but rejected, the use of political voting patterns in the Bernese Jura as an indication of separatist feeling. Both prior to and since the 1974 referendum, the RJ itself did not operate as a political party in the traditional sense, i.e., it did not put forward official RJ candidates in elections. Rather, it urged its members to support political candidates who supported the establishment of a new canton in the Jura, and to oppose candidates who were anti-separatist. This policy proved to be quite effective.

While certain political parties (such as the Christian Democrat party in the North Jura) have appeared, in the past, to have had higher proportions of their supporters who were separatist in sympathies than certain other parties, even the former have included,

Table A. *Changes in Electoral Divisions*

District	No. of communes	No. of electoral subdistricts
Courtelary	18	17
Delémont	23	23
Franches-Montagnes	17	10
Moutier	34	33
La Neuveville	5	5
Porrentruy	36	34
Total: 6 French-speaking districts	133	122
Laufen	12	12
Total: All districts of Bernese Jura	145	134

in their ranks, significant numbers of anti-separatists. The same observations apply to other parties (such as the Radical Party) which, on balance, have been unenthusiastic about the separatist cause. The votes garnered by traditional political parties were therefore considered to be of limited value for purposes of this study.[2]

It was finally concluded that by far the strongest single piece of available evidence of the relative strength of Jurassian separatist feeling was the percentage of voters in each commune who voted 'Yes' in the Bernese Jura referendum of 23 June 1974. This referendum was organized by the government of Canton Berne, and was designed to permit the inhabitants of the Bernese Jura to decide whether or not they wished to secede from Canton Berne and form a new Swiss canton. The results of this referendum were considered to be particularly significant, both because of the secret, democratic nature of the ballot, and the high level of voter participation. In summary, it was concluded that the percentage of 'Yes' votes (i.e., votes in favour of the establishment of a new Canton Jura) in a given commune in the 1974 referendum constituted the most appropriate dependent variable, given the other alternatives.

The 1974 referendum was held in the entire region (comprising seven districts[3] and 145 communes) of the Bernese Jura. The specific question posed to all Swiss citizens of voting age residing in the region was 'Do you wish to form a new canton?' Ninety per cent of those eligible to vote participated in the referendum.[4] Of these, 36,802 individuals voted in favour of, and 34,057 voted against, the establishment of a new canton, resulting in a narrow 52 per cent to 48 per cent 'Yes' majority vote. However, as indicated in Chapter 7, the 'Yes' vote varied greatly from commune to commune, and large percentages of 'No' votes were registered in certain communes. Four of the seven districts of the region, in fact, recorded overall 'No' majorities. The results of the 1974 referendum, on a commune-by-commune basis, were subsequently announced by the government of Canton Berne.

A study of this nature logically falls within the sub-field of electoral geography, a relatively new field of political geography. Early writers in this field include Siegfried (1913 and 1947), Wright (1944), and Goguel (1951). The newer school of electoral geographers includes Cox (1968), 1969), Prescott (1959, 1969, 1972), Reynolds (1969), and Busteed (1972, 1975). These writers, and others (including East (1937, 1948, 1960, 1962) and Pounds (1972), who have conducted research and published in the wider field of political geography), have focused on a wide variety of regions of the world. During the past twenty years, research in the field of electoral geography has included studies, among others, which have focused on Australia (Woolmington, 1966 and Glanville, 1970), Britain (Pelling, 1967), Canada (Anderson, 1966), Colombia (Blasier, 1966), the Netherlands (Nooij, 1969), the United States (Orr, 1969), and West Germany (Ganser, 1966). Little attention appears to have been paid to Switzerland specifically, however.

Electoral Divisions

In 1970 there were a total of 145 communes in the Bernese Jura as a whole. Of these, the six predominantly French-speaking districts contained a total of 133 communes, and the German-speaking district of Laufen contained twelve communes. One hundred and thirty-four 'electoral subdistricts' were established, by the cantonal authorities, in the region at the time of the 1974 referendum. These corresponded almost entirely to communal boundaries, except that in a few instances two (and sometimes three) adjoining communes were combined to form one electoral district.

Thus, in the district of Courtelary, the adjoining communes of Tramelan and Mont-Tramelan were combined into one electoral subdistrict. Franches-Montagnes' seventeen communes were reduced, by means of five combinations of two or three communes, to a total of ten electoral subdistricts. In the district of Moutier the communes of Sornetan and Monible were combined, and in Porrentruy the three communes of St-Ursanne, Montenol, and Montmelon were combined into one electoral subdistrict. There were no changes in the districts of Delémont, La Neuveville, and Laufen. (In summary, the changes were as shown in Table A).

Of the 133 communes (122 electoral districts) in the six predominantly French-speaking districts, seven communes (six electoral subdistricts) had a German-speaking majority at the time of the 1970 census. These communes were Ederswiler, Rebévelier, and Roggenburg in the district of Delémont, and Châtelat, Mont-Tramelan, Schelten, and Seehof in the district of Moutier. They are identified in Fig. 24 of the text.

Choice of the Independent Variables

Following his decision to use 1974 referendum data as his dependent variable, the writer next gave consideration to geographical factors which might reasonably be considered to be associated with the phenomenon of Jura separatism. Following his field research in the Bernese Jura (described earlier), he concluded that fourteen geographical factors might conceivably be related in some way to Jurassian separatist feeling. These factors involved:

(1) The French language.
(2) The Catholic religion.
(3) The proportion of the population whose ancestors were Jurassians, as contrasted with those whose ancestors came from German-speaking Swiss cantons, and from Canton Berne in particular. (Six theories relating to citizenship were developed and tested, in all.)
(4) Economic health.
(5) Depopulation (two theories concerning depopulation were developed and tested).
(6) Dependence on the agricultural sector.
(7) Distance from the city of Berne.
(8) Altitude above the city of Berne.

Data Collection

The federal government of Switzerland has obtained population data for each Swiss commune at approximately ten-year intervals since 1850, and some information is also available from more limited censuses which were conducted in 1837 and earlier. Data on the first language of each inhabitant of each Swiss commune are available from 1860 onwards. Certain religious data are available from 1850 onwards, and some data on citizenship have been included in Swiss censuses beginning in 1870.

Nevertheless, although, as indicated, certain basic data regarding total population, language, and religion were available from Swiss federal government sources, the greater part of the data obtained in this way was not in the form required, and had to be processed further by the writer. (For example, data on religion were normally provided, in officially published form, for the *entire* population of a commune. In industrialized communes, this total population would include large numbers of foreign 'guest-workers', who are predominantly Catholic and are not allowed to vote in Swiss elections.) In some instances, special requests for additional data breakdowns were made to Swiss federal government officials.

Citizenship data, which were obtained from the 1970 census, warrant some additional comments. The citizenship of a Swiss involves his relationship with that commune in which his ancestors resided during the early and middle years of the nineteenth century, when Swiss federal authorities first began to conduct censuses on a regular basis. Two examples will serve to illustrate the Swiss concept of citizenship.

Firstly, let us consider the hypothetical case of Josef Meier, aged 35, who is a resident of the commune of Brugg in Canton Aargau. Josef Meier is listed in official Swiss records as a citizen of the remote rural commune of Hergiswil, in Canton Lucerne. This is simply because his great great grandfather, Andreas Meier, was born in the commune of Hergiswil in 1829, and resided there until his death. However, his grandson (the present-day Josef Meier's grandfather), left Hergiswil in 1902. Josef Meier may never have lived in Hergiswil, but he is still recorded as a citizen of the commune.

On the other hand, let us consider the quite differnt hypothetical case of Franz Müller, aged 40. Franz Müller is both a resident and citizen of the same commune of Hergiswil which Josef Meier's ancestor left in 1849. This is simply because Müller's ancestors remained in the commune in Hergiswil, and Müller himself still lives there.

Because of the increasing geographical mobility of the population of Switzerland, individuals of the type represented by Franz Müller (i.e., individuals who are citizens of the commune in which they still reside) are becoming far less common. For this reason, the Swiss definition of communal citizenship may appear anachronistic to the non-Swiss observer. Nevertheless, this Swiss custom provides us with a useful indication of the degree to which a given Swiss community has experienced an influx of immigrants from elsewhere, in the past.

Such data are significant in any study of Jura separatism, because they enable us to measure the present-day residual effects, on a commune-by-commune basis, of the extremely heavy German-speaking Bernese immigration to many areas of the Bernese Jura in the late nineteenth and early twentieth centuries. We have already seen that the RJ considered these residual effects to be of great significance.

In the case of hypotheses involving the economic status of communes (i.e., variables relating to the commune's economic health, population growth or decline, and the degree to which the workforce was employed in agriculture), it was decided, following careful consideration, to use 'total population' figures, rather than data for Swiss citizens only, because the latter were not available. However, it may well be that 'total data', in this instance, were more indicative of the prosperity (or lack of prosperity) of an area in the Swiss context. A prosperous Swiss community which offers employment opportunities is likely to attract both Swiss citizens and non-Swiss citizens—the latter consisting almost entirely of foreign-born guest-workers.

State tax data for 1974 were obtained by the writer from the Bureau of Statistics of Canton Berne, and the average per capita tax paid per commune was compared to the average per capita tax paid for Canton Berne as a whole. An economic index was then calculated for each commune as a general index of economic prosperity, with the cantonal average being assigned a value of 100. Economic status indices for electoral districts which included two or more communes were calculated on a weighted average basis.

The altitude of each commune was recorded by the writer following a careful examination of large-scale local maps. In instances where a commune contained more than one settlement, with a separate altitudinal reading for each, a weighted average height, based on population density and distribution, was calculated. A weighted average height was also calculated where the map of a settlement included one or more altitudinal recordings. Finally, a weighted average height was calculated where communes were combined to form electoral subdistricts. The modern travel distance of each electoral subdistrict from Berne was also calculated with the aid of large-scale maps. The shortest travel distance was selected, whether this was by road or rail. Once again, a weighted average was used in the study where necessary.

Analysis of the Data

Following further consideration of the data, it was felt that the most appropriate way to begin the study was to ascertain the strength of the relationship between each geographical factor (or independent variable) and the intensity of Jurassian separatist feeling (the dependent variable). This would be done, firstly, by conducting a simple regression analysis involving each independent variable, in turn, with the dependent variable. Expressing this somewhat differently, an effort would be made to ascertain the degree to which the variation (or differences) in the 'Yes' vote between the various communes of the Bernese Jura could be explained (i.e. matched) by the variation in the scores recorded by a particular geographic factor for the same communes. The greater the ability of an independent variable (a geographical factor) to explain such a variation in the 'Yes' vote (Jura separatism), the greater the apparent association between them.

Following the completion of the series of simple regression analyses discussed in the previous paragraph, a number of step-wise regression analyses were undertaken by the writer. These were conducted by beginning with that geographical variable which most effectively explained the variation in the dependent variable (the 'Yes' vote), in an effort to determine the extent to which the remaining geographical variables were, in turn, successful in explaining the remaining variation in the 'Yes' vote.

A number of further analyses were subsequently conducted by the writer. Specifically, and in summary, the following additional analyses were conducted in the writer's study of the Bernese Jura:

(1) A Verson 8 SPSS bivariate linear regression analysis. The purpose of this analysis was to determine the degree to which variations, between subdistricts, in the values of a particular independent variable (such as, for example, the percentage of Swiss residents who were Catholics) explained (i.e., appeared to be associated with) variations, between Jura subdistricts, in the values of the dependent variable (the percentage of the voters who voted 'Yes' in the 1974 Jura referendum).

(2) An SPSS forward selection, step-wise multiple regression analysis. In this analysis, the dependent variable (the percentage 1974 'Yes' vote for each sub-district) was regressed on the fourteen independent variables. Beginning with the independent variable which had the highest R^2 value (i.e., which appeared to be more closely associated with Jura separatism than any other) this analysis sought to determine the degree to which additional independent variables, sequentially, were able to explain the remaining variations, between subdistricts, in the separatist vote.

(3) A principal components factor analysis, with iterations. The purpose of this analysis was to endeavour to identify, on a preliminary basis, certain factors or dimensions which might suggest interrelationships between certain independent variables (such as for example, between recent depopulation and low economic status). Evidence of such interrelationships might suggest the existence of even more basic, underlying causes of the phenomenon being measured than the independent variables first selected.

(4) A Varimax rotation of the factors identified earlier. This analysis was performed in order to produce a simple structure (the factor matrix) in which a particular independent variable (such as Catholicism) might load heavily on one factor (i.e., appear to be very closely related to it), and lightly on the remaining factors. Factors with certain minimum eigenvalues were selected for rotation. (The eigenvalue associated with each factor is the amount of total variance accounted for by that factor.)

(5) A second bivariate linear regression analysis, this time using, as independent variables, each of the *major factors* identified earlier, rather than the original fourteen independent variables. This analysis was conducted to ascertain the amount of variance in 'Yes' scores, between subdistricts, which could be explained by each identified factor.

(6) A second SPSS forward selection, step-wise multiple regression analysis, also using the identified factors as independent variables in place of the fourteen original independent variables.

Regional Groupings of Subdistricts

In studying Jura separatism as a geographical phenomenon, the data available to us can be studied on both an individual and aggregate basis. Firstly, because we have information available to us for each electoral subdistrict, we can study such data as, for example, the percentage of French-speakers in a subdistrict, compare it to the percentage of 'Yes' votes in the 1974 referendum, and reach certain tentative conclusions as to whether any relationship may exist between them *in that subdistrict*.

Secondly, on an aggregate basis, we can combine the basic data for subdistricts, to arrive at aggregate data for a larger area. Once again, with the aid of the computer, dependent and independent variables can be compared, and certain conclusions can be drawn regarding a possible relationship in the group of subdistricts (or region) *as a whole*.

Thirdly, and with the aid of the computer, both the individual and aggregative data can be examined to determine *patterns* within the larger region. The degree to which *variations*—from one subdistrict to another within a larger region—in the independent variable (for example, in the percentage of French-speakers) seem to explain the variations (or variance) in the dependent variable (the 1974 'Yes' vote) can be noted. Certain tentative conclusions can then be drawn with respect to the existence of a possible relationship between the independent (i.e. geographic) variable and the dependent variable (the percentage 'Yes' vote), indicating the strength of Jurassian separatist feeling.

In total, analyses were conducted for eleven regional groupings, as shown in Table B. Two warnings are in order here. Firstly, our examination of the variations in scores between subdistricts must not blind us to the fact that certain populous subdistricts account for a significant percentage of the total vote in a district, while scantily-populated subdistricts account for very little. For example, and by contrast, the Porrentruy and Roche d'Or subdistricts in the Porrentruy district of the region had 1970 voter populations of 4,330 and 28 respectively, out of a total district voter population of 15,615. Of these potential voters, 92 per cent (or 3,971 voters) participated in the 1974 referendum in the Porrentruy subdistrict, and 93 per cent (or 26 voters) participated in Roche d'Or (Appendix C: Table 3).

Table B.   *Analyses by Regional Groupings*

Grouping	No. of communes		No. of electoral subdistricts	
(1) The Bernese Jura as a whole (7 districts)	145		134	
(2) The French-speaking Bernese Jura (6 districts)	133		122	
(3) The North Jura (3 districts)	76	133	67	122
(4) The South Jura (3 districts)	57		55	
(5) The Courtelary district	18		17	
(6) The Delémont district	23		23	
(7) The Franches-Montagnes district	17	145	10	134
(8) The Moutier district	34		33	
(9) The La Neuveville district	5		5	
(10) The Porrentruy district	36		34	
(11) The Laufen district	12		12	

Secondly, great care must clearly be taken in interpreting data produced from groupings in which there are a limited number of observations. Having acknowledged this, however, it must also be recognized that, in studies of this type, certain interesting patterns can sometimes emerge even within such small groupings of subdistricts.

Post-thesis Research

Post-thesis research involved several visits by the writer to Canton Jura, the South Jura, Berne, Biel, Fribourg, and Zurich. Up-to-date statistical and other data were obtained, and discussions were held with informed observers in Canton Jura, Canton Berne, and elsewhere in Switzerland.

Notes

1. Berne serves, of course, both as the seat of government of Canton Berne *and* as the federal capital of Switzerland.
2. As indicated earlier in the book, separatist leaders were (and are) members of several different Swiss political parties.
3. A district consists of a number of communes, ranging, in the Bernese Jura, from five in the case of La Neuveville to thirty-six in the case of Porrentruy.
4. 1·3 per cent of those voting cast blank ballots.

APPENDIX B

SOURCES OF DATA USED IN THE FIGURES

Major sources of information for the figures in this text were *Atlas de la Suisse* (1972), produced by the Swiss Federal and Topographical Service, Wabern-Berne, and *Grand Atlas Suisse* (Jeanneret and Auf der Maur, 1982), published by Kümmerly and Frey, Berne. Another important source was the *'Planungsatlas'* series (1969, 1970, 1973), produced by the government of Canton Berne, which was particularly used in making possible the production of the maps indicating the centres, in the Bernese Jura, of the watch-making, light engineering, and metal-working industries.

Certain data for the historical maps were obtained from *Historischer Atlas der Schweiz* (Amman and Schib, 1958), and from *Histoire populaire du Jura bernois* (Amweg, rev. Prongué, 1974). Some of the data for the linguistic maps were obtained from *Sprachatlas der Deutschen Schweiz* (Hotzenkocherle and Trub, 1962), and from *Geographie der Schweiz* (Früh, 1932). The data used in Fig. 6 were taken, in part, from *The European Culture Area* (Jordan, 1973).

All maps dealing with percentages on a commune-by-commune basis (e.g., of German-speakers, of total population, of depopulation, of Catholics, etc. with the exception of referendum data) were produced by the author from census data obtained by him from the Swiss Federal Bureau of Statistics, from data obtained by special request, and from data which were processed further by the author. Maps dealing with the various Bernese Jura referendums, polls, etc. were produced by the author from data kindly supplied by the *Sécrétariat du Conseil-exécutif pour les affaires jurassiennes*, government of Canton Berne.

APPENDIX C

SUPPLEMENTARY TABLES

Appendix C: Table 1. *Selected Data for French-speaking Districts of Bernese Jura by District and Commune*

Courtelary district	A Population				B Population change, 1970 vs. 1960	C % of working population employed in agriculture, 1970	D German-speakers as a % of Swiss citizens				E Catholics as a % of Swiss citizens			
	1850	1910	1960	1970			1860[2]	1900	1930	1970	1860	1900	1930	1970
Corgémont	753	1,369	1,414	1,645	16·3	9	53	32	27	29	4	5	5	16
Cormoret	478	746	633	641	1·3	9	20	11	20	17	4	4	7	15
Cortébert	326	796	767	776	1·2	15	34	22	29	28	2	6	11	22
Courtelary	868	1,337	1,330	1,462	9·9	9	28	16	23	19	8	9	7	19
La Ferrière	796	630	507	445	−12·2	43	26	26	52	36	23	13	6	11
La Heutte	271	339	428	486	13·6	5	48	46	57	31	1	10	7	14
Mont-Tramelan	169	146	139	127	− 8·6	78	40	76	72	87	2	10	—	—
Orvin	659	760	796	1,034	29·9	14	10	22	13	16	—	3	3	7
Péry	560	1,201	1,304	1,486	14·0	4	36	31	26	22	8	16	9	16
Plagne	262	258	239	277	15·9	8	5	5	11	18	1	1	1	6
Renan	1,820	1,455	1,091	1,094	0·3	14	24	24	31	29	6	7	11	22
Romont	195	131	215	213	− 0·9	26	32	51	54	42	6	2	8	15
St-Imier	2,632	7,442	6,704	6,740	0·5	2	32	20	19	14	13	15	21	29
Sonceboz-Sombeval	565	1,183	1,404	1,446	3·0	6	33	33	27	15	4	12	9	16
Sonvilier	2,276	1,907	1,595	1,497	− 6·1	18	19	21	28	28	12	9	7	14
Tramelan-Dessous[1] Tramelan-Dessus[1]	2,551	5,267	5,567	5,549	− 0·3	5	8	11	15	16	4	14	14	22
Vauffelin	255	271	278	467	68·0	3	37	26	23	23	2	5	4	16
Villeret	970	1,507	1,125	1,057	− 6·0	7	36	19	14	18	9	6	11	18
Total	16,406	26,745	25,636	26,442	3·5	8	26	21	22	20	9	11	12	20

Appendix C: Table 1. *Continued*

Delémont district	A Population				B Population change, 1970 vs. 1960	C % of working population employed in agriculture, 1970	D German-speakers as a % of Swiss citizens				E Catholics as a % of Swiss citizens			
	1850	1910	1960	1970			1860[2]	1900	1930	1970	1860	1900	1930	1970
Bassecourt	759	1,105	2,284	2,985	30·7	4	—	7	10	7	99	90	90	89
Boécourt	655	642	706	756	7·1	13	1	—	12	7	100	100	89	83
Bourrignon	359	338	279	241	−13·6	57	8	13	14	11	98	98	82	85
Courfaivre	668	777	1,307	1,326	1·5	7	2	8	13	8	98	90	87	83
Courroux	1,173	1,455	1,667	1,788	7·3	12	15	29	26	13	94	81	74	73
Courtetelle	698	1,234	1,618	1,864	15·2	7	6	13	13	8	94	88	83	84
Delémont	1,650	6,161	9,542	11,797	23·6	2	28	41	28	10	92	64	62	74
Develier	590	549	709	955	34·7	19	3	15	26	13	98	86	68	74
Ederswiler	219	113	166	163	−1·8	33	100	96	90	96	91	89	87	82
Glovelier	537	710	969	997	2·9	9	—	13	11	6	99	87	87	91
Mettemberg	113	103	80	75	−6·2	19	—	1	8	7	100	100	95	96
Montsevelier	414	404	439	508	15·7	15	5	5	7	8	100	98	100	98
Movelier	386	286	384	338	−12·0	20	1	10	11	14	99	97	93	86
Pleigne	443	433	396	364	−8·1	46	12	22	18	21	91	90	84	81
Rebeuvelier	332	382	266	240	−9·8	30	10	26	22	14	96	88	82	74
Rebévelier	112	72	44	51	15·9	86	10	32	36	82	99	78	62	16
Roggenburg	412	243	260	232	−10·8	37	93	96	92	95	97	82	76	79
Saulcy	299	280	234	249	6·4	30	—	—	1	3	99	100	100	97
Soulce	441	371	274	227	−17·2	43	4	3	6	9	100	97	95	90
Soyhières[3]	279	592	550	491	−10·7	9	17	40	26	30	100	89	94	83
Undervelier	646	570	435	407	−6·4	21	10	18	17	17	98	83	79	73
Vermes	605	450	472	387	−18·0	38	27	33	39	31	92	91	78	73
Vicques	530	655	938	1,108	18·1	9	10	13	18	9	93	91	85	88
Total	12,320	17,925	24,019	27,549	14·7	8	14	25	22	12	96	81	77	80

Appendix C: Table 1. *Continued*

Franches-Montagnes district	A Population				B Population change, 1970 vs. 1960	C % of working population employed in agriculture, 1970	D German-speakers as a % of Swiss citizens				E Catholics as a % of Swiss citizens			
	1850	1910	1960	1970			1860²	1900	1930	1970	1860	1900	1930	1970
Le Bémont	612	522	360	307	−14·7	43	1	2	3	2	99	98	94	93
Les Bois	1,339	1,323	1,098	1,110	1·1	21	3	6	7	9	96	93	89	81
Les Breuleux	736	1,437	1,456	1,393	− 4·3	6	—	4	5	4	98	93	93	93
La Chaux	166	204	93	84	− 9·7	27	—	1	—	12	99	98	96	92
Les Enfers	203	186	142	100	−29·6	51	—	5	13	4	99	97	75	88
Epauvillers	293	259	201	195	− 3·0	46	—	2	3	6	100	99	99	89
Les Epiquerez	249	177	143	106	−25·9	73	4	7	22	18	100	93	82	78
Goumois	262	277	170	113	−33·5	33	2	7	24	38	99	95	72	67
Montfaucon	497	654	524	455	−13·2	32	—	7	7	10	100	97	85	88
Montfavergier	174	80	76	56	−26·3	50	3	—	—	32	96	100	94	69
Muriaux	801	810	461	392	−15·0	39	—	10	10	18	99	87	86	73
Le Noirmont	1,544	1,852	1,559	1,516	− 2·8	11	1	6	6	8	98	94	92	87
Le Peuchapatte	133	69	63	38	−39·7	83	—	1	1	26	100	96	89	76
Les Pommerats	357	364	266	224	−15·8	23	1	5	6	13	98	92	86	72
Saignelégier	754	1,679	1,636	1,745	6·7	6	2	9	10	10	98	88	82	82
St-Brais	463	410	292	261	−10·6	48	—	1	1	6	100	99	93	89
Soubey	391	311	187	208	−11·2	48	2	2	2	12	100	98	88	83
Total	8,974	10,614	8,727	8,303	− 4·9	20	1	5	9	9	98	93	88	85

Appendix C: Table 1. *Continued*

Moutier district	A Population				B Population change, 1970 vs. 1960	C % of working population employed in agriculture, 1970	D German-speakers as a % of Swiss citizens				E Catholics as a % of Swiss citizens			
	1850	1910	1960	1970			1860[2]	1900	1930	1970	1860	1900	1930	1970
Belprahon	126	147	133	193	45·1	14	18	56	37	22	6	14	10	26
Bévilard	294	808	1,604	1,952	21·7	2	40	16	15	12	4	11	8	22
Champoz	190	182	168	154	− 8·3	32	35	40	21	15	5	3	1	4
Châtelat	153	213	179	172	− 3·9	59	34	57	58	64	6	4	7	6
Chatillon	193	279	303	299	− 1·3	19	21	8	8	3	89	94	91	93
Corban	392	375	429	409	− 4·7	21	6	27	18	7	97	80	86	87
Corcelles	180	229	192	184	− 4·2	38	19	35	59	34	20	39	18	14
Courchapoix	271	238	305	318	4·3	27	7	23	12	5	94	80	90	89
Courrendlin	731	2,098	2,418	2,656	9·8	5	24	51	39	16	90	71	66	73
Court	581	1,207	1,493	1,550	3·8	8	42	37	32	14	91	13	12	10
Crémines	297	490	548	560	2·2	13	23	45	51	24	38	17	26	25
Eschert	208	313	322	358	11·2	10	36	52	42	19	8	18	13	24
Les Genevez	665	678	553	508	− 8·1	13	3	5	5	8	99	98	95	90
Grandval	261	314	393	426	8·4	14	29	26	42	21	13	15	9	13
Lajoux	571	571	566	525	− 7·2	24	2	10	9	4	100	96	92	89
Loveresse	227	421	322	287	−10·9	18	7	21	26	24	3	72	3	9
Malleray	471	1,421	1,838	1,969	7·1	3	32	28	19	10	19	11	7	25

Mervelier	490	452	548	527	− 3·8	18	6	17	13	8	100	96	92	89
Monible	132	76	27	29	7·4	62	40	32	11	34	1	4	—	7
Moutier	917	4,164	7,472	8,794	17·7	2	26	36	25	13	26	28	31	44
Perrefitte	236	403	519	569	9·6	9	40	30	29	22	10	15	14	30
Pontenet	121	246	231	203	−12·1	19	27	39	24	14	4	12	3	18
Reconvilier	361	2,139	2,567	2,784	8·5	2	33	29	17	15	7	14	14	21
Roches	277	289	265	323	21·9	17	46	46	42	40	15	18	15	18
Rossemaison	185	251	281	315	12·1	14	16	16	22	12	95	87	77	78
Saicourt	456	1,016	1,067	932	−12·7	13	29	47	53	22	22	11	11	27
Saules	143	190	202	191	− 5·4	26	3	26	28	27	2	2	1	8
Schelten	82	90	49	54	10·2	86	100	95	99	98	95	54	62	47
Seehof	202	125	105	86	18·1	63	95	97	96	91	92	52	18	16
Sornetan	299	184	129	131	1·6	38	30	35	38	28	—	5	5	7
Sorvilier	316	451	392	386	− 1·5	22	36	26	31	20	5	95	4	8
Souboz	200	209	150	132	−12·0	59	27	48	51	40	7	3	2	2
Tavannes	672	2,655	3,939	3,869	− 1·8	4	28	28	19	17	4	15	18	24
Vellerat	88	93	77	64	−16·9	10	—	11	12	15	100	92	78	76
Total	10,988	23,017	29,786	31,909	7·1	7	25	33	26	15	40	33	30	38

Appendix C: Table 1. *Continued*

Porrentruy district	A Population				B Population change, 1970 vs. 1960	C % of working population employed in agriculture, 1970	D German-speakers as a % of Swiss citizens				E Catholics as a % of Swiss citizens			
	1850	1910	1960	1970			1860²	1900	1930	1970	1860	1900	1930	1970
Alle	918	1,122	1,471	1,615	9·8	6	—	6	8	3	100	94	91	90
Asuel	444	342	253	265	4·7	21	4	6	2	7	99	97	96	91
Beurnevésin	347	255	177	204	15·3	28	3	9	18	9	99	96	84	88
Boncourt	647	1,020	1,493	1,528	2·3	6	3	9	7	5	98	91	93	93
Bonfol	1,263	1,304	992	888	−10·5	12	2	6	10	13	98	94	90	73
Bressaucourt	410	434	398	391	− 1·8	12	2	2	12	7	97	95	85	77
Bruix	453	549	589	614	4·2	16	—	2	6	3	100	98	95	95
Bure	798	653	558	593	6·3	17	2	3	9	3	98	97	94	94
Charmoille	599	507	494	480	− 2·8	31	4	9	16	13	98	97	87	83
Chevenez	952	843	768	678	−11·7	23	1	4	6	2	100	96	95	96
Coeuve	630	757	707	614	−13·2	16	—	1	5	5	99	100	97	97
Cornol	786	1,030	809	855	5·7	10	2	5	8	2	99	95	90	90
Courchavon	306	278	272	282	3·7	17	—	6	7	14	100	94	85	85
Courgenay	1,098	1,498	1,666	1,954	17·3	11	2	4	16	7	99	93	80	80
Courtedoux	499	703	621	651	4·8	14	1	4	4	7	98	96	93	84
Courtemaîche	426	779	735	661	−10·1	6	—	2	6	2	100	99	95	95
Damphreux	344	302	237	191	−19·4	32	1	1	9	9	100	100	94	90
Damvant	357	300	213	176	−17·4	22	—	2	7	6	97	97	95	93
Fahy	549	483	477	501	5·0	17	2	1	11	7	100	99	86	87
Fontenais	680	1,148	991	1,024	3·3	15	—	6	10	8	97	90	83	80
Frégiécourt	350	217	172	131	−23·8	32	—	16	21	4	100	86	62	77
Grandfontaine	471	434	350	338	− 3·4	24	—	2	7	6	100	99	94	97
Lugnez	292	262	265	231	−12·8	23	—	1	15	8	100	99	83	85

Miécourt	524	456	490	494	0·8	21	2	22	32	19	96	66	63	57
Montenol	80	65	80	76	− 5·0	46	—	1	3	1	100	98	100	100
Montignez	351	335	346	314	− 9·2	21	3	2	8	1	98	100	91	87
Montmelon	246	207	167	139	−16·8	70	2	2	19	9	96	98	79	92
Ocourt	381	227	171	157	− 8·2	53	9	5	32	30	98	92	70	61
Pleujouse	239	144	85	90	5·9	31	—	—	1	15	100	98	98	83
Porrentruy	2,880	6,591	7,095	7,827	10·3	2	4	11	15	8	90	80	78	80
Réclère	321	305	208	212	1·9	28	—	1	8	10	100	99	95	92
Roche d'Or	128	82	67	45	−32·8	80	—	—	1	11	99	100	96	87
Rocourt	272	213	175	144	−17·7	35	—	—	1	2	100	100	100	99
St-Ursanne	726	999	1,304	1,073	−17·7	5	—	5	7	8	98	93	92	87
Seleute	148	119	87	78	−10·3	61	3	9	25	5	95	92	81	71
Vendlincourt	644	643	668	621	− 7·0	14	—	7	17	11	100	93	83	76
Total	20,565	25,611	25,651	36,135	1·9	11	2	6	11	7	97	91	86	85
Total: 6 districts	73,090	108,149	118,764	126,094	6·2	9	14	18	20	13	61	54	51	56

[1] Tramelan-Dessous and -Dessus were joined together in 1952.

[2] Estimates for 1860 based on the ratio of German- and French-speaking households.

[3] Riedes-Dessus was removed from the jurisdiction of Courroux commune in 1856, and was added to Soyhières commune.

Source: Swiss Federal Bureau of Statistics.

Appendix C: Table 1. *Continued*

La Neuveville district	A Population				B Population change, 1970 vs. 1960	C % of working population employed in agriculture, 1970	D German-speakers as a % of Swiss citizens				E Catholics as a % of Swiss citizens			
	1850	1910	1960	1970			1860²	1900	1930	1970	1860	1900	1930	1970
Diesse	408	371	310	277	− 10·6	26	16	4	5	9	1	1	6	2
Lamboing	569	478	464	464	− 2·1	13	7	6	5	12	3	1	—	5
La Neuveville	1,719	2,296	3,216	3,917	21·8	4	27	30	32	28	5	9	8	18
Nods	811	709	473	464	− 1·9	34	15	14	10	13	1	1	—	4
Prêles	330	383	572	634	− 10·8	11	18	17	41	39	1	3	3	14
Total	3,837	4,237	5,045	5,756	− 14·1	6	20	21	24	25	9	6	5	14

Appendix C: Table 2. *Further Selected Data For French-speaking Districts of Bernese Jura by District and Commune*

Courtelary district	Citizenship of resident Swiss citizens, 1970			Voting behaviour		
	% Citizens of Bernese Jura	% Citizens of Old Canton	% Citizens of a German-Swiss canton	Results of poll of 5 July 1959: % 'Yes' vote	Results of referendum of 23 June 1974	
					'Yes' vote (%)	Participation (%)
Corgémont	24	53	64	24	32	91
Cormoret	32	43	49	31	25	92
Cortebert	32	49	54	37	27	88
Courtelary	37	43	53	26	26	93
La Ferrière	14	74	78	14	15	89
La Heutte	18	61	69	15	12	87
Mont-Tramelan	5	93	94	18	22	93
Tramelan	53	31	38	(18)	(22)	(93)
Orvin	59	29	36	41	25	81
Péry	34	42	55	16	21	86
Plagne	70	21	26	53	46	88
Renan	19	54	65	18	18	88
Romont	35	48	58	19	14	92
St-Imier	27	38	49	25	22	91
Sonceboz-Sombeval	32	39	49	43	38	86
Sonvilier	20	55	66	11	18	89
Vauffelin	35	33	43	43	29	83
Villaret	31	42	52	12	19	92
Total	35	41	50	24	23	90

Note: For Mont-Tramelan and Tramelan the voting behaviour figures (18, 22, 93) are bracketed together as a combined value for both communes.

Appendix C: Table 2. *Continued*

Courtelary district	Citizenship of resident Swiss citizens, 1970			Voting behaviour			Results of plebicites of 7, 14 Sept. and 19 October 1975: % 'Yes' vote
	% Citizens of Bernese Jura	% Citizens of Old Canton	% Citizens of a German-Swiss canton	Results of poll of 5 July 1959: % 'Yes' vote	Results of referendum of 23 June 1974		
					'Yes' vote (%)	Participation (%)	
Bassecourt	74	9	20	85	86	96	
Boécourt	73	11	21	85	87	94	
Bourrignon	70	16	29	76	77	95	
Courfaivre	66	17	29	76	83	94	
Courroux	62	25	33	58	75	94	
Courtételle	69	18	26	81	79	93	
Delémont	57	18	34	67	77	91	
Develier	54	28	41	58	72	94	
Ederswiler	74	17	26	33	45	77	
Glovelier	76	10	20	82	81	97	
Mettemberg	89	11	11	82	94	96	
Montsevelier	83	6	15	89	96	98	
Movelier	78	16	18	53	68	88	
Pleigne	68	19	31	91	94	97	
Rebeuvelier	55	32	44	52	65	89	
Rebévelier	18	80	82	38	35	92	17
Roggenburg	52	21	47	32	24	73	9
Saulcy	88	8	12	88	93	96	
Soulce	81	13	16	76	80	91	
Soyhières	55	17	42	71	67	91	
Undervelier	56	26	43	65	68	98	
Vermes	57	26	39	74	85	89	
Vicques	73	11	23	84	92	93	
Total	64	17	30	72	79	93	10

Appendix C: Table 2. *Continued*

Frenches-Montagnes district	Citizenship of resident Swiss citizens, 1970			Voting behaviour		
	% Citizens of Bernese Jura	% Citizens of Old Canton	% Citizens of a German-Swiss canton	Results of poll of 5 July 1959: % 'Yes' vote	Results of referendum of 23 June 1974 'Yes' vote (%)	Results of referendum of 23 June 1974 Participation (%)
Les Bois	70	15	21	69	70	95
Les Breuleux	86	6	9	82	81	96
La Chaux	76	11	24			
Le Peuchapatte	71	24	29			
Epauvillers	84	14	15	79	86	90
Epiquerez	66	18	19	79	86	90
Goumois	40	25	50	66	69	94
Montfaucon	81	10	16	85	77	95
Les Enfers	86	12	14	77	77	91
Le Noirmont	74	11	18	82	79	93
Les Pommerats	68	28	32	70	75	93
Saignelégier	71	15	21			
Le Bémont	87	12	12			
Muriaux	68	25	29			
St-Brais	88	4	11	74	92	93
Montfavergier	46	29	32	79	83	91
Soubey	66	24	27			
Total	75	13	19	76	77	93

Appendix C: Table 2. *Continued*

Moutier district	Citizenship of resident Swiss citizens, 1970			Voting behaviour			Results of plebicites of 7, 14 Sept. and 19 October 1975: % 'Yes' vote
	% Citizens of Bernese Jura	% Citizens of Old Canton	% Citizens of a German-Swiss canton	Results of poll of 5 July 1959: % 'Yes' vote	Results of referendum of 23 June 1974		
					'Yes' vote (%)	Participation (%)	
Belprahon	38	47	60	17	43	97	
Bévilard	34	44	54	27	34	93	
Champoz	51	41	43	0	5	95	
Châtelat	19	75	79	11	16	98	
Chatillon	79	8	17	88	87	97	90
Corban	75	15	24	83	93	95	97
Corcelles	25	62	75	5	12	94	
Courchapoix	91	6	6	83	97	95	100
Courrendlin	49	23	45	43	62	92	61
Court	31	52	63	30	31	91	
Crémines	30	45	63	20	26	94	
Eschert	20	63	76	8	18	92	
Les Genevez	85	8	9	80	91	93	97
Grandval	32	52	64	21	35	95	1
Lajoux	76	16	23	78	90	96	96
Loveresse	30	56	64	18	19	90	

Malleray	34	40	55	24	30	92	
Mervelier	84	8	15	76	85	93	93
Moutier	40	32	49	33	49	89	46
Perrefitte	30	53	66	24	40	91	1
Pontenet	32	51	57	49	23	96	
Réconvilier	34	45	56	24	23	92	
Roches	26	56	70	24	40	91	
Rossemaison	67	24	32	76	84	93	97
Saicourt	48	43	46	18	30	93	
Saules	32	49	67	25	15	89	
Schelten	—	60	100	33	42	68	
Seehof	2	58	85	0	15	87	
{ Sornetan	34	55	61	} 16	} 30	} 93	
{ Monible	52	41	48				
Sorvilier	30	59	67	46	35	89	
Souboz	37	45	61	19	14	98	
Tavannes	38	40	49	27	29	91	
Vellerat	40	34	50	76	80	100	
Total	42	37	50	34	43	91	91

Appendix C: Table 2. *Continued*

Porrentruy district	Citizenship of resident Swiss citizens, 1970			Voting behaviour		
	% Citizens of Bernese Jura	% Citizens of Old Canton	% Citizens of a German-Swiss canton	Results of poll of 5 July 1959: % 'Yes' vote	Results of referendum of 23 June 1974	
					'Yes' vote (%)	Participation (%)
Alle	82	10	15	72	73	96
Asuel	78	12	20	69	46	96
Beurnevésin	74	16	19	38	65	92
Boncourt	77	10	15	83	86	94
Bonfol	60	25	32	49	50	94
Bressaucourt	66	21	29	54	58	99
Buix	82	6	10	50	63	94
Bure	85	4	11	50	58	97
Charmoille	74	10	16	76	68	96
Chevenez	94	3	5	60	64	93
Coeuve	91	4	7	72	72	97
Cornol	75	15	19	80	73	94
Courchavon	67	19	28	65	59	89
Courgenay	67	21	27	55	55	94
Courtedoux	71	22	24	61	64	95
Courtemaîche	89	8	11	55	67	94
Damphreux	74	17	22	69	63	89
Damvant	77	13	20	67	76	93
Fahy	76	14	20	65	66	91
Fontenais	73	18	22	87	77	93
Frégiécourt	68	23	23	45	63	88

Grandfontaine	85	4	8	88	86	95
Lugnez	77	14	21	63	68	93
Miécourt	49	42	49	56	53	96
Montignez	79	15	16	54	56	95
Ocourt	61	28	35	72	52	89
Pleujouse	93	3	4	60	71	98
Porrentruy	67	14	25	64	68	92
Réclère	87	7	11	73	76	98
Roche d'Or	49	2	2	69	35	93
Rocourt	87	1	4	84	85	91
St-Ursanne	69	14				
Montenol	99	1	25	75	81	93
Montmelon	85	7				
Seleute	74	21	26	63	69	98
Vendlincourt	70	23	25	67	71	97
Total	73	14	21	66	68	94
Total: 6 districts	54	27	37	49	54	92

Source: Swiss Federal Bureau of Statistics

Appendix C: Table 2. *Continued*

Le Neuveville district	Citizenship of resident Swiss citizens, 1970			Voting behaviour		
	% Citizens of Bernese Jura	% Citizens of Old Canton	% Citizens of a German-Swiss canton	Results of poll of 5 July 1959: % 'Yes' vote	Results of referendum of 23 June 1974	
					'Yes' vote (%)	Participation (%)
Diesse	69	22	27	51	46	93
Lamboing	66	20	26	46	36	88
La Neuveville	24	36	57	28	33	86
Nods	63	28	31	54	42	85
Prêles	32	40	62	16	28	84
Total	35	34	51	35	34	87

Appendix C: Table 3. *Results of Simple Regression Analysis of Fourteen Geographical Variables for Eleven Areas of the Bernese Jura (dependent variable: 'Yes' vote in 1974 Jura referendum)*

Area studied with no. of observations	Theory no. 1: % of French-speakers		Theory no. 2: % of Catholics		Theory no. 3: % of Bernese citizens	
	R^2 value	Degree of significance	R^2 value	Degree of significance	R^2 value	Degree of significance
6 French-speaking districts (122)	0·25819	0·001	0·76636	0·0001	0·63609	0·0001
All 7 districts (134)	0·29290	0·005	0·53564	0·0001	0·41361	0·0001
North Jura (67)	0·26518	0·001	0·18378	0·001	0·14724	0·005
South Jura (55)	0·18984	0·001	0·80369	0·0001	0·59026	0·001
Courtelary (17)	0·28026	0·05	0·06011	*	0·42432	0·01
Delémont (23)	0·74849	0·001	0·36431	0·01	0·35927	0·005
Franches-Montagnes (10)	0·20851	0·25	0·21850	0·25	0·08600	*
Moutier (33)	0·20302	0·01	0·91699	0·0001	0·74000	0·001
La Neuveville (5)	0·82667	0·05	0·68369	0·1	0·56379	0·25
Porrentruy (34)	0·09629	0·1	0·17518	0·05	0·10925	0·1
Laufen (12)	0·04778	*	0·48996	0·05	0·20880	0·25

Appendix C: Table 3   *Continued*

Area studied with no. of observations	Theory no. 4: % of other German-Swiss citizens		Theory no. 5: % of total German-Swiss citizens		Theory no. 6: % of Communal citizens	
	R^2 value	Degree of significance	R^2 value	Degree of significance	R^2 value	Degree of significance
6 French-speaking districts (122)	0·07079	0·01	0·58285	0·0001	0·35005	0·001
All 7 districts (134)	0·16019	0·001	0·55456	0·0001	0·23627	0·001
North Jura (67)	0·00521	*	0·12726	0·01	0·07846	0·05
South Jura (55)	0·01824	*	0·48692	0·001	0·42376	0·001
Courtelary (17)	0·04748	*	0·45850	0·01	0·30249	0·05
Delémont (23)	0·10293	0·25	0·49373	0·005	0·13920	0·1
Franches-Montagnes (10)	0·32104	0·1	0·27184	0·25	0·22561	0·25
Moutier (33)	0·04690	0·25	0·62172	0·001	0·52906	0·001
La Neuveville (5)	0·76690	0·1	0·69025	0·1	0·59006	0·25
Porrentruy (34)	0·00053	*	0·08934	0·1	0·09907	0·1
Laufen (12)	0·44183	0·05	0·43296	0·05	0·22747	0·25

Appendix C: Table 3 *Continued*

Area studied with no. of observations	Theory no. 7: % of District citizens		Theory no. 8: % of Jurassian citizens		Theory no. 9: Economic status	
	R^2 value	Degree of significance	R^2 value	Degree of significance	R^2 value	Degree of significance
6 French-speaking districts (122)	0·50366	0·0005	0·65724	0·0001	0·02956	0·05
All 7 districts (134)	0·42488	0·0001	0·59615	0·0001	0·03694	0·05
North Jura (67)	0·09836	0·01	0·21260	0·005	0·00006	*
South Jura (55)	0·43109	0·001	0·56362	0·01	0·00001	*
Courtelary (17)	0·35869	0·05	0·36755	0·01	0·01919	*
Delémont (23)	0·16264	0·1	0·44484	0·005	0·08563	0·25
Franches-Montagnes (10)	0·22135	0·25	0·32552	0·10	0·28787	0·25
Moutier (33)	0·54296	0·001	0·65596	0·001	0·00827	*
La Neuveville (5)	0·55658	0·25	0·64944	0·1	0·91653	0·05
Porrentruy (34)	0·21029	0·01	0·32735	0·005	0·00234	*
Laufen (12)	0·31695	0·1	0·44466	0·05	0·08743	*

Appendix C: Table 3 *Continued*

Area studied with no. of observations	Theory no. 10: 13-year population change		Theory no. 11: Recent (3-year) population change		Theory no. 12: Agriculturalness	
	R^2 value	Degree of significance	R^2 value	Degree of significance	R^2 value	Degree of significance
6 French-speaking districts (122)	0·00068	*	0·04093	0·05	0·00001	*
All 7 districts (134)	0·01250	0·25	0·00164	*	0·00472	*
North Jura (67)	0·02347	0·25	0·02134	0·25	0·06601	0·05
South Jura (55)	0·01760	*	0·02832	0·25	0·00903	*
Courtelary (17)	0·10379	0·25	0·09217	0·25	0·15108	0·25
Delémont (23)	0·02688	*	0·01574	*	0·20002	0·05
Franches-Montagnes (10)	0·09790	*	0·39248	0·01	0·28334	0·25
Moutier (33)	0·03408	*	0·14208	0·05	0·05048	0·25
La Neuveville (5)	0·54375	*	0·63376	0·25	0·02377	*
Porrentruy	0·01284	*	0·01013	*	0·11870	0·05
Laufen (12)	0·00008	*	0·01246	*	0·00006	*

Appendix C: Table 3   *Continued*

Area studied with no. of observations	Theory no. 13: Distance from Berne		Theory no. 14: Altitude above Berne	
	R^2 value	Degree of significance	R^2 value	Degree of significance
6 French-speaking districts (122)	0·25051	0·001	0·09874	0·1
All 7 districts (134)	0·01682	0·25	0·02451	0·01
North Jura (67)	0·04538	0·1	0·01116	*
South Jura (55)	0·00093	*	0·09323	0·05
Courtelary (17)	0·16906	0·25	0·02672	*
Delémont (23)	0·01730	*	0·01398	*
Franches-Montagnes (10)	0·13615	*	0·00010	*
Moutier (33)	0·21473	0·01	0·10735	0·1
La Neuveville (5)	0·02377	*	0·15106	*
Porrentruy	0·01244	*	0·09754	*
Laufen (12)	0·20495	0·25	0·10586	*

* Indicates that the degree of significance falls below 0·25.

Appendix C: Table 4. *Varimax Rotated Factor Matrix for the Six French-speaking Districts of the Bernese Jura (122 observations)*

Independent variable	Factor 1 (Authochthonism)	Factor 2 (Culture)	Factor 3 (Pastoralization)	Factor 4 (Depopulation–Alienation)
FR	0·50979	−0·38597	0·52459	0·07583
CA	0·90252	−0·06233	−0·07035	0·12605
EC	−0·14594	−0·51410	−0·11737	0·04805
PC1	−0·15333	−0·42784	−0·05867	0·35810
PC2	−0·07837	−0·11476	0·02734	0·98878
DIS	0·26039	0·03260	−0·01182	0·49046
AG	−0·07363	0·82968	−0·13934	0·05847
HT	−0·41962	0·35214	0·24005	−0·15958
CC	0·68508	0·26282	0·30863	0·04762
CD	0·85660	0·17437	0·35792	0·04032
CJ	0·92833	0·06885	0·34100	0·03930
COC	−0·95754	0·05515	−0·11819	0·01016
COGC	−0·31801	−0·11550	−0·75369	−0·01781
CTGC	−0·90859	0·00844	−0·37416	0·00143
Transformation matrix				
Factor 1	0·93581	0·04315	0·34746	0·04084
Factor 2	0·04361	−0·79000	−0·09046	0·60483
Factor 3	0·01179	0·61043	−0·19771	0·76690
Factor 4	−0·34959	0·03753	0·91214	0·21065

Table 5. *Results of a Regression of Separatist Factors on 'Yes' Vote in 1974 Referendum: Bernese Jura and Subregions*

Area studied with no. of observations	Major factors which appear to be related to Jura separatism	Individual R² values	Degree of significance
All 7 districts (134)	Autochthonism (F1)	0·42800	0·001
	Culture (F2)	0·10422	0·005
6 French-speaking districts (122)	Autochthomism (F1)	0·60552	0·0001
North Jura (67)	Autochthonism (F1)	0·17220	0·005
South Jura (55)	Autochthonism (F1)	0·58388	0·001
Courtelary (17)	Autochthonism (F1)	0·37262	0·05
Delémont (23)	Autochthonism (F1)	0·22982	0·05
	Pastoralism (F2)	0·10857	0·05
Franches-Montagnes (10)	(NSF)	(NSF)	(NSF)
Moutier (33)	Autochthonism (F1)	0·33266	0·005
La Neuveville (5)	(NSF)	(NSF)	(NSF)
Porrentruy (34)	Autochthonism (F1)	0·08489	0·1
Laufen 912)	(NSF)	(NSF)	(NSF)

(NSF) Indicates no significant findings.

Appendix C: Table 6.   *Step-wise Regressions of 'Separatist Factor' on 'Yes' Vote in 1974 Referendum: Bernese Jura and Subregions*

Area studied with no. of observations	Factor	R² Values	Degree of significance
All 7 districts (134)	1. Autochthonism	0·42800	0·001
	2. All factors (4)	0·51037	0·1
6 French-speaking districts (122)	1. Autochthonism	0·60552	0·0001
	2. +Culture	0·68946	0·001
	3. All factors (4)	0·71542	*
North Jura (67)	1. Autochthonism	0·17220	0·005
	2. +Depopulation	0·23875	0·01
	3. All factors (5)	0·27570	*
South Jura (55)	1. Autochthonism	0·58388	0·001
	2. +Depopulation– Alienation	0·60077	0·25
	3. All factors (4)	0·61916	0·25
Courtelary (17)	1. Autochthonism	0·37262	0·05
	2. All factors (3)	0·46623	*
Delémont (23)	1. Autochthonism	0·22982	0·05
	2. Pastoralism	0·38402	0·05
	3. All factors (3)	0·9059	*
Franches-Montagnes (10)	(NSF)	**	—
Moutier (33)	1. Autochthonism	0·33266	0·005
	2. +Depopulation	0·66976	0·001
	3. All factors (3)	0·77456	0·005
La Neuveville (5)	(NSF)	**	—
Porrentruy (34)	1. Autochthonism	0·08489	0·1
	2. All factors (3)	0·30654	0·25
Laufen (12)	(NSF)	**	—

(NSF) Indicates no significant findings.
  * Indicates that the degree of significance falls below 0·25.
 ** Indicates R² value is extremely low.

BIBLIOGRAPHY

Amman, H. and Schibm, K. (1959). *Historischer Atlas der Schweiz*, H. R. Sauerlander, Aarau.

Amweg, G. (1928). *Bibliographie du Jura bernois*, le Jura, Porrentruy.

Amweg, G. (revised by Prongué, B.) (1974). *Histoire populaire du Jura bernois*, Éditions jurassiennes, Porrentruy.

Anderson, G. (1966). Voting Behaviour and the Ethnic-Religious Variable: A Study of the Election in Hamilton, Ontario, *Canadian Journal of Economics and Political Science*, Vol. 32, 27–37.

Archer, J. See Reynolds and Archer.

Armattoe, R. (1944). *The Swiss Contribution to Western Civilization*, Dundalgan Press, Dundalk.

Association romande pour la défence de la langue française (ed.) (1975). *Menace sur la frontière des langues*, Neuchâtel.

Aubry, G. *et al.* (1977). *Jura bernois, 1952–1977: dans le sens de l'histoire: vingt-cinq ans de lutte*, Force démocratique, Tavannes.

Aubry, G. (1977). *Le Temps des imposteurs*, Éditions Agecopresse, Tavannes.

Aubry, G. (1978). Konfession und Kirchen im Jura heute, *Jura-Perspektiven*, Evangelische Zeigschaft für Kultur und Politik, Vol. 27, 311–48.

Aubry, G. (1983). *Sous la coupole pas sous la coupe!*, Éditions Agecopresse, Tavannes.

Avebury, Lord (1906). *The Scenery of Switzerland and the Causes to Which it is Due*, Macmillan, London.

Auf dem Weg zum Kanton Jura (1978). *Politische Rundschau* Vol. 57, 1–37. Special issue on the new canton by several contributors.

Bandelier, A. *et al.* (1973). *Bibliographie jurassienne 1928–1972*, Société jurassienne, Porrentruy.

Banks, J. C. (1971). *Federal Britain?* Harrap, London.

Barber, B. (1974). *The Death of Communal Liberty: A History of Freedom in a Swiss Mountain Canton*, Princetown University Press, Princeton.

Bassand, M. (1975). The Jura Problem, *Journal of Peace Research*, Vol. 2, 139–50.

Bassand, M. and Fragnière, J. (1976). *Les Ambiguités de jurassiennes*, Éditions Georgi, St-Saphorin.

Bassand, M., D'Epinay, C., and Thoma, P. (1976). *Un essai de démocratie culturelle: le centre culturel jurassien*, Herbert Lang, Berne.

Baumlin, K. and Altermatt, U. (eds.) (1978). *Jura-Perspektiven, Evangelische Zeigschaft für Kultur und Politik*, Vol. 27, 232–35.

Baumlin, R., Borel, A., Favre, A., and Steinlin, C. (1971). *Expertise sur une autonomie scolaire jurassienne*, Conseil-exécutif du canton de Berne, Berne.

Bax, B. (1966). *The Rise and Fall of the Anabaptists*, American Scholar Publications, New York.

Becquet, C. (1963). *L'Éthnie française d'Europe*, Nouvelles éditions latines, Paris.

Beer, G. de (1949). *Travellers in Switzerland*, Oxford University Press, London.

Béguelin, R. and Schaffter, R. (1964). *Berne à l'heure du choix*, Rassemblement jurassien, Delémont.

Béguelin, R. (1967). *L'Autodétermination*, Rassemblement jurassien, Delémont.

201

Béguelin, R. (1968). *Les Voies de la négociation*, Rassemblement jurassien, Delémont.

Béguelin, R. (1972). *Le Réveil du peuple jurassien: 1947–50*, Rassemblement jurassien, Delémont.

Béguelin, R. (1973). *Un faux témoin: la Suisse* (second edition), Éditions du Monde, Paris.

Béguelin, R. (1978). Speech at Thirty-first fête du peuple jurassien, Delémont, 30 September 1978.

Béguelin, R. and Charpilloz, A. (1982). *Les Racines de l'unité jurassienne*, Rassemblement jurassien, Delémont.

Béguelin, R. and Schaffter, R. (1974). *L'autodisposition du peuple jurassien et ses conséquences*, Rassemblement jurassien, Delémont.

Béguin, P. (1948). *Le Balcon sur l'Europe*, La Baconnière, Neuchâtel.

Bernel, A. (1955). *Le Droit du code civil française applicable au Jura bernois*, Fornara, Geneva.

Bender, H. (1970). *The Anabaptists and Religious Library in the Sixteenth Century*, Historical Series No. 16, Facet Books, Fortress Press, Philadelphia.

Berne, government of (1969). *Planungsatlas 1: Bevölkerungsstatistik*, Kantonales Planungsamt, Berne.

Berne, government of (1970). *Planungsatlas 2: Wirtschaft 1*, Kantonales Planungsamt, Berne.

Berne, government of (1973). *Planungsatlas 3: Historische Planungsgrundlagen*, Kantonales Planungsamt/Universität Bern, Berne.

Bessire, P. (revised by Prongué, B.) (1977). *Histoire du Jura bernois et de l'ancien évêché de Bâle*, Éditions de la Prévôté, Moutier.

Bez, J. du (1977). *Brins de malice et grains de sel* (second edition), W. Gassmann, Bienne.

Bezirkskommission Laufental. (1976). *Das Laufental: Eine Bestandesaufnahme*, Volksfreund, Lauten.

Bezirkskommission Laufental. (1978). *Erggänzender Bericht der Bezirkskommission Laufental*, Volksfreund, Laufen.

Bickel, W. (1947). *Bevölkerungsgeschichte und Bevölkerungspolitik der Schweiz seit dem Ausgang des Mittelälters*, Buchergilde Gutenberg, Zurich.

Bickel, W. (1973). *Die Volkswirtschaft der Schweiz*, Säuerlander Verlag, Aarau.

Bietenholz, P. (1971). *Basle and France in the Sixteenth Century*, University of Toronto Press, Toronto.

Billigmaier, R. (1950). Aspects of the Cultural History of the Romansh People of Switzerland, unpublished Ph.D. thesis, Stanford University.

Billigmaier, R. (1979). A crisis in Swiss Pluralism: The Romansh and their Relations with the German- and Italian-Swiss in the Perspective of a Millenium, Mouton, The Hague.

Blache, V. de la (ed. de Martonne, E.) (1959). *Principles of Human Geography*, Constable, London.

Blasier, C. (1966). Power and Social Change in Colombia: The Cauca Valley, *Journal of Inter-American Studies*, Vol. 8, 366–410.

Boesch, H. and Hofer, P. (1963). *Villes Suisses à vol d'oiseau*, Kummerly and Frey, Berne.

Bogdanor, V. (1979). *Devolution*, Oxford University Press, Oxford.

Bonjour, E. (1946). *Swiss Neutrality: Its History and Meaning*, George Allen and Unwin, London.

Bonjour, E., Offler, H., and Potter, G. (1970). *A Short History of Switzerland*, Clarendon Press, Oxford.

Bonnaud-Delamere, R. (1966). L'Immigration helvétique dans les principautés de Murbach et de Lure après la guerre de trente ans, *Annales litteraires de l'Université de Besançon*, Vol. 76, 72–89.

Bottinelli, P. (1978). *Ma question jurassienne*, Éditions Publipress, Bienne.

Bouquet, J. (1975). Pays de Vaud et évêché de Bâle en 1814: le problème de la compensation, *Revue Suisse d'histoire* Vol. 25, 88–120.

Breton, R. (1970). The Geography of Languages as a basis for the Geography of 'Ethnies', *21st International Geographic Congress: Selected Papers*, Vol. 3, Calcutta.

Breton, R. (September–October, 1975). La Place de la géographie des langues, *Annales de Géographie*, No. 465, Librairie Armand Colin, Paris.

Bridel, M. (1952). *La Démocratie directe dans les communes suisses*, Polygraphischer Verlag, Zurich.

Brocard, A. (pref) (1977). *Une centenaire; la ligne CFF Delémont–Delle: 1877–1977*, Éditions jurassiennes, Porrentruy.

Brooks, R. (1918). *Government and Politics in Switzerland*, World Book Co., New York.

Brooks, R. (1930). *Civic Training in Switzerland: A Study of Democratic Life*, University of Chicago Press.

Brown, L. (1969). Spatial Competition, Information Flows and Opinions: *Proceedings of the Annual Meeting of the American Political Science Association*, New York.

Burckhardt, W. (1931). *Kommentar der Schweizerschen Bundesverfassung, vom 29. Mai 1874* (Third edition), Stämpfli, Berne.

Burschweiler, C. (1939). *Bilder zur Bevölkerungsgeschichte, in Die Schweiz im Spiegel der Landesausstellung*, Vol. 1, Atlantis Verlag, Zurich.

Burger, M. (1969). A propos de la limite norde du francoprovençal, *Colloque de dialectologie francoprovençal Neuchâtel*, Faculté des lettres, Neuchâtel, Libraire Droz, Geneva.

Busteed, M. (1972). Northern Ireland: Geographical Aspects of a Crisis, School of Geography Research Paper No. 3, Oxford University.

Busteed, M. (1975). *Geography and Voting Behaviour*, Oxford University Press, London.

Campbell, D. B. (1980). Nationalism, Religion and the Bases of Conflict in the Swiss Jura, in W. Chandler and M. Fleming, (eds), *Proceedings of the Workshop on the Smaller European Democracies and European–Canadian Comparisons*, European Politics Group, London, Ontario.

Carter, H. and Thomas, U. (1969). The Referendum on the Sunday opening of Licensed Premises in Wales as a criterion of a Culture Region, *Regional Studies*, Vol. 3, 61–71.

Chancellerie d'État, Berne (1963). *Rapport du conseil-exécutif du canton de Berne sur l'évolution des relations de l'état de Berne avec la partie jurassienne du canton*, Berne.

Chancellerie d'État, Berne (1974). *Constitution du canton de Berne*, Berne.

Chancellerie d'État, Berne (1979). *Constitution du canton de Berne* (contains modifications resulting from the establishment of Canton Jura), Berne.

Chancellerie de la Constituante jurassienne (1978). *Jura: votre avenir*, Delémont.

Charpilloz, A. (1976). *Le Jura irlandisé* (second edition), Éditions Bertil Galland, Vevey.

Charpilloz, A. and Grimm-Gobat (1982). *La Romandie dominée*, Favre, Lausanne.

Chorley, R. and Haggett, P. (eds.) (1969). *Progress in Geography*, St Martin's Press, New York.

Chorley, R. and Haggett, P. (1970). *Network Analysis in Geography*, St Martin's Press, New York.

Christe, J. (1975). *A cârre di füe (Au coin du feu)*, Éditions Pro Jura, Delémont.

Claude, I. L. (1955). *National Minorities: An International Problem*, Greenwood Press, New York.

Claus, P. (1972). *Anabaptism: A Social History: 1525–1816*, Cornell University Press, Ithaca.

Clout, H. (ed.) (1975). *Regional Development in Western Europe*, John Wiley, London.

Clout, H. (1976). *The Regional Problem in Western Europe*, Cambridge University Press, Cambridge.

Codding, G. (1961). *The Federal Government of Switzerland*, Riverside Press, Cambridge, Mass.

Cole, J. and Wolfe, E. (1974). *The Hidden Frontier: Ecology and Ethnicity in an Alpine Valley*, Academic Press, New York.

Comité de coördination et d'action contre l'éclatement du Jura (1974). *Message aux citoyennes et citoyens du district de Moutier*, Moutier.

Comité de Moutier (1948). *La Question jurassienne présenteé au gouvernement du canton de Berne*, Delémont.

Comment, A., Huber, H., and von Greyerz, H. (1948). *Gutachten Über die Vereingungurkunde des Jura mit dem Kanton Berne an den Regierungsrat des Kantons Bern*, Staatskanzlei des Kantons Bern, Berne.

Conseil-exécutif du canton de Berne (1963). *Rapport sur l'évolution des relations de l'État de Berne avec la partie jurassienne du canton*, Berne.

Conseil-exécutif du canton de Berne (1968). *Rapport de la commission des 24 sur les données actuelles du problème jurassien*, Berne.

Conseil-exécutif du canton de Berne (19 September 1972). *Rapport sur la création de régions de l'aménagement du statut du Jura*, Berne.

Conseil-exécutif du canton de Berne (1972). *Évolution des relations financières de l'état cantonal bernois avec ses régions*, St Gallen.

Coupland, R. (1954). *Welsh and Scottish Nationalism*, Collins, London.

Cox, K. (1968). Suburbia and Voting Behaviour in the London Metropolitan Area. *Annals of the Association of American Geographers*, Vol. 58, 111–27.

Cox, K. (1969). The Voting Decision in a Spatial Context, *Progress in Geography*, Vol. 1, London.

Coxe, W. (1780). *Sketches of the Natural, Civil and Political State of Switzerland in a Series of Letters*, Cadell, London.

Crevoisier, J. and Béguelin, R. (1980). *La Question jurassien en 1980*, Rassemblement jurassien, Delémont.

Crone, G. (1967). *Background in Political Geography*, Dufour, Chester Springs, Pennsylvania.

Crossland, N. (1979). The Everlasting League: A Survey of Switzerland, *The Economist*, 3 February.

Dellenbach, E. (1966). *Violence au pays des grandes joux*, Imprimerie du Progrès, Tramelan.

Deutsch, K. (1942). The Trend of European Nationalism: The Language Aspect, *American Political Science Review*, Vol. 36, 533–41.

Deutsch, K. (1963). *The Nerves of Government*, Free Press, London.

Deutsch, K. (1969). *Nationalism and Its Alternatives*, Alfred Knopf, New York.

Deutsch, K. (1975). *Nationalism and Social Communication* (second edition), MIT Press, Cambridge, Mass.

Deutsch, K. (1976). *Die Schweitz als ein paradigmatischer Fall politischer Integration*, P. Haupt, Berne.

Deutsch, K. and Weilenmann, H. (1965). The Swiss City Canton: A Political Invention, *Comparative Studies in Sociology and History*, Vol. 3, 393–408.

Deutsch, K. and Foltz, W. (eds.) (1966). *Nation-Building*, Atherton Press, New York.

Deutsch, K. and Merritt, R. (1970). *Nationalism and National Development: An Interdisciplinary Biography* (second edition), MIT Press, Cambridge, Mass.

Diem, A. (1979) *Western Europe: A Geographical Analysis*, Wiley, New York.

Doka, C. (1973). *Switzerland's Four National Languages*, Pro Helvetia, Zurich.

Doka, C. (1973). *Switzerland in its Cultural, Social and Political Aspects*, Pro Helvetia, Zurich.

Domeniconi, R. (1968). *Le Jura en chiffres et graphiques*, Rassemblement jurassien, Delémont.

Domeniconi, R. (1974). *Jura: le plébiscite du 23 juin 1974*, Rassemblement jurassien, Delémont.

Domeniconi, R. (1978). *Le Canton de Jura: statistiques, graphiques 1970–1975*, Assemblée constituante de la République et canton du Jura, Delémont.

Domestici, R. (1969) La Question jurassienne, Mimeographed DES thesis, University of Nice.

DuBois, P. (ed.) (1983). *Union et division des Suisses: les relations entre alémaniques, romands et tessinois aux XIXe et XXe siècles*, Editions de l'Aire, Lausanne.

Earle, E. (ed.). (1950). *Nationalism and Internationalism*, Columbia University Press, New York.

East, G. (1937). The Nature of Political Geography, *Politica*, Vol. 2, 259–86.

East, G. (1948). *The Geography Behind History*, Thomas Nelson, London.

East, G. (1960). The Geography of Land-Locked States, *Transactions and Papers, Institute of British Geographers*, Vol. 28, 1–22.

East, G. (1962). *A Historical Geography of Europe* (fourth edition), Thomas Nelson, London.

Egger, E. and Blanc, É. (1974). *Education in Switzerland*, Swiss Educational Documentation Centre, Geneva.

Ehinger, P. (ed.). (1977). La Question du Jura dans l'optique radicale, *Revue politique, économique et culturelle*, Vol. 56, 1.

Ernst, F. (Transl. Palmer, C.) (1951). *European Switzerland, Historically Considered*, Fretz and Wasmuth, Zurich.

Esman, M. J. (ed.) (1977). *Ethnic Conflict in the Western World*, Cornell University Press, Ithaca.

Estall, R. and Buchanan, R. (1973). *Industrial Activity and Economic Geography*, Hutchinson, London.

Ezekiel, M. and Fox, K. (1959). *Methods of Correlation and Regression Analysis* (third Edition), Wiley, New York.

Fabre, D. (transl. Lloyd, J.) (1961). *Switzerland*, Viking Press, New York.

Fallet, M. (1930). *Les Origins de l'industrie de la montre dans le Jura bernois actuel*, La Bonne Presse du Jura, Porrentruy.

Federal Government of Switzerland (1969). *Premier rapport de la commission confédérée de bons offices pour le Jura*, Berne.

Fell, R. (1964). Les Grands Problèmes ferroviaires, *Intérêts du Jura*, Vol. 35, 132–50.

Fell, R. (1976). *Un Canton du Jura: pourquoi?*, Rassemblement jurassien, Delémont.

Feller, R. (1965). *Wie der Jura Bernisch würde (1918)*, Paul Haupt, Berne.

Fishman, J. (1970). *Sociolinguistics*, Newbury House, Rowley, Massachusetts.

Fishman, J. (1972). *The Sociology of Language*, Newbury House, Rowley, Massachusetts.

Fishman, J. (1972). *Language and Nationalism: Two Integrative Essays*, Newbury House, Rowley, Massachusetts.

Fleure, H. (1941). Notes on the Evolution of Switzerland, *Geography*, Vol. 26, 169–77.

Fleury, R. (1968). *L'Affaire Fleury*, Éditions Jura, Porrentruy.

Flückiger, F. (24 February, 1977). Unité jurassienne? Notion de 'peuple' et celle d'"état', (Talk delivered to *L'Association des amis du Jura bernois*, Berne.)

Force démocratique (1976). *Aux autorités des cantons suisses de la Conféderation*, Tavannes.

Force démocratique (1976). *Les Événements de Moutier: 1–8 Septembre, 1975*, Tavannes.

Force démocratique (1977). *Dans le sens de l'histoire: vingt-cinq ans de lutte*, Moutier.

Forster, P., Zimmerman, H., Frei, O., and Müller, K. (1974). *Schwierige Selbstbestimmung im Jura: Hintergründe eines Minderheitenproblems*, Buchverlag Neue Zürcher Zeitung, Zurich.

Frei, O. and Müller, K. (1965). *Der Hintergründe der Jurakrise*, Buchverlag Neue Zürcher Zeitung, Zurich.

Frei, O. (1970). Der Jura—Konflikt in der Schweiz, *Monat*, Vol. 22, 56–61.

Friedrich, C. and Cole, T. (1967). *Responsible Bureaucracy: A Study of the Swiss Civil Service* (second edition), Russell and Russell, New York.

Froidevaux, A. (1977). *Dossier sur l'assemblée constituante de la république et canton du Jura*, Société jurassienne d'émulation, Porrentruy.

Froidevaux, C. (1977). *Roland Béguelin, ou la conscience du Jura*, Pierre M. Favre Publications, Lausanne.

Froidevaux, L. (1962). *Mes quatorze jours de prison*, Éditions du Jura Libre, Delémont.

Früh, J. (1932). *Geographie de Schweiz* (3 Volumes), Buchdruckerei Zollikofen, St. Gallen.

Furer, J. (1982). *Romanche: du bilingualisme à la fin de la discrimination*, Institute de science politique de l'université, Lausanne.

Ganser, K. (1966). A Division of the City of Munich into Social Areas by means of Voting Behaviour of Political Electors, *Münchener geographische Hefte*, Vol. 28, 87–103.

Gasser, A. (1977). *Der Jura und der Kanton Bern*, Buchdruckerei Volksfreund, Laufen.

Gasser, A. (1978). *Berne et le Jura: 1815–1977*, Éditions Imprimerie Fédérative, Berne.

Gautschi, K. (1973). *An Outline History of Switzerland*, Pro Helvetia, Zurich.

Geiger, P. and Weiss, R. (1973). *Atlas de folklore suisse*, Société suisse des traditions populaires, Basle.

Gerber, S. (ed.) (1978). *Informations-Blätter: Schweizerischer Verein fur Täufergeschichte*, Isaac Zurcher, Berne.

Gieré, G. (1956). *Die Rechtsstellung des Rätoromanischen in der Schweiz*, Keller, Winterhur.

Gilg, P. (1974). Die Entwicklung der Jurafrage seit 1947, *Reformatio* 23, 274–7.

Gilliard, C. (transl. Hartley, D.) (1955). *A History of Switzerland*, George Allen and Unwin, London.

Girard, B. (1976). *Renaissance d'un état*. Éditions Naiade, Porrentruy.

Girod, R. Allardt, E. and Littunen, Y. (eds.) (1964). *Geography of the Swiss Party System in Cleavages, Ideologies and Party Systems*, Helsinki.

Glanville, T. (1970). Spatial Biases in Electoral Distribution, unpublished thesis, University of Melbourne.

Goguel-Nyegaard, F. (1951). *Géographie des élections françaises de 1890 à 1951*, Librairie Armand Colin, Paris.

Goodey, B. (1968). The Geography of Elections: *An Introductory Bibliography, Monograph No. 3*, Centre for the Study of Cultural and Social Change, University of North Dakota.

Gottman, J. (1952). *La Politique des états et leur géographie*, Librairie Armand Colin, Paris.

Gottman, J. (1969). *A Geography of Europe* (fourth edition), Holt Rinehart, Winston, New York.

Gottman, J. (1973). *The Significance of Territory*, University Press Of Virginia, Charlottesville, Virginia.

Graedel, A. (1950). La Question jurassienne, in *Die Schweiz* (yearbook of the New Helvetic Society), 43–58.

Gregor, D. B. (1982). *Romontsch: Language and Literature*, The Oleander Press, Cambridge.

Grosjean, R. and Domericoni, R. (eds.) (1970). *La Question jurassienne: documents*, Rassemblement jurassien, Delémont.

Groupe bélier (ed.) (1969). *Jura en marche*, Porrentruy.

Groupe bélier (1976). *République et canton du Jura: lignes directrices pour l'élaboration de la constitution*, Porrentruy.

Gruner, E. (1943). *Das bernische Patriziat und die Regeneration*, Herbert Lang, Berne.

Gruner, E. (1968). Die Jurafrage als Problem der Minderheit in der schweizerischen Demokratie, *Civitas*, Vol. 17, 523–37.

Gunzinger, C. and Moine, D. (1976). *L'Assemblée constituante jurassienne*, Éditions du Brise-Vent, Delémont.

Gutersohn, H. (1958). *Geographie der Schweiz in drei Bänden: Vol. 1: Jura*, Kummerly and Frey, Berne.

Haggett, P. and Chorley, R. (eds.) (1967). *Models in Geography*, Methuen, London.

Haggett, P. (1975). *Geography: A Modern Synthesis* (second edition), Harper and Row, London.

Hanhart, J. (1978). *Jura total: ses 1326 ans d'histoire et de civilisation*, Éditions de la Prévôté, Moutier.

Harder, H. (1978). *Der Kanton Jura: Ursachen und Schritte zur Losung eines Schweizer Minderheitenproblems*, Peter Lang, Frankfurt.

Hay, A. (1970). La Suisse romande dans l'économie suisse, *Revue économique et sociale*, Vol. 28, 9–14.

Hechter, M. (1974). The Political Economy of Ethnic Change, *The American Journal of Sociology*, Vol. 79, 1151–78.

Hegnauer, C. (1947). *Das Sprachenrecht der* Schweiz, Schultess, Zurich.

Henchoz, P. (1969). *Mirages sur la Suisse*, la Baconnière, Neuchâtel.

Henecka, H. P. (1974a). *Die jurassischen Separatisten, Studia Ethnologica, Vol. 3*, Verlag Anton Hain, Meisenheim.

Henecka, H. P. (1974b). Der Jurakonflikt gesehen, *Reformatio*, Vol. 23, 257–74.

Henry, R. (1906). *La Suisse et la question des langues*, Stampfli, Berne.

Herak, M. and Stringfield, V. T. (eds.) (1972). *Karst Areas of the Northern Hemisphere*, Elsevier, Amsterdam.

Héraud, G. (1963). *L'Europe des ethnies*, Presses d'Europe, Paris.

Héraud, G. (1973) *Contre les états: les régions d'Europe*, Presses d'Europe, Paris.

Héraud, G. and Béguelin, R. (1965). *Europe–Jura: 150ᵉ anniversaire du Congrès de Vienne*, Rassemblement jurassien, Delémont.

Herold, C. (1948). *The Swiss Without Haloes*, Columbia University Press, New York.

Hoover, E. (1948). *The Location of Economic Activity*, McGraw-Hill, New York.

Hotzenköcherle, R. and Trüb, R. (1962). *Sprachatlas der deutschen Schweiz: Band 1*, Francke Verlag, Berne.

Houston, J. (1953). *A Social Geography of Europe*, Duckworth, London.

Huber, H. (1968). *How Switzerland is Governed*, Schweizer Spiegel Verlag, Zurich.

Huber, H. (1963). Routes jurassiennes, *Intérêts du Jura*, Vol. 34, 222–9.

Hudson, J. C. (1972). Geographical Diffusion Theory, *Northwestern University Studies in Geography, No. 19*, Evanston, Illinois.

Hughes, C. (1954). *The Federal Constitution of Switzerland*, The Clarendon Press, Oxford.

Hughes, C. (1962). *The Parliament of Switzerland*, Cassell, for the Hansard Society, London.

Hughes, C. (1975). *Switzerland*, Ernest Benn, London.

Huguelet, F. (1967). *Pourquoi je suis autonomiste* (second edition), Rassemblement jurassien, Delémont.

Hürlimann, M. (1931). *Die Schweiz*, Atlantis Verlag, Zurich.

Imhof, E. *et al.* (1965–78). *Atlas de la Suisse*, Service topographique fédéral, Wabern-Berne.

Inglehart, R. and Woodward, M. (1977). Language Conflicts and Political Community, *Comparative Studies in Society and History*, Vol. 10, 27–45.

Jackson, W. and Samuels, M. (eds.) (1971). *Politics and Geographic Relationships* (second edition), Prentice-Hall, Englewood Cliffs, New Jersey.

Jackson, W. and Bergmann, E. (1973). *A Geography of Politics*, W. C. Brown, Dubuque, Iowa.

Jacquet, N. (1969) *Die Jura-Frage als gesamtschweizerische Angelegenheit*, Basler Berichthaus, Basle.

Jeanrenaud, E. (1953). L'Horlogerie à St-Imier, *Intérêts du Jura*, Vol. 24, 153–8.

Jenkins, J. R. G. (1980). A Geographic Study of Jura Separatism in Canton Berne, Switzerland, and Its Implications for the Swiss Confederation, 2 vols., unpublished D.Phil. Dissertation, University of Oxford.

Jobin, A. (1964). *La Question jurassienne*, La Chaux-de-Fonds, Madeleine Jacot.

Jordan, T. (1973). *The European Culture Area: A Systematic Geography*, Harper and Row, New York.

Joy, R. (1972). *Languages in Conflict: The Canadian Experience*, The Carlton Library, No. 61, McClelland and Stewart, Toronto.

Junod, R. (1974). La latinité du Jura-Sud-est en danger, in Béguelin R. and Schaffter, R. *L'Autodisposition du peuple jurassien et ses conséquences*, Rassemblement jurassien, Delémont.

'Le Jura bernois se présente'. (1979). Special issue of the *Journal du Jura*, Biel/Bienne, 25 August.

Jura-Sud Autonome (ed.) (1975). *Les Relations financières entre le Jura-Sud et l'état de Berne*, La Neuveville.

Kamer, P. (1975). *Switzerland: Geography, History, State* (second edition), Pro Helvetia, Zurich.

Kasperson, R. and Minghi, J. (1969). *The Structure of Political Geography*, Aldine Publishing Co., Chicago.

Kendrew, W. (1957). *Climatology* (second edition), Oxford University Press, London.

Kendrew, W. (1953). *The Climates of the Continents* (fourth edition), Oxford University Press, London.

Kerr, H. H. (1974). *Switzerland: Social Cleavages and Partisan Conflict*, Sage, London and Beverly Hills.

Klassen, W. (1973). *Anabaptism: Neither Catholic nor Protestant*, Conrad Press, Waterloo, Ontario.

Kohler, F. and Prongué, B. (1974). La Députation jurassienne: 1922–1974, *Les Intérêts du Jura*, Vol. 45, 256–84.

Kohn, H. (1956). *Nationalism and Liberty: The Swiss Example*, Allen and Unwin, London.

Kreisel, W. (1974). Zum Problem der Waldhufen-Siedlungen am Beispiel des schweizer Juras, *Geographica Helvetica*, Berne, Vol. 29, 97–108.

Kristol, A. (1976). La Densité des liaisons matrimoniales le long de la frontière entre le français et le francoprovençal dans le Jura suisse, *Vox Romanica*, Vol. 35, 51–83.

Kubly, H. (1964). *Switzerland*, Life World Library, New York.

Laubscher, O. (1945). *Die Entwicklung der Bevölkerung im Berner Jura insbesondere seit 1850.* Neuenschwandetsche Verlagsbuchhandlung, Weinfelden.

Lebau, R. (1975). *La Suisse*, Masson, Paris.

Leeman, W. (1939). *Landeskunde der Schweiz*, Eugen Rentsch, Zurich.

Lejeune, Y. (1978). La Secession du nouveau canton du Jura aux traits internationaux du canton de Berne, *Revue générale de droit international public*, Vol. 82, 1051–74.

Lewis, P. E. (1965). The Impact of Negro Migration on the Electoral Geography of Flint, Michigan: 1932–1962: A Cartographic Analysis, *Annals of the Association of American Geographers*, Vol. 55, 1–25.

Ligia Romontscha/Lia Rumantscha (1980). Eingabe an den schweitzerischen Bundesrat, Chur.

Lijphart, A. (1973) Linguistic Fragmentation and Other Dimensions of Cleavage, Paper presented at the Ninth World Congress of the International Political Science Association, Montreal, 1973.

Lebsiger, G. (1968). La Population suisse dans son cadre naturel et politique, unpublished doctoral thesis, University of Grenoble.

Luck, J. M. (ed.) (1978). *Modern Switzerland*, Society for the Promotion of Science and Scholarship, Palo Alto, California.

Lugon, C. (1983). *Quand la Suisse française s'éveillera*, Perret-Gentil, Geneva.

Lunn, Sir A. (1963). *The Swiss and Their Mountains*, Rand McNally, Chicago.

Lüthy, H. (1966). Politische Problem der Mehrsprachigkeit in der Schweiz, *Civitas*, Vol. 5, 39–47.

Lüthy, H. (1969). *La Question jurassienne*, Texte intégral du rapport (forum à la télévision entre Gonzague de Reynold, Pierre Béguin, Herbert Lüthy, et Olivier Reverdin), Rassemblement jurassien, Delémont.

Lüthy, H. (1972). *Une proposition pour le Jura*, la Baconnière, Neuchâtel.

McCracken, K. (1970). *The Rise of the Swiss Republic* (reprint of 1901 work), AMS, New York.

McDonald, J. (1978). Europe's Restless Regions, *Focus* (American Geographical Society), Vol. 28(V), 1–16.

McRae, K. (1964). *Switzerland: Example of Cultural Coexistence*, Canadian Institute of International Affairs, Toronto.

McRae, K. (1983). *Conflict and Compromise in Multilingual Societies: Switzerland*, Wilfrid Laurier University Press, Waterloo.

Maillat, D. and Pellaton, J. (1975) *La Région Centre-Jura: étude des potentialités et des objectifs de développement*, Groupe d'études économiques, Université de Neuchâtel, Neuchâtel.

Martin, W. (1974). *Histoire de la Suisse* (seventh revised edition) Librairie Payot, Lausanne, Switzerland. [Includes additional chapter by Pierre Béguin.]

Martonne, E. de (transl. Laborde, E.) (1961). *A Shorter Physical Geography*, Christophers, London.

Mayer, K. (1951). Cultural Pluralism and Linguistic Equilibrium in Switzerland, *American Sociological Review*, Vol. 16, 156–63.

Mayer, K. (1952). *The Population of Switzerland*, Columbia University Press, New York.

Mayer, K. (1968). The Jura Problem: Ethnic Conflict in Switzerland, *Social Research*, Vol. 35, 707–41.

Mayer, K. (1977). Groupes linguistiques en Suisse, *Recherches sociologiques*, Vol. 8, 23–24.

Maylan, R. (1951). *Géographie économique de la Suisse*, Librairie Payot, Lausanne.

Merazzi, C. (1979). Letter to *Journal du Jura*, Biel, 18 October.

Meuron, L. de (1979). *Lettre ouverte à Roland Béguelin*, editions Liberté et vérité, Neuchâtel.

Meyer, K. (transl. Briod, B.) (1952) *La Suisse, état polyglotte: antécédents historiques de la paix linguistique au sein de la Confédération la Baconnière*, Neuchâtel.

Meylan, J., Gottraux, M., and Dahinden, P. (1972). *Communes suisses et autonomie communale*, Imprimeries populaires, Lausanne.

Michel, G. and Wiest, A. (1930). *La Suisse*, Fraguère Frères, Fribourg.

Miljan, T. (1976). *The Minority and Politics in a Bicultural Society: The Case of Finland*, Workshop on the Politics of Multicultural Societies, Louvain.

Moeckli, G. (1968). Le Jura et les trafics ferroviaires CFF et BLS en 1967, *Intérêts du Jura*, Vol. 39, 225–229.

Moine, V. (1965). L'École jurassienne dans le cadre de la legislation bernoise, in *150 Jahr Berner Jura: 1815–1965*, Volksfreund, Laufen.

Monbaron, M. (1974). *Aspects de la géologie jurassienne*, Éditions Pro Jura, Moutier.

Monkhouse, F. (1974). *A Regional Geography of Western Europe* (fourth edition), Longman, London.

Moritz, J. (1976). *Le Comité de Moutier, 1947–1952*, Rassemblement jurassien, Delémont.

Moser, A. (1953). Le Séparatisme jurassien du point d'une des finances publiques, Mimeographed paper, Berne-Muri.

Moser, A. and Ehrensperger, I. (1983). *Arts et monuments Jura bernois, Bienne et les rives du lac*, Buchler, Wabern.

Moser, U. (1983). *La Démocratie aliénée*, Rassemblement jurassien, Delémont.

Müller, C. (Preface by Wahlen, Fritz-Traugott) (1965). Sprache und Sprachgrenze in Jura, in *150 Jahre Berner Jura: 1815–1965*, 57–96, Volksfreund, Laufen.

Müller, K. (1969). *Der Jura: Ein unbewältigtes Minderheitenproblem*, Der Zürcher, Zurich.

Müller, K. (1975). Kann die Jurafrage überhaupt gelost werden? *Neue Zürcher Zeitung*, Zurich.

Müller, K. (1976). Die Jurafrage und ihre Bewältigung, *Neue Zürcher Zeitung*, 7 January, Zurich.

Natan, (1970). *Swiss Men of Letters: Twelve Literary Essays*, Wolff, London.

Netting, R. (1972). Of Men and Meadows: Strategies of Alpine Land Use, *Anthropological Quarterly*, Vol. 45, 132–45.

New Helvetic Society (1978). *Oui au canton du Jura (Annuaire 1978)*, Vol. 49, Buri Druck, Berne.

Nooij, A. (1969). Political Radicalism among Dutch Farmers, *Sociologia Ruralis*, Vol. 9, 43–61.

Nussbaumer, C. (1934). *Die Rechtslage der Katholiken in Berner Jura: Nach bernischen Staatsrecht und Katholiken dargestellt*, Walter, Olten.

Obler, J. Steiner, J., and Dierickx, G. (1977). *Decision-Making in Smaller Democracies*, Sage Publications, Beverly Hills, California.

Oechsli, W. (transl. Paul, E. and C.) (1922). *History of Switzerland 1499–1914*, Cambridge University Press, Cambridge.

Orr, D. (1969). The Persistence of Gerrymandering in North Carolina Redistricting, *South Eastern Geographer*, Vol. 9, 39–54.

Paratte, H. (1980). *Jura Acadie*, Rassemblement jurassien, Delémont.

Peel, R., Chisholm, M. and Haggett, P. (eds.) (1975). *Process in Physical and Human Geography*, Heinemann, London.

Pelling, H. (1967). *The Social Geography of British Elections: 1885–1910*, London.

Petitpierre, Max *et al. Laufental—Woher? Wohin?* Athenaeum Verlag, Lugano.

Philippe, V. (1978). *Le Jura république, 23ᵉ canton suisse*, Éditions 24 heures. Lausanne.

Pinson, K. (1935). *A Bibliographical Introduction to Nationalism*, Columbia University Press, New York.

Pounds, N. (1972). *Political Geography* (second edition), McGraw-Hill, New York.

Prescott, J. (1959). The Function and Methods of Electoral Geography, *Annals of the Association of American Geographers*, Vol. 49, 296–304.

Prescott, J. (1965). *The Geography of Frontiers and Boundaries*, Aldine Publishing Co., Chicago.

Prescott, J. (1969). Electoral Studies in Political Geography, in Kasperson, R. and Minghi, J. (eds.) *The Structure of Political Geography*, Aldine Publishing Co., Chicago.

Prescott, J. (1972). *Political Geography*, Methuen, London.

Prescott, J. (1978). *Boundaries and Frontiers*, Croom Helm, London.

Price, G. (1969). *The Present Position of Minority Languages in Europe: A Selective Bibliography*, University of Wales Press, Cardiff.

Prongué, B. (1972). *L'Esprit 'national' du liberalisme jurassien et le but national du radicalisme suisse (1846–1848)*, Éditions jurassiennes, Porrentruy.

Prongué, B. (1973). *Histoire populaire du Jura de 1943 à 1973*, Éditions jurassiennes, Porrentruy.

Prongué, B. (1974). *Le Jura et le plébiscite du 23 juin 1974*, Éditions jurassiennes, Porrentruy.

Prongué, B. (1975). *ADIJ 1925–1975*, Association pour la défense des intérêts du Jura, Moutier.

Prongué, B. (1976). *Le Jura de 1936 à 1975*, Éditions de la Prévôté. Moutier.

Prongué, B. (1978a). Histoire jurassienne et réalités politiques, *Civitas*, Vol. 17, 487–501.

Prongué, B. (1978b). L'Unité jurassienne: une question posée à la Suisse, *Jura-Perspektiven*, Evangelische Zeigschaft fur Kultur und Politik, Vol. 27, 291–348.

Rabl, K. (1980). Fragen der Verwirklichung des Grundsatzes der Selbstbestimmung der Völker eidgenossens chaft (Républic et Canton du Jura), in Adamovich, L. and Pernthaler, P. (eds) *Auf dem Weg zur Menschenwürde und Gerechtigkeit: Festschrift für Hans R. Klecatsky, Braumüller*, Vol. 2, 781–807, Vienna—dargestellt am Beispiel der Entstehung des 23. Kantons der Schweizerischen.

Rais, J. (ed.) (1975). *Bibliographie jurassienne 1974*, Société jurassienne d'émulation, Porrentruy.

Rantala, O. (1967). Political Regions of Finland, *Scandinavian Political Studies*, Vol. 2, 117–40.

Rappard, W. (1936). *The Government of Switzerland*, Von Nostrand, New York.

Rappard, W. (1948). *Collective Security in Swiss Experience: 1291–1948*, Allen and Unwin, London.

Rassemblement jurassien (1954). *Déclaration de principe sur la constitution et sur les lignes directrices de la politique de l'état jurassien*, Delémont.

Rassemblement jurassien (1955). *La Force financière du Jura*, Delémont.

Rassemblement jurassien (1959). I. *Prise de position sur le scrutin cantonal du 5 juillet 1959:* II. *Programme jurassien d'action No. II*, Delémont.

Rassemblement jurassien (1969). *Status du Rassemblement jurassien*, Delémont.

Rassemblement jurassien (1970). *La Question jurassienne: documents*, Delémont.

Rassemblement jurassien (1974a). *Guide des communes jurassiennes*, Delémont.

Rassemblement jurassien (1974b). *23 juin, 23ᵉ canton*, Delémont.

Rassemblement jurassien (1977a). *Constitution de la république et canton du Jura*, Delémont.

Rassemblement jurassien (1977b). *Trente ans de la lutte pour la liberté du peuple jurassien*, Delémont.

Rassemblement jurassien (1981). *'Livre blanc' sur les relations entre le Rassemblement jurassien et les autorités suisses*, Delémont.

Rees, H. (1974). *Italy, Switzerland and Austria: A Geographical Study*, Harrap, London.

Rennwald, J. C. (1977). *Combat jurassien: alientation ethnique et nouvelle culture politique*, Institut de science politique, Lausanne.

République et Canton du Jura (1983). *Annuaire officiel: 1983–1984*, Le Franc-Montagnaro, Saignelégier.

Reusser, F. (1945). L'Industrie jurassienne de l'horlogerie et des machines, ses préoccupations et ses perspectives d'avenir à la fin de 1945, *Intérêts du Jura*, Vol. 16, 172.

Reverdin, O. (1967). *Introducing Switzerland* (second edition), Swiss Office for the development of Trade, Lausanne.

Reymond, F. (1965). La Question jurassienne et l'évolution du mouvement séparatiste: 1949–1964, in *Schweizerisches Jahrbuch für politische Wissenschaft*, Berne, 32–3.

Reynold, G. de (1968). *Destin du Jura*, Éditions Rencontre, Lausanne.

Reynolds, D. (1969). Spatial Dimensions of Electoral Behaviour, 65th *Annual Meeting of the American Political Science Association*, New York.

Reynolds, D. and Archer, J. (1969). An Inquiry into the Spatial Basis of Electoral Geography, *Discussion Paper No. 11*, University of Iowa, Ames.

Richardson, K. (1978). Swiss Passion Makes a Rift in Alps, *The Sunday Times*, 24 September.

Riley, R. C. (1973). *Industrial Geography*, Chatto and Windus, London.

Roberts, M. and Rumage, K. (1965). The Spatial Variations in Urban Left-Wing Voting in England and Wales, *Annals of the Association of American Geographers*, Vol. 55, 161–78.

Rohr, J. (1972). *La Suisse contemporaire: société et vie politique*, Librairie Armand Colin, Paris.

Rougemont, D. de (1965). *La Suisse ou l'histoire d'un peuple heureux*, Hachette, Paris.

Rougemont, D. de and Muret, C. (1946). *The Heart of Europe: Switzerland*, Duell, Sloan and Pearce, New York.

Roy, D. (1974). *Projet de budget pour la république et canton du Jura*, Gassmann, Biel.

Ruffieux, R. and Prongué, B. (1972). *Les Petitions du Jura au canton de Berne durant le XIXe siècle*, Éditions universitaires, Fribourg.

Ruffieux, R. and Prongué, B. (1978). Le Canton du Jura à travers les travaux de l'assemblée constituante, *Annuaire suisse de science politique*, Vol. 18, 195–9.

Rundle, S. (1946). *Language as a Social and Political Factor in Europe*, Faber and Faber, London.

Salis, J. de (1970). *Switzerland and Europe: Essays and Reflections*, Wolff, London.

Sanguin, A.-L. (1983). *La Suisse: essai de géographie politique*, editions Ophrys, Gap.

Sanguin, A.-L. and Gauthier, P. (1977). La Forme territoriale de la Suisse, *Geographica Helvetica*, Vol. 1, 21–8.

Schaffter, R. (1965). *Les Rélations entre les jurassiens et la Confédération suisse vues à travers les événements de 1815*, Rassemblement jurassien, Delémont.

Schaffter, R. (1967a). *Despotisme démocratique ou négociation?* Rassemblement jurassien, Delémont.

Schaffter, R. (1967b). *1947–1967, vingt ans de lutte, Rassemblement jurassien, Delémont*.

Schaffter, R. (1968). *Les Impératifs de la liberté*, Rassemblement jurassien, Delémont.

Schaffroth, P. (1978). Die Jurafrage: Ein europäisches Problem? *Europäische Rundschau*, Vol. 6, no. 3, 53–7.

Schaller, J. (1958). L'Industrie jurassienne. Son importance industrielle des districts jurassiens, *Intérêts du Jura*, Vol. 29, 165–74, 201–17, 245–59.

Schäppi, P. (1971). *Der Schutz sprachlicher und konfessioneller Minderheiten im Recht von Bund und Kantonen*, Schulthess Polygraphischer Verlag, Zurich.

Schindelholz, G. (1973). *Les Sects et communautés dissidentes du Jura*, Éditions transjuranes, Porrentruy.

Schmid, C. L. (1981). *Conflict and Consensus in Switzerland*, University of California Press, Berkeley.

Schwander, M. (1971). *Jura: Argernis der Schweiz*, editions, Pharos, Basle.

Schwander, M. (1977). *Jura: Konfliktsoff für Jahrzehnte*, Benziger, Zurich and Cologne.

Schweizerische Bankgesellschaft (1976). *Die grössten Unternehmen der Schweiz im Jahre 1975*, Zurich.

Schweizerische Bankgesellschaft (1979). *Schweizerisches Wirtschaftsjahr*, Zurich.

Service topographique fédéral (1972). *Atlas de la Suisse* (sixth edition), Wabern-Berne.

Shafer, B. (1955). *Nationalism: Myth and Reality*, Harcourt Brace, New York.

Shaub, M.-A. (1972). *Une contribution à la solution du problème jurassien*, Association suisse des amis du Jura libre, Berne.

Siegfried, A. (1913). *Tableau politique de la France de l'Ouest sous la troisième république*, Librairie Armand Colin, Paris.

Siegfried, A. (1947). *Géographie électorale de l'Ardèche*, Paris.

Siegfried, A. (1956) *La Suisse: démocratie-témoin* (third edition), La Baconnière, Neuchâtel.

Smith, D. (1966). A Theoretical Framework for Geographical Studies of Industrial Location, *Economic Geography*, Vol. 42, 95–113, April.

Société de secours en faveur des victimes de la lutte pour la patrie jurassienne (1967). *Histoire et procès du front de libération jurassienne*, Delémont.

Société jurassienne d'émulation (ed.) (1973). *Bibliographie jurassienne: 1928–1972*, Porrentruy.

Société jurassienne d'émulation (ed.) (1979). *Bibliographie jurassienne: 1973–1979*, Porrentruy.

Soloveytchik, G. (1954). *Switzerland in Perspective,* Oxford University Press, London.

Sorell, W. (1973). *The Swiss: A Cultural Panorama of Switzerland,* Wolf, London.

Statistisches Bureau de Kantons Berne (1966). *Structure économique des communes du canton de Berne, 1966,* Berne.

Statisches Handbuch des Kantons Bern (various years), Francke, Berne.

Stauffer, P. (1974). Series of four articles on the subject of Jura separatism, *Journal de Genève,* 17–20 June, Geneva.

Steinberg, J. (1976). *Why Switzerland?* Cambridge University Press, Cambridge.

Steiner, F. (1978). *Laufental—Woher? Wohin?,* Athenaeum, Lugano.

Steiner, R. (1947). Industrie et commerce du Jura bernois au début du XIXe siècle, *Intérêts du Jura,* Vol. 18, 159–65.

Steiner, R. (1964). Le Trafic transalpin et le Jura, *Intérêts du Jura,* Vol. 35, 115–22.

Stephens, M. (1976). *Linguistic Minorities in Western Europe,* Gomer Press, Llandysul.

Storey, A. (1902). *Swiss Life in Town and Country,* George Newnes, London.

Stucki, L. (1971). *The Secret Empire: The Success Story of Switzerland,* Herder and Herder, New York.

Swiss National Tourist Office (1973). *The Swiss Universities,* Zurich.

Swiss Office for the Development of Trade (1974). *Switzerland and its Industries,* Lausanne.

Taylor, P. J. and Johnson, R. J. (1979). *Geography of Elections,* Penguin, Harmondsworth.

Theakstone, M. and Harrison, R. (1970). *The Analysis of Geographic Data,* Heinemann, London.

Thilo, E. (1941). *Note sur l'égalité et sur l'usage des langues nationales en Suisse,* Roth, Lausanne.

Thomas, R. (1968). *The Geography of Economic Activity,* McGraw-Hill, New York,

Thürer, G. (transl. Heller, R. P. and Long, E.) (1970). *Free and Swiss: The Story of Switzerland,* Wolff, London.

Trudgill, P. (1975). The Application of Geographic Techniques and Theories to Linguistic Problems, *Progress in Geography,* Vol. 7, 227–52.

Université populaire jurassienne. (1980). *Rapport d'activité, 1979–1980,* Porrentruy.

Veiter, T. (1971). *Le Droit de libre disposition du peuple jurassien,* Wilhelm Braumüller, Stuttgart.

Viatte, L. (1908). La germanisation du Jura, *Actes de la Société jurassienne d'emulation,* second series, Vol. 15, 61–77.

Von Burg, D. and Farie, C. (1978). *Le Jura au quotidien: portrait d'un Franc-Montagnard de sa famille et de son entourage,* Tribune editions, Geneva.

Wagner P. (1958). Remarks on the Geography of Language, *Geographical Review,* Vol. 48, 86–97.

Warburton, R. (ed. Smith, A.) (1976). Nationalism and Language in Switzerland and Canada. in *Nationalist Movements,* Macmillan, London.

Webb, F. (1909). *Switzerland and the Swiss,* Pitman, London.

Weber, M. (1962). *L'Éthique protestante et l'esprit du capitalisme,* Plon, Paris.

Weigert, H. (1957). *Principles of Political Geography,* Appleton-Century-Crofts, New York.

Weilenmann, H. (1925). *Die vielsprachige Schweiz: Eine Lösung des Nationalitätenproblems,* Rhein-Verlag, Basel.

Weilenmann, H. (1951). *Pax Helvetica,* Eugen Rentsch, Zurich.

Weilenmann, H. (1961). Political Problems of Poly-Ethnic States: The Example of Switzerland, *Fifth World Congress of International Political Science Association*, Paris.

Weilenmann, H. (1966). National and Personality Structure, in Deutsch and Foltz, *Nation-building*, Vol. 44.

Weilenmann, H. *et al.* (1963). La Question linguistique en Suisse, *Res Publica*, Brussels, Vol. 4, 225–74.

Weinreich, U. (1952). Research Problems in Bilingualism, with Special Reference to Switzerland, unpublished Ph.D. dissertation, Columbia University.

Welsh, P. (1966). Plurilingualism in Switzerland, 2 vols. mimeo. A Study prepared for the Royal Commission on Bilingualism and Biculturalism, Ottawa.

Wheare, K. (1968). *Federal Government: The Workings of Federalism in the United States, Switzerland, Canada and Australia* (fourth edition), Oxford University Press, New York.

White, P. (1974). *The Social Impact of Tourism on Host Communities: A Study of Language Change in Switzerland*, School of Geography Research Paper No. 9, Oxford University.

White, P. (1976). Aspects of the Effects of Tourism and Economic and Social Geography of Small Host Communities, unpublished D. Phil. Thesis, Oxford University.

Wicks, J. (1974). William Tell's Other Island, *Financial Times*, 18 June 1974.

Wiegandt, E. (1979). Unity through Diversity in Switzerland, unpublished paper, Graduate Institute of International Studies, Geneva.

Wildhaber, L. (1981). Ederswiler und Vellerat: Zur Gebietsveränderung im Bundesstaat, in *Recht als Prozess und Gefüge: Festschrift für Hans Huber zum 80, Geburtstag*, Stampfl, Berne.

Wilhelm, J. (1965). La Question jurassienne, *Civitas*, Vol. 20, 224–36.

Wilhelm, J. (1967). *La Romandie sous tutelle*, Rassemblement jurassien, Delémont.

Windisch, U. and Willener, A. (1976). *Le Jura incompris: fédéralisme ou totalitarisme?*, Éditions Delta, Vevey.

Windisch, W. (1983). D'un fédéralisme entropique à un fédéralisme de la complexité active: dimensions culturelles des relations entre majoritaires et minoritaires: le cas du Jura, in DuBois, P. *Union et Division des Suisses*, 213–29.

Woolmington, E. (1966) *A Spatial Approach to the Measurement of Support for the Separatist Movement in Northern New South Wales*, University of New England Monograph Series, No. 2, Armidale, New South Wales.

Wright, J. (1944). Training for Research in Political Geography, *Annals of the Association of American Geographers*, Vol. 34, 190–201.

Zeisel, H. (1957). *Say It with Figures*, Harper and Row, New York.

Ziegler, J. (transl. Middleton, Rosemary) (1979). *Switzerland: The Awful Truth*, Harper and Row, New York.

Znaniecki, F. (1952). *Modern Nationalities: A Sociological Study*. University of Illinois Press, Urbana.

INDEX

217